RACE AND THE UNIVERSITY

RACE AND THE UNIVERSITY

A Memoir

George Henderson

Foreword by David W. Levy

With Contributions by Sterlin N. Adams,
Sandra D. Rouce, and Ida Elizabeth Mack Wilson

UNIVERSITY OF OKLAHOMA PRESS : NORMAN

This book is published with the generous assistance of the Wallace C. Thompson Endowment Fund, University of Oklahoma Foundation.

Library of Congress Cataloging-in-Publication Data

Henderson, George, 1932–
    Race and the university : a memoir / George Henderson ; foreword by David W. Levy ; with contributions by Sterlin N. Adams, Sandra D. Rouce, and Ida Elizabeth Mack Wilson.
        p. cm.
    Includes bibliographical references and index.
    ISBN 978-0-8061-4129-9 (hardcover : alk. paper)
    1. Afro-American Student Union (University of Oklahoma) — History. 2. African American college students — Oklahoma — Norman — Societies, etc. — History. 3. University of Oklahoma — History — 20th century. 4. College integration — Oklahoma — Norman — History. 5. Norman (Okla.) — Race relations. I. Adams, Sterlin N. II. Rouce, Sandra D. III. Wilson, Ida Elizabeth Mack. IV. Title.
LD4326.2.H46 2010
378.766'37 — dc22
2010000156

The paper in this book meets the guidelines for permanence and durability of the Committee on Production Guidelines for Book Longevity of the Council on Library Resources, Inc. ∞

3 4 5 6 7 8 9 10

For George Henderson, Jr., our family's Atlas.
He held us up on his broad shoulders
and showed us how to love and respect
one another, and strangers too,
in good times and bad.

Contents

Illustrations

Foreword

David W. Levy

O ne of the few times when events on the campus of the University of
Oklahoma captured national attention (not counting football) occurred during the five years following the end of World War II. Then the
interest centered on a small group of intrepid African Americans who
had somehow taken it into their heads that just because they were citizens
of the state of Oklahoma, they had a right to attend the state university in
Norman. From September 1945 until June 1950, they struggled against
the constitutional and legislative fortifications of segregation, against
a traditional and entrenched bigotry in much of the population, and
against a powerful state officialdom committed to resisting integration.
Although there were numerous sympathetic whites among the University's students, faculty, and administrators, the ultimate victory was mostly
the result of the patience, dignity, and courage of those African Americans. Before it was over, they were required to make two well-publicized
trips to the United States Supreme Court.

In this book, George Henderson, a longtime member of the University's faculty, presents a picture of the racial situation on the campus
seventeen years after that victory. Arriving as a young African American
professor in 1967 (only the third black member of a Norman faculty of

more than five hundred), he found a town and a campus that was, despite
some notable exceptions, far from welcoming. The traumatic ordeal of
simply trying to find a house where he and his family could live was a
sufficient indication of the atmosphere he had to confront in town. As far
as the University itself was concerned, he quickly came to see it as a place
of "white privilege, black separatism, and campus-wide indifference to
bigotry." The days of open and vicious opposition to blacks entering the
University might be over, but race relations on the campus left a good
deal to be desired. "Although blacks and whites shared the same geography and the same academic curriculums," Henderson recalls, "the sense
of being equal members of the same community had not been achieved."
The testimonies of three African American students, whose reminis-
cences of life at the University during these years are included in these
pages, echo Henderson's view of what the situation was like.

If the new professor of education and sociology had come to Norman
expecting to spend his life tranquilly teaching and writing, he promptly
learned that additional responsibilities were about to devolve upon him.
Expectations of him — both on campus and in the state's black community — were high. Almost unwillingly, he and his wife, Barbara, found
themselves deeply engaged in the twin tasks of quietly helping individual
black students adjust and succeed in an unfriendly climate and of par-
ticipating in the large and sometimes dramatic group efforts to improve
race relations at the University. The Henderson home became a refuge
for lonely and sometimes discouraged students, and the young professor
became an adviser and guide to African American students who wanted
to do something about racial tensions in Norman and at the University.
How they went about it is the subject of this account.

Starting with the creation of the Afro-American Student Union in
November 1967, black students — together with supportive whites on the
faculty and in the student body — began to address the tangled questions
of race. They had to walk a difficult line. On the one hand, it was imperative that they understood the uneasiness and anxiety of many of the white
students who were suddenly faced with the prospect of real integration
for the first time in their lives. On the other hand, they could not let that
sympathetic understanding stand in the way of determined action. They
also had to carefully choose from the spectrum of possible tactics — quiet
diplomacy with University officials, personal relationships, written state-

ments, public demonstrations. From the start, they were determined to avoid violence, for both philosophic and strategic reasons. But, as Henderson shows, there was little unanimity among them, and their efforts over the next few years were characterized by lively and thoroughgoing internal debate. Henderson does not attempt to disguise these divisions within the movement but portrays them as thoughtful and democratic attempts to reach wise decisions.

One of the most interesting aspects of this story is the extent to which the most thoughtful participants in the struggle were guided by the works of a handful of theorists, activists, and social scientists whose books and articles they read and discussed. Those who think that the civil rights conflicts on the campus were fueled entirely by blind anger over injustice and ill treatment will be surprised by Henderson's insistence that those involved studied and discussed the teachings of writers and reformers before deciding how to proceed. Here again there were spirited divisions of opinion, but readers will emerge with a respect for the serious and honest deliberations that were an integral part of the efforts undertaken during these years.

A strong case can be made for the argument that the four years chronicled in this memoir constituted a turning point in the history of race relations at the University of Oklahoma. In one sense, the movement away from black isolation and white indifference (or worse) was symbolized by the election, in the spring of 1970, of the first African American president of the student body. But there were other signs as well that those earnest and determined students and their mentors and friends on the faculty were able to bring about changes in institutional practices and private feelings that were important and permanent. Few readers will find reason to disagree with Henderson's assessment. "We were ordinary people," he insists, "who sometimes did extraordinary things."

Preface and Acknowledgments

I was only going to stay in Oklahoma for two or three years. Then I would move on to a better place. More than forty years later, I am still here. I came for a job and it turned into a career. But that is not why I stayed. I could have had a career in one of the dozen or so other universities that tried to recruit me. I stayed because of some very special people whom I would not have found elsewhere. Together, we made the University of Oklahoma a better place. So, as you will find out in this book, I found my destiny. Or better yet, I found my dignity.

Much of what I tell you is drawn from my memories of the most formative period of my career at the University of Oklahoma: August 1967 to December 1971. Again and again something happened to temporarily dishearten or anger me during that period. But mainly, those things cemented my resolve not to give in to hatred. It was a time when African Americans in the University were desperately searching for soul mates. And we found each other. With calculated abandon, we conjured up new lives for ourselves and vowed not to surrender our hope of achieving racial equality. The fusion of academic data with former students' recollections and other information into this narrative is done to present the complexities of interactions that defined and shaped my teaching, research, and community service. Seldom were things simple; almost never were they easy to do equitably.

Portions of this book were written first in my mind with fits and starts of information that cried out for remembrance. That African Americans — and other minorities — at the University of Oklahoma survived against great odds is the subtext of those thoughts. How we survived is the main narrative. I realized a few years ago that if I, or someone else, did not put our recollections of those times down in writing, the essence of our survival would be lost to future generations. And that would be a tragic loss. African Americans in particular, and other minority peoples in general, would have no knowledge of what prompted the University to commit itself to becoming one of the nation's most culturally diverse institutions. They would not even know why they enjoy the rights and privileges that are theirs today.

Under the best of circumstances, a clear accounting of what happened such a long time ago is difficult to retrieve. Aggregates of people and their behavior did not come easily or quickly to me when summoned. The risk in all recollections is that so much is lost to time. Factual aspects of those interactions fade in and out of my consciousness like an old-time movie — frequently in fuzzy black-and-white ruminations — and other times in clear, precise, full-color memories. Distortions surely fill in some of the missing pieces. This process, at once frustrating and exhilarating, has been used since members of *Homo sapiens* dared reconstruct their lives for examination. These retrievals sometimes seem incomplete because they are. The recalled parts do not always fit neatly, and some of them are bloated or inconsequential. This is especially true of conversations drawn from my memory or someone else's. Therefore what has taken shape in this narrative is an effort that will gratify nitpickers.

For several years, Norris G. Williams invited me to describe to assemblies of incoming black students, and older ones too, what turned out to be the first large-scale black student rebellion at a historically white university in Oklahoma. The annual oral history telling began in 1977, when Norris was coordinator of the University's Black Student Affairs Program; it continued when he became director of Minority Student Services in 1980; and it ended in 2003, when he was appointed director of the Henderson Scholars Program. During those years, I checked and double-checked my recollections by reading personal communications and news stories. In addition to examining copies of the *Oklahoma Daily* and *Sooner*

Yearbooks, I also talked to scores of people who were at the University during that time. I did not want my story to lead down a faulty historical path that would leave the reader with something less than a valid understanding of my perceptions of selected aspects of University of Oklahoma history.

Not every important event is included in this book. But I have tried to include enough information to convey the depth and essence of the black students' rebellion and other peripheral activities. I hope that I have provided a useful snapshot for people who wish to revisit those years, as well as for others who are finding out about them for the first time. In any case, I offer for your examination a historical potpourri. Some of the bits and pieces are not very interesting on their own. When they are examined together and within their social contexts, however, I believe that they become meaningful conceptual overviews. They are, in a sense, an educational gumbo. On several occasions, institutional fairness intersected with our sense of fair play; and the result was a satisfactory outcome. During those times, at least, the African American students and I had fulfilling University experiences.

We were ordinary people who sometimes did extraordinary things, but there was considerably more to it than that. We were able to overcome the incalculable horror of being ridiculed by our critics and even demonized by a few of them. There were numerous instances when our adversaries were wrong about us. None of our adversaries was more memorable than the others—they all missed or misread important things about us. Our rebellion was worth the risks we faced. What really mattered to me was that we tried to abolish as many vestiges of racial segregation and discrimination in the University as we could.

Finding supportive friends and new roles for us was no small challenge. At the same time, the academic bar had been set so low for us that condescending onlookers often praised our mediocre performances. In other instances, our efforts to extricate ourselves from this morass came off like a poor B movie: serious, yet off the mark so much that the final results were comical or farcical. Something unsettling almost always seemed to happen. But no matter how serious those encounters were, there was usually a bit of dark humor or comic relief in them. When I became involved with the students, my career morphed into more than what I expected it would be. I developed the full range of my voice as a teacher and an activist. Along the way, I came to terms with what I believed about the University of Oklahoma, and what I wanted to believe about it.

As we pushed forward with new grievances and circled back to revisit old ones, we became some of the most successful gadflies in the University's history. Sometimes I was center stage and the African American students supported me from backstage; at other times our roles were reversed. Notwithstanding flashes of racial equality, there was always segregation and discrimination. Without question, the lucky or the shrewd among us were the few tokens of success. But the African Americans who lived on the edge of mainstream acceptance did not have an abundance of appreciation for their own academic worth. When their stifled anger turned into full-blown outrage, their riveting attention to the smallest grievances left no wiggle room for apologists. So this is their story too. It is cobbled from memories of times when we dared to rebel against white privilege, black separatism, and campus-wide indifference to bigotry. For the most part, though, this is a story of change.

On November 20, 2003, I had the honor of being inducted into the Oklahoma Hall of Fame. The right for ethnic minorities to receive opportunities, awards, and honors at the University of Oklahoma today was partially paid for many years earlier. Simply put, the initial down payments were made with declarations, petitions, sit-ins, negotiations, and casualties. Another ingredient was just as important as the protest activities: we had allies from other ethnic groups. Personally, the awards, honors, and citations for meritorious service I received while working full-time at the University were the result of my successful involvement with students, faculty, and staff. Therefore I will feel so much better, less inflated, and less bothered for accepting the booty after I tell you about the multiracial giants who lifted me high enough to reach the Oklahoma Hall of Fame.

During those early years, I found guidance in these lyrics written by Johnny Mercer: "You've got to accentuate the positive. / Eliminate the negative. / Latch on to the affirmative. / Don't mess with Mister In-between." I spent a lot of time accentuating the positive aspects of racial integration, trying to eliminate my own negative beliefs and behavior that impeded it, latching on to hopeful people and things, and not messing with wishy-washy people. So my story goes. But never in the wildest fancies of my mind did I imagine that my life would unfold the way that it did.

In many ways, my induction into the Oklahoma Hall of Fame was a tribute to people that I call "friends and loved ones." In the following acknowledgments, I have drawn from my induction speech, for it captures my innermost feelings about people whose steadying encouragement and advice sustained me long enough to have a successful career at the University of Oklahoma.

My journey began long before I came to Oklahoma. I am indebted to my parents, Kidd and Lula Henderson, and my stepmother, Rose Henderson. They believed in me before I believed in myself.

The central figure in my story is my wife, Barbara Beard Henderson. For more than fifty years, she has been my most ardent supporter, trusted adviser, best friend, and soul mate. Without her love, approval, and encouragement, I probably would not have come to Oklahoma, and I certainly would not have stayed without her. Much of my life has been a George and Barbara collaboration.

We have seven wonderful children, five beautiful grandchildren, and a spoiled great-grandson. All of our children and grandchildren gave me permission to take some of the time allocated to them and use it to pursue school and community goals. Each of them cares passionately about helping oppressed people.

Then there are my extended family members at the University of Oklahoma. Scores of precious people, like Melvin B. Tolson, Jr., welcomed me to Oklahoma and gave life to my dream of social justice. David and Molly Boren have been the wise, caring heads of my University family. Throughout the years, administrators, faculty, staff, and students have supported me in my quest for fairness and inclusion of all groups. I am a better person as a result of being a member of the OU family. Nor will I forget the many other persons scattered throughout Oklahoma who have been my mentors, role models, and cheerleaders. Some of them have stood in my shadow, and others have shared public spotlights with me. All of them have helped me to love and cherish Oklahoma and its citizens.

Several individuals deserve my gratitude for helping me write this book. At the top of the list is my wife, Barbara. Her faith in me and her timely suggestions, recollections, and encouragement kept me on task.

Melvin Tolson, Jr. reviewed the initial manuscript for the accuracy of my descriptions of interactions in which we both participated. Without his assistance, I would have omitted several seminal events. Comments and suggestions from the following individuals helped me further refine the manuscript: Oklahoma librarians Jennifer Greenstreet, Larry Johnson, Christopher Kennedy, and Michael E. Owens; professors James P. Comer (Yale University), Martha Biondi (Northwestern University in Illinois), Clarence Lang (University of Illinois at Urbana-Champaign), Emmett G. Price III (Northeastern University in Massachusetts), and LaQueta L. Wright (Richland Community College in Dallas); and author Dennis Kimbro (Atlanta). Betty Leverich typed the first two drafts of the manuscript and told me what made sense to her and what didn't, and Lisa Henderson, Joy Henderson Baldwin, Michael W. Ridgeway, and Jake Tullius also critiqued the initial manuscript. I very much needed their comments.

I had tremendous assistance when I was collecting the data cited in this book. Specifically, I am referring to the following University personnel: Dunni Okediji, my very competent research assistant; Debra L. Copp in the Athletics Department; Patricia A. Kessler in the Office of the Provost; Mary A. Smith in the Henderson Scholars Program; and Jennifer Needham in the Open Records Department. I am also grateful to Shirley Marshall and Carol Coles, employees of the City of Norman, for their assistance. I cannot say enough good things about the insightful recollections written by Sterlin Adams, Beth Wilson, and Sandy Rouce. Their narratives provide colorful and valuable descriptions of what the University of Oklahoma was like to them during an unmatched period of race issues, rebellions, and reconciliation.

Revised excerpts of my selected course lectures that were printed in *Human Relations: From Theory to Practice* (University of Oklahoma Press, 1977) make up portions of chapter 2; and my brief ouster from the Afro-American Student Union that is described in chapter 7 is reprinted from *Our Souls to Keep: Black/White Relations in America* (Intercultural Press, 1999).

Vanity aside, most manuscripts greatly benefit from the oversight of talented editors. My manuscript was no exception. Acquisitions editors Kirk Bjornsgaard and Jay Dew, special projects editor Alice Stanton, and copy editor Rosemary Wetherold enhanced my manuscript in numerous ways. Upon hindsight, I now realize that saying "Thank you" to them did not adequately convey my heartfelt gratitude. Hopefully, the sentiment of this paragraph will hit the mark.

RACE AND THE UNIVERSITY

CHAPTER ONE

The Setting

In August 1967, as an associate professor of sociology and of education, with joint appointments in the Department of Sociology and the College of Education, I began what would eventually be an almost forty-year career at the University of Oklahoma. That August, I became the third full-time African American professor at the University's Norman campus. Melvin B. Tolson, Jr., assistant professor of modern languages, and Lennie Marie Muse-Tolliver, associate professor of social work, had the distinction of being the first and the second, respectively, and Marie Mink, assistant professor of nursing at the Oklahoma City health sciences campus, was the University's first African American full-time professor. The four of us were trailblazers. There was something inconspicuous and yet attractive about being part of the University. Especially in my first four years there, I became a twentieth-century pioneer in more ways than even my friends or I could have imagined, considering that I grew up in an urban slum.

Life before Oklahoma

I was born in Hurtsboro, Alabama, on June 18, 1932. Like most other sharecropper families in Hurtsboro, we lived in abject poverty. There were no creature comforts in the small two-bedroom wooden shack that was home for three generations of us — my father's parents, my parents, and me. Although my parents gave me few material things, they did give me an abundance of love. They also instilled in me the American dream, telling me that they wished I would grow up healthy, get a good education, land a high-paying job, and pull our family out of poverty. Contrary to frequently cited social science literatures of the time, poor children were often expected to rescue their families from poverty. That expectation certainly wore heavy on my young mind.

When I was six years old, my parents and I moved to East Chicago, Indiana. Actually, we *fled* from Hurtsboro. The precipitating event was similar to thousands of other ones that caused countless black families to leave the South. My father had a fistfight with a white man who swore that he would put him in his "black place": hanging at the end of a rope. It was not an idle threat. The Ku Klux Klan probably would have lynched him. Consequently, we fled from the racism of the South to its northern version in East Chicago, where some of our relatives lived.

In the city, we lived in a series of musty, dimly lit, poorly insulated, and otherwise unhealthy houses and apartments. Each of them held a never-ending series of cockroaches, rats, bedbugs, and other uninvited things that fascinated me during the day and scared me awake at night. In short, I was living in places that were better habitats for rodents and insects than for people. I was a slum dweller in every sense of the term. But so were most of the other children in my community. Throughout the early years of my childhood, I believed that only black people were really poor. When I was ten, a chance encounter with two scrawny white boys my age shattered that myth. I smelled and dressed the part of a poverty-stricken person, but those boys smelled more rancid than me and their clothes were more ragged.

I asked one of them, "Who are you?"

He said, "We ain't nobody but poor white trash."

My family was on and off public welfare rolls for ten years. At the beginning of each school year, my parents were given store vouchers to buy me a new school outfit: one pair of shoes, four pairs of socks, two pairs of pants or overalls, three or four shirts, assorted underwear, and a winter coat. Each outfit had to last me for the whole year; there were no replacements. Unfortunately, they never lasted that long. By early spring, my outer garments had holes in them. When parts of an outfit wore out, my mother patched them as best she could with a mishmash of pieces of cloth, and before the year ended, my clothes had patches over patches. However, my mother could not patch the holes that wore into the soles of my shoes. I tried placing torn newspaper and cardboard over them, but it was all for naught. The newspaper and cardboard could not keep out rain or snow for very long. By the middle of winter, my socks had holes in the bottom of them that matched the holes in the bottom of my shoes.

Elementary school itself was even more trying for me. My father had completed the ninth grade, and my mother dropped out of school in the eighth grade. Neither of them had graduated from high school, because they spent more time helping their parents plant and pick cotton and other crops than attending school. Although education was more impor-tant to them than farming, survival trumped school. Besides, they were not given a choice between school and working in the fields. Years later, when we lived in East Chicago, my parents told me that I must try to be a good student. They also told me that they would not be able to help me complete school assignments. With virtually no educational guidance from my parents, I began my formal schooling functionally illiterate. After several failed attempts by impatient first- and second-grade teachers whose only mission, I thought, was to expose my ineptness as a reader, they gave up on me. My second-grade teacher shook her head and told my mother, "George is not a slow learner. He is no learner."

I still have flashbacks of the excruciating embarrassment that teacher inflicted on me by forcing me to read out loud in the class. The good readers mocked my mispronounced words. The poor readers were thank-ful that it was I, not them, who had been chosen to be the public example of a dumb student, as my snickering classmates referred to me. Help came not a moment too soon. Midway through the third grade, I learned to read. I was delivered from academic hell. The teacher who taught me to read also taught me to read slowly. From then on, as I passed to each new grade, a kindly teacher was waiting to give me her special attention. It was as though I was their reclamation project of the decade.

After years of searching, my father finally got a steady job in a brick-making factory in East Chicago. I was in the eighth grade at the time. Our family's lifestyle improved slightly, and I got a few more clothes and toys. But we were still poor. Our family's earned income was too much for us to be on welfare and too little for us to be middle class. He had joined the ranks of the working poor, and we rose no higher up the socioeconomic ladder. It was up to me to take us to the next level. Watching my father struggle to make ends meet gave me an epiphany: there were only a few ways people like us could change our situation, and not all of them were good.

I made a list of what I thought were the five things I could do to alter my own lifestyle. I could join the U.S. Army, become a successful criminal, be sent to prison, go to college, or die. The military, crime, prison, and death did not appeal to me; that left college as the default escape route. There was one glaring problem with this option, however. I didn't have a clue about what college entailed. If I could somehow manage to earn a college degree, I would be the first person in my family to accomplish that feat. Two elementary school teachers were the major forces behind my academic transformation. My grades and self-esteem improved significantly because of the remedial homework they assigned me and the one-on-one tutoring I got from them. Three years later, my high school track coach taught me techniques that optimized my sprinting abilities. I graduated from East Chicago Washington High School in 1950 as a National Honor Society inductee. I was also the star sprinter on the track team. Running fast and having an overall 3.55 grade point average got me a combined track and scholastic scholarship to Michigan State Agricultural and Mechanical College.

During my second year at Michigan State, 1951, I met and fell in love with Barbara Ann Beard. We got married a few months later. In 1953 the Korean Conflict interrupted my education; I received a notice from my draft board to report for military service. To avoid going into the army, I volunteered for the air force. Two years later, in 1955, I was given an honorable discharge. Barbara, our two children, and I moved to Detroit, where I worked full-time and also attended Wayne State University full-time. Ten years and six different professional jobs later, I had earned three academic degrees from Wayne State (a B.A. and an M.A. in sociology, and a Ph.D. in educational sociology). Only two of my college professors were black; the others were white. So the good, the bad, and the ugly teachers were mostly white. As I began to achieve excellence in my studies, I learned that being black did not make me an inferior college student; nor did being white make my classmates superior ones. Accomplishment, not ethnicity, was the distinguishing marker. Good grades helped me get several meaningful jobs.

George and Barbara Henderson on their first date at Michigan State College, 1951.

I was a social worker in Detroit's Big Brother/Big Sister program (1957–59); and a community organizer in outreach programs of the Detroit Housing Commission (1960–61), the Detroit Urban League (1961–63), and Wayne State University (1963–65). When I completed the doctorate, I became assistant director of intercultural relations (1965–66) and assistant to the superintendent (1965–67) of the Detroit Public Schools. From 1961 to 1967, I was also an adjunct instructor at Wayne State, the University of Michigan, and Harper Hospital School of Nursing. In 1967 I received a job offer to become a full-time professor at the University of Oklahoma. My life then took several decidedly novel turns.

A Friendly Warning

Leonard Moss, chairman of Wayne State University's Department of Anthropology and Sociology, asked me to decline the teaching position at the University of Oklahoma. "You won't like it there. It's a small redneck school in a backward state. If you want to go to a suburban school and live a nice quiet life, let me find you a better place," he pleaded. "You shouldn't begin your career in a second-rate university in the boondocks of Oklahoma. Besides, it's not a place where your social values and professional abilities will be appreciated."

Leonard was my mentor, adviser, and friend. But this time he was just flat-out wrong, I thought. He even tried to get my wife to talk me out of going to "that horrible place," as he described it to her. It was evident that he did not believe my going to the University of Oklahoma would be career enhancing. In his words, "it would be a dumb-ass job" into which I could not disappear, in storybook fashion, and live happily ever after. He did not hesitate to tell people that he expected me to become more than an associate professor at a second-tier school anywhere. He thought that my varied professional employment made me attractive to first-tier schools. And it did.

But the mere thought of getting my first full-time university job anywhere was exhilarating. Location was only a secondary concern. After I signed my University of Oklahoma contract, a race riot erupted two blocks from where I lived. There were street fights, gun battles, murders, looting, and arson. Suddenly the location of a job became very important to me. I wanted to work somewhere far away from riot-prone cities. The job in Oklahoma seemed like a godsend. So, in spite of Leonard's warning, I believed that I would indeed be happy in Norman, Oklahoma. I would perform my professorial duties — teach classes, produce scholarly publications, and provide service through university, community, and professional organization committees — and thrive. I was extremely unschooled in the histories of Norman and the University of Oklahoma.

The City of Norman

What was there not to like about the city of Norman or the University of Oklahoma? Why was Leonard so negative? Norman was situated in the center of the state, about thirty minutes or so from the Will Rogers World Airport. I would have convenient access to local, regional, national, and international destinations. And the quality of life would be markedly better than Detroit's. For someone like me who had spent most of his life in big cities, suburban living seemed a welcome respite from unkempt streets, garbage-strewn alleys, inadequate schools, high crime rates, and environmental pollution. There were other amenities too, including pastures and farms within the city limit. However, Leonard was correct concerning the readiness of Norman to accept me. He had spent time there during the 1940s and had experienced firsthand the community's antiblack sentiments and behavior, conditions that had existed there much earlier.

In the formative years of Oklahoma Territory, White Cappers, a racist group, began running blacks out of the region. According to Mozell C. Hill by late September 1896 all of the African Americans had been run out of Norman.[1] The systematic expulsion of blacks from most of the white Oklahoma communities continued after the territory became a state in 1907. The *Guthrie Daily Leader* reported on December 17, 1907:

> Members of a negro colony 13 miles northeast of Norman on a 220-acre ranch owned by Dowd and Cook, residents of this place, have been threatened with murder if they do not leave. Notices have been sent out by a "Ku Klux Klan" which styles itself "community," and is causing consternation among the negroes. Anticipating a night attack by the whites, the negroes are arming. Notices signed "mysterious community" have been posted on

the negro cabins, and repeatedly left in their mailboxes. They say that the negroes will be given until December 28 to gather crops and leave the country. . . . It is unwritten law that negroes do not stay in this town after the sun goes down.

In the 1950s and 1960s, Norman became a haven for white parents who lived in the Oklahoma City metropolitan area but did not want their children to attend racially desegregated public schools. It was common knowledge that most property owners in Norman would not even rent to blacks. In 1967, for example, John R. Sadberry, a black University of Oklahoma graduate student and a Vietnam veteran, was turned down three times by Norman landlords, and Willie Wilson, another black graduate student, was turned down twenty-eight times. Both of them finally moved into University housing. Their experiences were typical for black renters. Two years earlier, the citizens of Norman had defeated an open housing ordinance. Notwithstanding being classified as a southwestern state, Oklahoma was in all other ways southern, especially in terms of its laws and racial customs.

Even though I had imagined how contentious the desegregation of southern white communities might be, I had never been personally involved in the process. Therefore my decision to live in Norman was nothing more to me than moving from theory to practice. As I found out later, the transition would be difficult for me as a professor, and it would be excruciating for me as a husband, a father, and a son-in-law. Indeed, it was one thing for me to jump into a hostile fire of community race relations; it was something else very troubling to pull my family in with me.

After I returned the signed employment contract to University president George Lynn Cross, he arranged for Barbara to visit Norman in order to buy a house. That befuddled several faculty members who could not imagine giving their wives that much power. When they became acquainted with her, they understood why I did not come back to Norman with her to find a house. Her poise and business abilities blew away their doubts. When she told the faculty representatives that she wanted to see property only in Norman, and not in northeast Oklahoma City, where most of the black people in the area lived, it became clear to them that they were going to be involved in desegregating one of the most racially segregated cities in Oklahoma.

Because our family was large by then (ten), the search initially centered on older houses near the campus. None of them appealed to Barbara. She wanted to see contemporary houses that were in better repair. At her request, she was shown several houses scattered throughout Norman. After an exhaustive search, she narrowed the field to three houses on the west side of town, and she made a down payment on her first choice. When she returned to Detroit, all of the family members looked at the pictures of what was going to be our new home. Except for the two youngest children, Lisa and Dawn, who could care less where they lived as long as it was with the rest of us, we were ecstatic. We soon would be suburban dwellers.

Or would we? Within a week after Barbara returned to Detroit, I received a frantic telephone call from someone whom my secretary, Clorice Chomick, identified as "a man from Oklahoma."

"Dr. Henderson," a rather timid voice began. "I'm the owner of the house your wife has made a down payment on."

He abruptly stopped talking. After a few seconds of empty silence, I injected, "I'm glad to hear from you. It is a beautiful house, and we're looking forward to moving in."

There was more silence. I could hear him clearing his throat. "The realtor forgot to tell you that I recently made more than $1,500 worth of improvements in the house. . . . I'll need the additional money as part of your down payment," he blurted out, as though he was fearful that I would verbally attack him or do something worse.

His request for additional money irritated me. But Barbara did in fact tell me that she thought the house had undergone rather extensive renovations. Without hesitating, I responded, "Exactly what amount should I write on the check, and who should I send it to?"

More silence, then a faint groan. "Brother Henderson, I've got to level with you. Prominent political families live in the neighborhood and they don't want you to move into it. Would you please not buy the house?"

Now I was beyond being irritated. I was way beyond angry. I could feel blood rushing to my face as my body stiffened and I shouted, "I'm not your brother. As for your house, you can keep it. I'll void the deposit payment check."

Who in the hell were those people who didn't want us to live in their neighborhood? I should have made the owner honor the agreement. Instead of listening to my head, I listened to my broken heart and canceled the deal. I didn't panic, though, because Barbara had two backup houses for us to select from. Or so we thought. In less than three days, the realtors for the other two houses telephoned me and said that their properties were no longer on the market. (I learned later that wasn't true.)

With no other housing options lined up, I notified President Cross that I would not be joining the University, because I could not find a suitable house to move into. He assured me that he was looking forward to having me on the faculty, and he asked me to give the University time to find a house for us. Richard "Dick" Hilbert, chair of the Sociology Department, and his colleagues — mainly Professors Fred Silberstein and David Whitney — launched a search. They canvassed several neighborhoods, looking for a house in a neighborhood where most of the residents would accept a black family. They found one. The owners, Larry P. and Virginia E. Martin, were out of the country. He was director of the University's Extension Department. Dick Hilbert approached the realtors who had listed the property to see if it was still available.

This time Dick Hilbert suggested to Barbara that he accompany her when she inspected the Martin house. Forty years later, he told me: "I thought if anyone in the neighborhood saw Barbara and me together, they would think she was my maid. Some of the people in the neighborhood had black maids. It would be reasonable for the residents to think I brought my maid with me for her to see how much work she would have to do if I bought the house."

If that was indeed what the residents thought, it worked. Barbara liked the house, paid the deposit for it, and moved in three weeks later — before the few bigots in the neighborhood found out that their new neighbors were black. I stayed in Detroit for three more weeks to finish my contract with the Detroit Public Schools and also to assist with post-riot cleanup plans for the schools.

Barbara and I had settled for a house that was not our first, second, or third choice. It was only minimally adequate in terms of space, but it had the potential for being reconfigured. Three years later Fred D. Shellabarger, professor of architecture at the University, redesigned our house and recommended a contractor to do the work. He also supervised the renovations, but he would not accept payment for any of his work. He said, "It is my gift to you and Barbara." Nothing like that had ever happened to us before.

The realtors who sold Barbara and me a house were fine representatives of what I liked about Norman. Indeed, Sally A. Matthews, Sam M. Matthews, and Edward "Mokey" Webb, owners of Sallie's Real Estate, were three of countless citizens of Norman who valued being fair more than being keepers of an archaic "white people only" community norm. I cannot accurately convey the bravery of the people at Sallie's Real Estate who made Barbara and me the first African American homeowners in Norman. Doctoral student Herbert Inhaber described a tiny portion of the upheaval our presence triggered. In a "Cabbages and Kings" column in the *Oklahoma Daily* on May 8, 1968, he wrote that one of my neighbors called the agency and asked, "What are you trying to do with niggers? My family has had them as servants for years and they'll steal everything in sight." Some of the other reactions were no less hostile:

> Another neighbor called to complain and sold his house.
> A woman living in the Town and Country District (a distance from the new residents) called to ask Sallie's: "Did you sell to the nigger family? You'd better not sell our area to them."
> A less abusive but nonetheless worried neighbor asked: "Just what is going to happen to my property?"
> An instructor at the University queried: "What are you trying to do to our neighborhood?"
> A long-time friend of Webb's told him: "I'll never speak to you again."
> Webb's life was threatened on the telephone.
> After a meeting at the municipal library, a man almost started a fistfight by telling the three realtors: "You're a sorry bunch of people — you're not fit to live in this town."

In May 1973 the agency's listings dropped below an economically sustainable level. Without much fanfare Sallie's Real Estate ceased to exist. It took six years after the bigots had blacklisted it for the agency to go out of business. That was six years too long for their detractors who, in their narrow minds, believed that the owners of Sallie's were traitors. But they were heroes to me. I owed Sally, Sam, and Mokey a debt of gratitude that could never be fully paid. They were the real stars in this historic story, and history matters.

Community relationships are based largely on history. My family had no history as residents in Norman. We were unknown entities. In fact, to an untold number of Norman residents, we were their worst nightmare come true. Doom-and-gloom rumors of immediate declining property values, an increase in the local crime rates, and a mass exodus of white people out of the city preceded our arrival. The negative forecasts caused a sizable number of people to panic. Clearly, their behavior reflected an unbridled fear of Americans who happened to be of African descent. If my family was not the deadly plague, as one of my neighbors described us to his minister, we were certainly God's punishment to him. I was glad there were open-minded residents of Norman who did not share those apocalyptic beliefs. Bald-faced bigots are a distinct minority in today's climate of political correctness, but there was an overabundance of them in the 1960s.

Fortunately, numerous individuals welcomed us to Norman in 1967. Several of them, including many I had met during my job interview, were more than cordial. The most vocal and sincere of our non-neighbor supporters were University of Oklahoma faculty members. As an example, during a coffee break with John "Jack" Renner, professor of education, and me, David Whitney chuckled and said, "I guess the people of Norman now know who *we* invited to dinner—and is going to stay! It's long past time we opened this town and had black homeowners."

"It sure is," Jack agreed. "We've finally joined the ranks of racially open cities."

It was a small opening but significant nevertheless. In terms of numbers, my family was among the largest in Norman. Barbara and I brought our seven children—George Jr., Michele Alicia, Lea Ann, Faith Elaine, Joy Lynne, Lisa Gaye, and Dawn Noel—and her mother, Ora Beard, to Norman with us. To bigots, we became the black community of Norman.

What some people might have called small courtesies were extended to members of my family and me. To us, however, they were grand gestures. As an illustration, Loree Schwartz was the first neighbor to welcome us. Her fruit-and-candy gift basket was chock-full of tasty snacks. Another example occurred in 1968. My daughters attended a tea party at the University's Boyd House, the president's residence. Cleo Cross, their hostess, fed the girls and allowed them to play with dolls and toys that belonged to her daughter, Mary-Lynn. The tea party was a highlight of our daughters' summer. To them, it was like getting a Christmas present in July. We received more unexpected good news when Dr. Mary Abbott, one of the most highly respected and sought-out physicians in Norman, volunteered to be our children's pediatrician.

Several other people, especially civic leaders and University personnel, invited us into their homes. Barbara and I attended more dinner parties during our first three years in Norman than we had during any three years in Detroit. The number of dinners that we were invited to grew quickly and exponentially. It became clear to us that we would either eat our way into social acceptance or we would become the best-fed wannabes in the history of Norman. Luckily, our weights held constant as the number of our friends increased.

One dinner party in particular stands out in my mind. David and Carol Burr, our congenial hosts, arranged for us to dine with Bud Wilkinson, the University's renowned football coach. I was as much intrigued by Coach Wilkinson's reputation of being a nice person as I was impressed with his stellar coaching record. I asked him why he had allowed Prentice Gautt to join the team as a walk-on and become the school's first black scholarship player. His answer surprised me. "I didn't allow Prentice to do anything," he said. "He earned everything he got. It was obvious to me a little later than it was to most of the white players on the team that Prentice was not only a gifted athlete but he was also a fine person. It was a simple decision for me. I wanted to win games and Prentice could help our team to win."

That was a remarkably revealing answer. I wasn't ready to stop probing. "Surely there were some football boosters and other people who didn't want you to break the color barrier."

He nodded.

"What changed your mind?"

He seemed to relish the opportunity to tell me the rest of the story. "Prentice changed my mind," he declared. "He dominated his competition on our practice field. A couple of the players came to me and said that our team would be greatly improved with Prentice in the starting lineup. They said that winning games would mean more to our fans than them watching Prentice sit on the bench. And then they scored their final points by reminding me that any athlete who would give us a better chance to beat the University of Texas was certainly worth playing."

We both laughed. After a brief silence, he said, "Segregation is a politician's game and I always believed that it was a fool's game. Any white coach with half a brain who had seen talented Negro boys play in segregated games was either blind or a hopeless bigot or a liar if he said that they weren't as good as the white boys he could only play because of laws that kept Negroes out of white schools. I suppose that if I had compiled a less acceptable win-loss record when Prentice played for me, we would not be having this conversation. I would have been fired. Prentice made me look very good in the eyes of football fans who, in their minds, lived their fantasy lives running up and down the field scoring and blocking with him."

Coach Wilkinson's honesty and sense of fair play were refreshing. Uneasy with the focus on himself, Bud commented that he was glad that I had joined the faculty. Then he deftly punted the conversation to me: "How in the world did you and Barbara get up enough nerve to buy a home in Norman? I have been eagerly looking forward to talking with you."

I told him why I decided to come to Oklahoma. We talked for almost two more hours. That was one hour more than Barbara and I had planned to stay at the Burrs' house, and it was much longer than Bud had planned to stay. Only an early flight out of town the next morning caused a reluctant Bud Wilkinson to end our conversation. It was a good evening for Barbara and me. We had spent uninterrupted time with a University of Oklahoma legend, and, equally important, we spent time with David and Carol Burr. The dinner was an omen of other good things to come.

Layer after layer of Norman society was peeled back so that Barbara and I might be enclosed within it. Each intimate dinner was filled with inquisitive people who were tactfully probing for our personal beliefs, values, and goals. They all seemed to be trying to discreetly find out if Barbara and I would be good additions to their in-groups or if we were misfits they would have to jettison as quickly as we were granted an audition. Most of them decided that we were acceptable. Barbara and I gradually became members of several previously all-white cliques and groups. Although we became bona fide black tokens in a white society, we did not take pleasure in that exclusive status. We made it clear to our new friends that we hoped other minorities would become members too. That probably made us seem like ingrates to some people or arrogant to others. That was not our intention. We wanted to encourage integration.

While Barbara and I were making our rounds on the social circuit, our school-age children were adjusting to being students in the University's laboratory school, on the North Campus near the Norman Airport. "Uni," as it was commonly called, was housed in decrepit World War II wooden barracks. The saying "Don't judge a book by its cover" certainly applied to that little school, which was spearheaded by Professor Jack Renner. Its wonderful mixture of multicultural students were taught by some of the most dedicated, talented teachers in Oklahoma. Modeled after John Dewey's discovery-learning concepts, Uni was a pedagogical marvel. Real learning took place there, fostering civility, creativity, and academic excellence. A bonus was that my children were, for the most part, spared the racial hostilities that characterized the Norman public schools.

During the darkest, most contentious times of our residency, strangers reached across the community's enormous racial divide to make us feel wanted. Without those people we would not have been able to survive the bitterness surrounding our arrival. Even so, none of their friendly acts could wash away completely the horror of receiving obscene and threatening telephone calls, garbage and a makeshift cross thrown on our front yard, raw eggs splattered on our cars, and epithets yelled at us by strangers in cars speeding past our house. Also, police officers stopped me a couple of times at night and asked me why I was in the neighborhood. That was not unique to me, however. Blacks who rented apartments or houses in Norman were given similar hostile treatment.

Most of the black students who did not live in University housing rented property near the campus or in east Norman. That was not accidental. Because the vast majority of the high-status people lived in west Norman, sellers, landlords, and real estate brokers conspired to restrict black renters to east Norman. Therefore my family's presence in west Norman was a huge irritant to a lot of people. Our detractors' behavior probably reflected how the majority of the white people in Norman defined black people in general. Invectives uttered by whites were showered on blacks as though we were aliens from a another planet. As a whole, we were denied most community privileges such as housing, employment, social clubs, and courteous treatment in public stores and restaurants. So we created our own self-contained enclaves, and we went to Oklahoma City for the social and religious services that we could not duplicate in Norman.

Barbara and I let the students use our house as a refuge, a home away from home. Announced or unannounced, they came to cook meals or just to be with a black resident family in a predominantly white town. A few of them dropped by to spend time with Barbara's mother, whom they called "Grandma." Several of the undergraduates—mainly those who came from large families—stopped by to play with our youngest children, whom they considered to be their adopted sisters. But the treat the students all seemed to enjoy the most was Barbara's and her mother's home cooking. None of the students were strangers once they stepped inside our door. They became members of our extended family.

With no white barbers or beauticians willing or wanting to cut or style their hair, the black students found barbers and hairdressers within their own subcommunity or in Oklahoma City. The same thing pertained to dining out. Undeterred by the limited access they had to public dining places, the students cooked their own lavish meals and held their own weekend parties. They dined out in each other's houses and apartments. Consequently, most of them, especially the undergraduates, had a flourishing social life. They studied hard and played hard. House and apartment parties substituted for white fraternity and sorority parties; pickup games took the place of University intramural contests; and friends became day care providers.

On November 1, 1967, *Oklahoma Daily* editor Hanay Geiogamah made a rare comment pertaining to racial discrimination against mixed couples or groups in restaurants: "Discrimination in a university city such as Norman? Hard to believe as it is, it is nonetheless true. . . . It is disheartening to learn that members of non-Caucasian races are barred from a restaurant because they are in the 'mixed' company of a Caucasian. . . . In this sense the reported discrimination around Campus Corner is morally without foundation because it is inconsistent, and this inconsistency is quite probably a worse sin than the actual hard core discrimination."

A cursory review of *Oklahoma Daily* editorials that were published before Geiogamah's uncovered only a handful that focused on discrimination of any kind. Racism was an abhorrent truth that most people in the University and the residents of Norman chose to ignore in public. The punishment for talking about it was meted out through silence, stares, glares, chiding, or ostracism. Such punishments were extremely hurtful experiences for longtime Norman residents. It was more accept-able to publicly flaunt one's political or philosophical sentiments than one's antiracism beliefs. The comfort levels of Norman's white citizens seemed to be highest when conversation centered on sports, clothing trends, parties, local politics, and beauty contests.

After the 1950s, few mass meetings to discuss racial equality were held as they had been earlier, but some white people in Norman were well-read on racial issues. In 1967, for example, local bookstores sold a large num-ber of books on race relations, including new releases by George Breit-man, Stokely Carmichael and Charles V. Hamilton, Harold Cruse, Martin Luther King, Jr., and Carl Oglesby and Richard Shaull.[2] Although the intellectual pot was stirred, there were only a few open forums, mainly at the University, in which the implications of the books were discussed.

The paucity of public dialogue on race relations was not in keeping with Norman's late 1940s and 1950s history, however. Plenty of debates in those days centered on racial desegregation, including the U.S. Supreme Court cases *Sipuel v. Board of Regents of the University of Oklahoma* (1948) and *McLaurin v. Oklahoma State Board of Regents for Higher Education* (1950). George W. McLaurin was the first black student admitted to the University of Oklahoma; Ada Lois Sipuel Fisher was the school's first black law school student. Their cases were among the U.S. Supreme Court decisions that required historically white colleges and universities to provide the same treatment to black students that they gave to white students. Clearly, discriminatory treatment of blacks enrolled in the University violated the spirit and the letter of the Court's rulings.

Most people in Norman and in the University could not move inter-racially in any direction they chose. They lived in parallel communities, one white and one black, where tightly drawn informal racial boundaries greatly restricted their contact. Therefore the University and the city of Norman took on qualities of something regrettable that seemed to mirror a surreal novel or a dark play. The absence of black neighbors and em-ployees was Norman's hallmark. When I moved there, the self-proclaimed liberals bragged about the progress of race relations as much as they fretted about its slow pace. And they were disheartened by large-scale anti-black sentiments that were common throughout Oklahoma. From my perspective, this was a challenging situation by any measurable standard.

Humaneness itself at times seemed to have been under assault as more and more people in and outside the University were too willing to abandon racial rapprochement in favor of social isolation. Besides, tough times had befallen University and community leaders who wore the imaginary racial integration label. That racial segregation existed is not the major point I want to make. That most white people did not accept blacks as equals was the bigger tragedy. Still, the majority of blacks believed in Martin Luther King, Jr.'s dream of one nation characterized by liberty and justice for all of its citizens. It was a dream of happiness.

Peace, equality, and serenity did not come to my mind, though, after I became accustomed to Oklahoma. The Civil War was more like it. Hundreds of thousands of men fought and died in that war to free Africans from slavery. Some of those former slaves and their offspring migrated to Oklahoma and were denied freedom there. In the 1960s, only foolish people would have bet that blacks would in the long run be accepted as equals by a substantial number of white people in communities like Norman. It was the kind of bet that bookmakers would have gladly taken, and they would have seldom lost. When I signed my contract and moved to Norman, I had figuratively placed a long-shot bet on the city of Norman and the University of Oklahoma. Was I a foolish person? Leonard Moss had thought so. I was hell-bent on proving him wrong.

Black Hope or Hype?

Hidden deep beneath chamber of commerce propaganda featuring friendly white Oklahomans were disillusionment and rage among countless black citizens who had reached out in vain for their friendship. When blacks tried to get better housing, a better quality of education, and worthwhile employment, precious few white people helped them. Even so, except for the Tulsa race riot in 1921, there were no major incidents of black Oklahomans engaging in race riots, not even in self-defense. A plausible explanation for this circumstance is that people who made up distinct racial minorities, such as blacks in Oklahoma, had been conditioned through majority-group abuse to suffer quietly and to be nonviolent during interracial conflicts. In those instances, discretion was more than the better part of valor. It was a matter of survival.

Most black citizens did not have to be constantly told how to behave. They seldom liked the situation, but they knew their socially assigned places. More than enough stories about beatings, even a few killings, of uppity blacks had been passed down from one generation to the next. In the early days, sadistic whites were creatively cruel when punishing blacks, and blacks devised imaginative nonviolent ways to defy their white oppressors. Yet whatever separated them — race, slavery, social class — I believe that black and white Oklahomans were bound tightly together in at least one important way: they needed each other to justify their own self-righteous indignation about being thought of as modern-day *Grapes of Wrath* characters. That idea, of course, is a matter of opinion. In any case, they did not want to become irrelevant as human beings. If I had not looked more closely at that drama, I would not have seen or fully appreciated the outstanding black people who were too often hidden in the shadows of bigots.

As it happened, several of those black people found me, rather than vice versa. At various formal and informal gatherings, black citizens throughout Oklahoma introduced themselves to me and graciously reached out to members of my family as though we were longtime Oklahoma residents. The first people to do that lived in the greater Oklahoma City area. Being ignorant of Oklahoma black history at the time, I did not know that several of them were among the most prominent citizens in our nation. They included civic club members and politicians Dr. Charles N. Atkins and Hannah D. Atkins; Urban League board member Dr. Frank B. Cox; Dr. A. L. Dowell, plaintiff in the federal lawsuit that led to the desegregation of the Oklahoma City Public Schools; Ada Lois Sipuel Fisher, plaintiff in the federal lawsuit that forced the University of Oklahoma to admit blacks to its law school; attorney John E. Green, the second African American to graduate from the OU Law School; civic club leaders and state education committee members Ira D. Hall and Rubye M. Hall, the first African American to earn a master's degree in speech pathology at the University of Oklahoma; religious and civil rights leader Reverend W. K. Jackson; public school teacher and administrator Sylvia A. Lewis; Clara S. Luper, a public school teacher and the leader of the first civil

Clara Luper addresses Henderson class about black-white relations, 1968. Western History Collections, University of Oklahoma Libraries.

rights sit-in in Oklahoma; renowned Oklahoma public school administrator F. D. Moon; Russell M. Perry, copublisher of the *Black Dispatch*; and Jimmy Stewart, president of the Oklahoma City branch of the NAACP. Through their innumerable and astounding accomplishments, they gave human faces and voices to the amorphous black people in Oklahoma who were usually relegated to abstractions in news media stories. Each of my new friends welcomed me and my family and wished only the best for me at the University of Oklahoma.

When they told me that they expected great things from me, I thought they were referring to my teaching accomplishments only. Rubye Hall set me straight. She laid out their expectations quite explicitly in October 1967 after my presentation at a meeting of the Oklahoma Federation of Colored Women's Clubs: "We Negroes in Oklahoma City are counting on you to help the Negro students at the University of Oklahoma, my alma mater, to improve things for themselves and their friends down there. . . .

And when you get some extra time, we have a few projects in Oklahoma City and throughout the state that we want you to help us with too."

"Wow," I said to myself while driving back to Norman. A lot of fine people who didn't know me very well had extremely high hopes for me — their anointed black warrior at the University of Oklahoma. I was honored, pleased, and afraid of the challenge in equal measure — at times simultaneously. What if I did not live up to their expectations? It seemed that nothing raised hope higher or dashed it more quickly among black Oklahomans than a new black professor at one of the state's historically white colleges or universities. Reputations were made or destroyed there. The careers of errant black professors who did not quickly live up to the abilities others imagined them to possess were often tarnished and buried before they even had a chance to develop. And those professors lost their right to speak as representatives of Oklahoma black people. I did not want to be one of those academic casualties, but I did not want to refuse the challenge either. So I told all of my well-wishers that I needed their support, patience, and counsel. They gave me all of those things — and more. They gave me courage.

Describing in great detail several of his civil rights experiences, Jimmy Stewart cautioned me to not be discouraged when my small victories melted away into bitter losses. "That's what happens in Oklahoma race relations," he said. "We win some battles and lose some. But we never give up." Then he added for good measure, "We've got your back, Doc." Sure enough, on many different occasions he and the others intervened to quash efforts within and outside the black community to write me off as black carpetbagger.

With friends like Jimmy Stewart, Clara Luper, and the others, I was ready to be a linchpin in our pursuit of whatever changes we could make in higher education and the community of Norman. With my eyes and mind opened wider, I allowed myself to be drafted and pushed and pulled deep into the Oklahoma civil rights waters that my new friends had been swimming in for many years. My challenge, as I imagined it, was to endure situations that would probably be laced with slivers of facts and tons of presumptions — situations in which truths would frequently become casualties of lies. Jimmy told me how hard it had been for him to become accepted as a fair-minded civil rights leader by most white people, who read distorted newspaper stories about him. Those individuals preferred to believe the undocumented negative portions of the stories and discount the positive documented portions.

It occurred to me that I might destroy myself in trying to achieve the expectations that other people had for me — not literally of course, but the thought was unsettling nevertheless. Soon, though, I would revel in the audacity of my commitment to help improve race relations in Oklahoma, and I would grin at the individuals lying in wait to thwart me. My University and community activist life in Oklahoma began almost from the moment I arrived in Norman. I received too many requests for my involvement in various projects and too little time for planning. I have never been very good at saying no to requests for me to participate in programs concerning racial issues. During my first year in Oklahoma, I gave speeches at thirty public meetings, conferences, and workshops.

Through those diverse activities, I was able to firmly establish my professional credentials as a teacher and a community activist, to hone my presentation skills, and to become a plausible spokesperson for some black groups. My community activist reputation throughout Oklahoma began rather innocently in 1967. Five of my colleagues in the College of Education invited me to attend an annual statewide continuing education conference for public schools teachers and administrators that was held at our university. The four featured speakers were faculty members from the academic disciplines of education, philosophy, sociology, and psychology. I gladly accepted the invitation because the theme of the conference was "Educating Urban School Children."

Initially I felt like an interloper among the more than three hundred participants. But warm greetings from a dozen or so black teachers erased any doubts I had about being accepted. I was smack in the middle of waves of multiracial educators who obviously were well acquainted with each other. As one of them told me, the conference was an excellent place to get new information, occasional inspiration, continuing education credits, and a small stipend — not necessarily in that order. But a lot more than that was going on there.

When the plenary session began, I made my way up the stairs to an amphitheater-like room and found a vacant seat in the last row. As the all-white panelists described several cultural problems confronting black children, I became increasingly irritated by what I thought were a dozen overgeneralizations and two outright false statements. My discomfort peaked as the final presenter, who was also the moderator, summarized the most salient points that had been made. Then he opened the session for comments and questions. Four members of the audience praised the speakers for their insightful presentations. At that moment, I broke a promise to myself to keep quiet. I raised my hand to speak.

"I disagree with a couple of statements made by all of you," I said in an irritated voice. The room fell deadly silent. Most people in the audience were in disbelief that anyone, let alone a total stranger, would disagree with the eminent panelists.

The moderator asked me, "What specifically do you take issue with, sir?"

"First," I began in a calm voice, "low-income or inner-city children don't have a problem giving birth to children out of wedlock. Their major problem is that they don't get married, or don't wait to get married, before becoming parents."

A smattering of mummers ensued, and a very audible "Right on!" came from one of the black teachers. Suddenly the lecture hall was abuzz with side conversations. The moderator quickly regained control by asking me, "And what is your second point of disagreement?"

"Second, I take serious issue with calling children born out of wedlock 'illegitimate.' Every child that I know or have heard of has a mother and a father. That, in my estimation, makes them legitimate. If we must label someone, let's call the parents 'illegal.' The children in these situations have enough to overcome without being publicly stigmatized through our labels of them."

A visibly shaken white participant, sitting in the seat directly in front of me, turned around to face me and, without giving the moderator a chance to respond, asked me who I was and why I was at the conference. When I answered his questions, he was still not satisfied. Agitated, he asked me again, much more loudly, "Why are you *really* here?"

In a serious voice and with a contrived otherworldly look, I said, "Before I left Detroit to accept a position here at the University of Oklahoma, I attended a national meeting of black people. We divided up the United States and I got Oklahoma. I'm here to take care of my people." The forum room burst into laughter and applause. But several of the white participants were not sure that I was joking. News of my arrival at the University spread quickly. I had become an overnight attraction, at best, or a subversive, at worst. I overheard a black teacher at the conference describe me to a white friend: "There's a new Negro sheriff in town."

The University Community

Shortly after I began teaching in August 1967, a group of black students asked me what I was going to do about "our situation." They rattled off some shocking data regarding the Norman campus: relatively few black students were enrolled at the University, there were no black administrators or coaches, and only ten or so blacks were employed there, as extension specialists and in lesser staff positions. Guinnevere Hodges, a sophomore, said to me, "Welcome to our plantation, Dr. Henderson."

The black students were well aware of their places, and most of them were careful not to step out of them. Dick Hilbert told me during my job interview that the University's black students as a whole were not very assertive. Once I became acquainted with most of them, I recognized something very familiar about them. They were similar to other black collegians I knew at historically white colleges and universities: they were disillusioned with their isolated lives; and they yearned for much more inclusion in campus and community life. The University of Oklahoma and the city of Norman had become airtight cages with only very limited social and educational opportunities available to them.

The first campus-related research that I conducted was to determine the extent of the black students' involvement in University activities. There were fewer than one hundred black students enrolled at the Norman campus in 1967; approximately 12 percent of them were graduate students. Only a small number of blacks were involved in the University's academic, social, and athletic programs. Blacks who were not involved were conspicuous by their absence—constantly and intentionally left out. Of special notice to me was the paucity of black females in University organizations. It was impossible for anyone to put a good spin on the situation. As a whole, the black students were, except for the athletes, the kind of people W. E. B. Du Bois and Ralph Ellison might have called "invisible men and women." At the intersection of campus-wide procedures and pronouncements designed to enfranchise all students were a substantial number of left-out ethnic minorities.

At our first University of Oklahoma football game, in 1967, Barbara and I got a shocking dose of racial insensitivity disguised as friendship and fairness. The Sooners were playing Washington State University. It was a toughly fought contest with lots of jarring blows. During a key third-down play, a Washington State player slipped past the line of scrimmage and blindsided Granville Liggins, our star noseguard. The hit delivered to Liggins could be heard up in the stands where I was sitting. An irate white fan leaped to his feet, flailed his arms, and shouted, "Ref, stop that nigger from hurting our colored boy. Give him a penalty for unnecessary roughness."

The people around him cheered. Stunned, I turned and stared at the overexcited University of Oklahoma fan. He smiled at me and flashed a thumbs-up gesture, signaling to me that he had come to our player's defense. He either didn't understand the gravity of his comments or he didn't care. He had publicly insulted Barbara, Granville, the Washington State player, and me during his intemperate outburst. We won the game 21–0, but he lost my respect 4–0.

Infrequent newspaper stories about blacks in non-sports activities were boring to uninterested white readers who believed that black scholars got exactly what they deserved: very little recognition. Those people missed the deeper meaning of the omissions. It was amazing to me that so many blacks at the University were able to endure the slights and achieve as much as they did. For most of them, though, their college lives were a series of emotional obstacle courses that they barely cleared, with discomfort inherent in each hurdle. This is not to say that every achievement was a struggle; it only seemed to be. An untold number of the high achievers were able to move on to other challenges instead of sitting comfortably on the edge of their successes. Even so, racial bigotry decimated the ranks of the students. Although official statistics were not kept by racial or ethnic identity, several administrators told me that the attrition rate was highest for black sophomores at the University—hovering, depending on the speculator, at around 50 to 60 percent. They were an academic endangered species. But that was only a part of the picture.

Minority-group staff members told me that they, too, had watched their campus situations slide from benign neglect to just plain neglect. Their complaints to the appropriate administrators were usually dismissed as unfounded, a response that obviously destabilized whatever sense of inclusion the staff members might have had. For many of those individuals, unfortunately, the tension between hope to be accepted and despair at being rejected had long ago faded. Now only despair remained. Like injured passengers in a wrecked vehicle on a crowded highway, they waited for someone, anyone, to rescue them. After hearing their stories, I knew for sure that I would try to help as many of them as I could.

Acknowledging Our Common Bond

Once the black students, more so than the black staff members, became aware of my presence, their rekindled hope for better University outcomes seemed to be everywhere among them. But not all of the students readily accepted me. The cautious ones had every right to be leery of me, the new black hope. In the past, glimmers of improved University race relations had been initiated by faculty members who recommended black students for scholarships and jobs, and extinguished by administrators almost as fast as they were recommended. Those mishaps, too painful for black students to rehash in conversations with me, were precisely what had to be aired and resolved if the students were ever going to have closure. Whenever I broached the subject of past failures, most of the students spent little time on them, as though they had forgotten what happened. They withheld information in order to move forward, not backward, in their perspective. They had dug deep subconscious holes in which they buried those unpleasant memories.

As members of the University community waffled between extremes of civility and incivility, the tangled web of academic freedom and racial segregation and discrimination exposed the frayed edges of black-white social relationships. It was an all too familiar scenario. Still, it startled me. Although blacks and whites shared the same geography and the same academic curriculums, the sense of being equal members of the same community had not been achieved. It seemed at times that concerned people could only lament their missed opportunities to unite. Weary students occasionally spoke out on behalf of other members of their respective ethnic groups. With each passed-up opportunity to connect, they burrowed deeper into their separate subcultures. They had grown tired of playing hide-and-seek and seldom finding each other, and they stopped trying. That said, this was hardly the time for me to abandon them. I felt a need to become even more involved with those students, but I did not want to be off-putting.

Despite our age differences, scores of alienated black students realized that we lived parallel lives. I had been educated in a historically white college and a historically white university, so I understood clearly the agony of being a black student in the University of Oklahoma. Inventive black students, and white ones too, found ways to make meaningful connections with me. I became a surrogate father, uncle, brother, cousin, friend—whatever they needed at the time. These interactions conveyed something important pertaining to them, such as what they would like to do or become. My experiences were all there for other people to learn from. With a dash of hope and a lot of wishful thinking, several of the students saw me as one of their faculty champions.

Jockeying for public support for racial integration on the crowded stage of public opinion was tricky business. I remember telling several disgruntled students, "Like it or not, as long as we were here, we're all we've got—black and white together." I shuddered to think what would happen if we did not find ways to cease being separate and distinct subcommunities. Along the way to change, I surmised, there would be numerous complex interactions between our cultural beliefs and behavior. To make our community gel, we would have to avoid as many hurtful actions and cruel words as we could.

One common trait that we all seemed to have was the uncanny ability to misunderstand each other—to extract animosity out of incomplete sentences, and to dismiss as insincere any questions involving each other's complicity in the campus-wide malaise that some of us attributed to racism. Because race and oppression had been inextricably entwined for what to me seemed like forever, it further seemed to me that it might take that long to unravel them. That raised serious questions in my mind about the importance of democracy at the University of Oklahoma. It was a sad commentary about our school that so many people lived at the outer edge of equality. Almost all of the black people—and a significantly smaller proportion of white students, faculty, and staff—were fed up with bigotry coated over with insincere niceties. Nonetheless, as flimsy as they were, niceties were often the only pseudo-common ground on which we could all stand.

Barbara and I were among the very few blacks in Norman who crossed racial divides and got to know intimately people from other racial groups. Therefore only a few of us enjoyed the pleasures of interracial friendships. Individuals who did not cross the divide offered various reasons for the sorry state of the University's race relations. Predictably, seldom were the reasons self-incriminating. Blame was conveniently passed to foes and friends alike. In campus conversations that focused on race relations, castigation was more likely than praise. Most of the discussants demeaned themselves while trying to devalue other people. For those and other reasons, successful diversity initiatives had generally eluded the University community. This was especially true in terms of black-white relations.

I realized early on that it would not be easy for those of us who wanted to get the University to be more responsive to black people's inclusion issues. A breakthrough came the last two weeks in October 1967. Mixed in with sensational *Oklahoma Daily* stories about trivial things were three announcements concerning racial issues: I gave a speech titled "The History of the Negro in America" at a United Christian Fellowship meeting in Oklahoma City. At the Weekend University program, civil rights worker Vernon E. Jordan, Jr., College of Law assistant dean Robert L. Richardson, and I discussed "The Negro Revolution: Civil Rights or Civil Strife?" The most important of the three announcements was that the first official meeting of the Afro-American Student Union was scheduled for November 28, 1967.

As I prepared to leave my office for the Thanksgiving holiday break, Lynn Lester, a white senior, stopped by and said, "I'm glad you're here. If I can do anything to help you, let me know."

I had been thinking about black students, and a white student was thinking about me. What an irony! A voice within me said that I was going to get a lot of help from people like Lynn. Yes, there was plenty for me to like about Oklahoma. The words of a Bob Dylan song seemed very appropriate at that moment: "The times they are a-changin'."

As bleak as some aspects of the University were, I thought that it was the most progressive higher education institution in Oklahoma. But an untold number of people throughout the state did not share that view. They believed that the University was a modern version of Sodom and Gomorrah. At the very least, they firmly believed that it was unquestionably a sinful place where too many bad things, such as excessive parties and fornication, happened.

During one of my classroom discussions that focused on students' perceptions of community norms, a discontented white coed who was in the process of transferring to another university, said, "This school is the only place I know that has such a large number of weirdoes [a code term for hippies, feminists, and radical minorities]. They don't even hide their blasphemy. Worst yet, they're egged on by so-called liberal teachers and administrators." She was looking directly at me, and she did not blink an eye. I did not think of the University as a safe haven for weirdoes. Her observation took me aback. Nor did I did think of myself or other people similar to me as being blasphemers. Iconoclasts, yes, but not blasphemers. I wanted to believe that she was not representative of most other Oklahomans.

Robin Cook, a student in the course, challenged me to open my eyes and mind wider: "Spend a little time on the South Oval during a weekend and watch the people in the cars that drive by." I was so busy looking inward at myself that I had not spent much time looking outward at the campus.

Nothing could have adequately prepared me for what I saw on a Sunday afternoon. Cars full of adults and small children drove slowly past the short stretch of property adjacent to the Lindsey Street boundary of the University's South Oval. Some of the children in the cars that I could see clearly had pressed their faces to the windows as they stared at and pointed to long-haired white coeds and bearded white male students dressed like poor sharecroppers. They were sitting on the grass playing with animals or catching Frisbees or chasing after each other. Another group of students was composed of African Americans who were sprawled in a semicircle, listening to music and eating food. The two discrete groups seemed to be unaware of each other. The gawking visitors were looking at what to them might have been the equivalent of a very small zoo. A couple of the children threw bananas at my feet. I guess they thought that I, too, was one of the animals in their imaginary zoo.

The North and South Ovals would acquire very different associations for me than that of a child's fantasy menagerie. They would become places where people gathered to inaugurate a president, mourn the deaths of their slain heroes, and protest a myriad of conditions at the University and in the larger society. Indeed, the temporary platforms erected on the Ovals for speakers would become the stages upon which I would strut and fret before large crowds. In subsequent months, I would deliver some of my most effective and ineffective speeches there. During the process, I would become a visibly active member of the University of Oklahoma community. Nothing happened in later years to persuade me to change my mind concerning the potential for successful interventions in the University and in Norman. If the right people — I hoped I was one of them — used the right tactics, good things could happen.

CHAPTER TWO

Lessons for Rebels

The seed for my commitment to community activism had been planted before I moved to Oklahoma—at a lecture on cultural anthropology at Wayne State University in 1963. I don't remember the name of the professor, but I will always remember the substance of his talk. He had just returned to the United States from a field study in the "bush," as he called the remote African site. My doctoral classmates and I were enthralled by his description of the behavior of an indigenous African people. He told us about watching two men guess the gender of an unborn child of a pregnant woman within their vision. The men made a wager. One of them took a machete, cut the woman's stomach open, examined the dead fetus, and collected his winnings. At first I was quietly horrified; I didn't know if he was spoofing us or not. But suddenly I couldn't control myself.

I blurted out, "What did you do?"

My classmates were aghast. We had been told over and over again what the proper protocol was: record our observations; don't get personally involved. The professor glared at me, "What did I do, Mr. Henderson? Unlike what you probably would have done, I did what any good researcher would do. I recorded what had taken place."

I had known then that I was not going to be a good social or behavioral scientist in the traditional sense. The urge within me to take action when human lives were threatened was stronger than the need to record those things as they happened and publish them in refereed journals. I had no interest in being a nonparticipant observer when lives or careers were involved. Perhaps I was a closet "social engineer," or maybe I was a social worker in denial of my vocational leaning. In any case, I felt a strong need to make my cultural values and beliefs transparent through my behavior both inside and outside the classroom.

A Few Years of Seasoning

During the last seven years that I lived in Detroit, I was an active member of several interagency committees and a consultant to two African American grassroots leaders. I have fond memories of serving on those committees, especially the one chaired by Monsignor Clement Kern, pastor of Detroit's Most Holy Trinity Church. The committee's sole purpose was to help Monsignor Kern improve the quality of life for low-income residents of the Corktown area. In return for the coalition members' assistance, Monsignor Kern arranged for us to hear civil rights presentations by activists who worked in other states. One of the guest speakers was the renowned labor organizer César Chávez. His spellbinding speech described effective public protest tactics that had gotten better wages and decent working conditions for itinerant farm laborers.

Jean Washington and Lena Blevins were the grassroots leaders with whom I worked. Jean coordinated property beautification contests for neighborhood block clubs. She also served on a couple of public agency oversight committees. In 1962 Jean invited me to her home to help her and a third person revise the block club beautification contest categories and judging standards. The third person was Rosa Parks, the woman who sparked the 1955 bus boycott in Montgomery, Alabama. After the revisions were made, I chatted with Mrs. Parks about the problems inherent in nonviolence as a tactic to combat racial segregation. When I returned home that night, I could barely wait to tell Barbara about the invigorating conversation I'd had with Mrs. Parks. Barbara gleefully informed me that Jean had introduced her to Mrs. Parks earlier that day. I was Jean's formal consultant; Barbara was her informal consultant.

Lena Blevins was the founder and president of a public housing tenants association. At her request, I accompanied Lena to grievance meetings with public housing officials. It was educational for me to observe her patience, tact, and persistence as she spoke forcefully without wilting. She was able to get faulty elevators replaced, laundry room equipment repaired, and additional streetlights in hazardous locations on the project grounds. The association members wanted their families to live in a clean, safe environment, not the squalor and crime-infested ones that characterized most of the other public housing complexes. As a last resort, Lena and I got assistance from city councilman Mel Ravitz, who was also one of my Wayne State professors, to resolve stalemates.

The interagency committees greatly increased my knowledge of social networking, and being a consultant to the grassroots leaders made me more politically astute and street-smart. My experiences as a community activist improved my teaching, and vice versa. Although I had become a seasoned agent of change in Detroit, there was much more for me to learn, and Oklahoma was an ideal place for me learn some of those lessons.

Before the Afro-American Student Union was formed to combat racism on the University of Oklahoma's Norman campus, many of the black students had already been involved intellectually in what Louis Lomax called the Negro revolt.[1] They had read and debated among themselves numerous seminal protest theorists. A few of the students had been involved in civil rights activities in their hometowns. So, too, had a few of their teachers, including me. Contrary to popular misconceptions, though, we were not blind followers of any single theorist. While searching for relevant strategies, we found relevance in several theorists. Activists at the University of Oklahoma, like activists everywhere, were informed and guided by a series of famous and not-so-famous philosophers and social scientists. Some of their writings taught and inspired me personally, some of their works were assigned reading in my classes, and others were independently read and discussed by some of the black students that I mentored.

Saul Alinsky

In his 1947 manifesto, *Reveille for Radicals*, Saul Alinsky defined a radical as "that person to whom the common good is the greatest social value," and a liberal as a person who "puts his foot down firmly on thin air."[2] Alinsky postulated that a democracy operates on the basis of pressure groups and power blocs. If the poor are not organized into a self-determining mass, he cautioned, they would be effectively excluded from the democratic process. He also asserted that people are not inherently bad, but only morally ambivalent and susceptible to becoming bad through dehumanizing conditions. The hope for humanity, he concluded, depends on people getting to know each other as human beings.

Alinsky's second book, *Rules for Radicals,* was published in 1971. It showed that his love of democracy and his belief in self-determination and power had not changed substantially. The book also explained his rationale and tactics for community renewal. His last years were spent teaching others (mainly the "have-a-little, want-mores") to be radicals who would eventually, he hoped, change the world from what it was to what it could be by organizing the masses of have-nots to take power away from the haves.[3]

As a strategist for the "people's army," Alinsky moved along almost the entire continuum of change tactics, stopping short of physical violence. He took a practical approach to the question of ends and means: ends are what people want and means are how they get them. He approached the selection of a tactic in a situational manner that depended on the characteristics of his adversaries. There were rules for Alinsky-type radicals who wanted to be agents for change. And certain central concepts of action operated regardless of the place or the time.

Alinsky the organizer characterized himself as an architect and an engineer who created a new order from the old. According to him, the essential difference between a leader and an organizer is that leaders want power for themselves, while the organizer's raison d'être lies in securing power for others to use for their own good. Alinsky outlined thirteen rules to be used as weapons against social injustice: (1) Power is not only what you have that can be used against your foes but what they think you have. Make them think that you have more power than you actually do. (2) Use change tactics that your people feel comfortable with. (3) Whenever possible, use tactics that make your adversaries uncomfortable. (4) Make your adversaries live up to their own laws, rules, and procedures. (5) Ridicule is a potent weapon. (6) A good tactic is one that your people enjoy implementing. (7) A tactic that drags on too long becomes a drag. (8) Keep the pressure on with different tactics and actions, carefully selected for particular purposes. (9) A threat is usually more terrifying than the thing itself. But don't threaten something you are not willing to do. (10) Apply constant pressure. (11) Every negative thing has a positive side. (12) Have a well thought-out alternative to the situation or procedure that you are trying to change. (13) Pick a target, freeze it, personalize it, and polarize it.[4]

Our first big test of Alinsky's strategies occurred in fall 1968. Led by Willie Wilson, a team of four black students attended a lecture in an American history course that they were not enrolled in. They had gotten word that the instructor was going to give the obligatory lecture on slavery. If true to form, he would, as had other instructors, point out that not everything was bad for slaves. Midway through the apologist portion of the lecture, Willie stood up and shouted, "Bull crap. There was nothing good about being a slave. What if I enslaved your mother, would she be happy? Would you want my great-grandchildren to tell your children how good life was for her?"

The instructor was speechless. His mouth opened wide, but no words came out. The mere sight of the four black strangers standing at the back of the room intimidated him. Unquestionably, the tactic made the instructor uncomfortable or, more precisely, afraid. Before he could regain control, another black student glowered at him and shouted, "According to OU policy, you should not demean students. Or don't you consider black people students? Oh, I forgot that we are happy darkies."

Feeling sympathy for the instructor and irritated by the interruption of the lecture, a white male student turned to face the interlopers and said in a stern voice, "Leave our class and go somewhere else to create trouble. . . . We paid our money for this class. You didn't."

The other students enrolled in the class, including two black students, were becoming uneasy with the direction in which the confrontation had started to drift. A couple of the white students sided with Willie and his team. Four white coeds left the class. One of them was in tears. The tactic had dragged on too long. One of the black outsiders grabbed Willie's right arm and pulled him toward the door. They left the room, and the people who remained in it were frozen in their places for two or three minutes.

The general consensus of students who piloted a few of Alinsky's rules—use a tactic that your people feel comfortable with, use a tactic that makes your adversary uncomfortable, and ridicule is a potent weapon—

agreed during debriefing that they were partially effective. Nevertheless the confrontation might have been even more effective if the target had been the chairman of the History Department. The instructor was an easy target. In fact, he was too easy and that gave him the aura of a helpless victim, which in turn probably placed the black students in the role of oppressors. At least now the students would be able to factor in some of those things.

As for which of Alinsky's tactics were better for us than the others, it is futile to speculate. Much depended on the situations, the people involved, and the specific community or organization forces. We used all of his tactics at one time or another. The joy of a tactic always came from satisfactory results.

Frantz Fanon

The writings of Frantz Fanon focused on the harsh realities of racism and oppressive tyrants. Central to his thoughts was the belief that conflict — even violent revolution — is the prerequisite for freedom from colonialism. During the last year of his life, Fanon worked furiously to finish his most renowned work, *The Wretched of the Earth*, which earned him the reputation of being a spokesman for millions of colonized peoples. He discussed elaborate theories and strategies for the overthrow of colonial dictators, and the book became a handbook for revolutionaries throughout the world.

The seeds of Fanon's transformation into a theorist of black revolution were sown in *Black Skin, White Masks*, in which he described in detail the frustration, anger, and alienation of black people in a white world.[5] He carefully described the effects of colonization on people who were systematically stripped of their language, culture, and history. Even though he specifically focused on black Algerians who were brainwashed by the French into feeling inferior to them, his observations were relevant to African Americans too. Quoting Aimé Césaire, he said: "I am talking of millions of men who have been skillfully injected with fear, inferiority complexes, trepidation, servility, despair, abasement."[6]

Fanon maintained that black intellectuals ought to provide the initial liberation ideology and cogent rebellion strategies for the rest of the black population during the prerevolutionary period. But all too often they are more concerned with their own assimilation into the colonialist society than leaving it. Therefore they block mass black resistance to white injustice through appeals for nonviolent reform. Furthermore, he cautioned, black intellectuals often attempt to mollify their black brothers and sisters with references to white values and ethics and a constant warning that black people are neither militarily nor politically prepared to successfully resist their oppressors.

Winning independence, Fanon concluded, is not enough to maintain freedom. Black people must be prepared to counter the greed of their own bourgeoisie as well as the maneuvers of their former oppressors to infiltrate their ranks and dominate them again. The goals of the revolution — freedom and equality — will be lost without constant vigilance. For those reasons, Fanon reiterated that the newly freed peoples must turn their backs on status quo goals and create a new order of things; they must turn over a new leaf, work out new concepts, and recreate themselves as new people.

Fanon's books contributed greatly to my own understanding of the psychology of oppression. James "Jim" Todd II and I discussed a few of Fanon's most intriguing ideas during a protracted conversation in 1970. Jim was frustrated by his inability to explain to several of his white classmates the psychology of oppressed black Americans. "Their blank stares and shrugged shoulders speak volumes," he lamented.

Almost at my wits' end, I said rather dismissively, "Louis Armstrong gave a brilliant answer when a puzzled white reporter asked him what jazz was. Do you remember the answer?"

"Yes, I remember what he said. He said that if you have to ask what jazz is, you would never know what it is."

"Will that be a sufficient reply for you to give your classmates?"

"Come on, Doc, get serious."

I was very serious, but Jim wasn't accepting any of my glib retorts that day. So I tried a different tack: "When you strip away Fanon's words and use your own, what would you as a Fanon follower say to those perplexed white folks?"

He carefully weighed his words. "I would tell them that all people, including black Americans, must have dignity and self-respect intact enough to willingly trudge through life. We must be free to encounter our white classmates as equals. When that doesn't happen, we become something less than fully human. We become our society's caged animals. Like any caged animals that want to be free, we will attack you in order to be free. The psychology of oppressed blacks is the psychology of all human animals. We will use any means necessary to have life, liberty, and equality."

It was a good summary, by a gifted speaker.

If Alinsky was our tactician, Fanon was our fire. His books were widely read by black collegians throughout the United States. It was not a far stretch for most of the black students at the University of Oklahoma to identify with the colonized people of Africa that Fanon so desperately wanted to be equal to their white oppressors. Furthermore, blacks at the University were aware that a violent revolution in Oklahoma during the 1960s and 1970s would probably have caused a catastrophic white backlash. That had happened during the 1921 race riot in Tulsa. So we opted to focus on Fanon's strategies for achieving black solidarity and positive self-images. There was little attraction among blacks on our campus for a violent revolution. Compromise and conciliation were, contrary to Fanon's strategy, more appealing to us. In truth, most of the black students and I were prisoners of our own bourgeoisie desire to get, not destroy, white privileges.

Malcolm X

Malcolm X became a persuasive teacher and organizer for the Nation of Islam and later established the nonsectarian, politically oriented Organization of Afro-American Unity, a foundation for an Afro-American revolt in America. His strategies evolved from his wealth of street-life experiences and from a firm historical base; his tactics were those of unification among the black people of America and with the peoples of the Third World; his goal was the liberation of black people in America and of all humanity oppressed by white colonialism and capitalism. His policies of enlightenment and mobilization of a united organization of Afro-Americans provided the blueprint for the first stage in the 1960s black revolution.

Malcolm X held fast to his belief in racial separatism and advocated the removal of African Americans to Africa far in the future. Before we return home to Africa, he said, we have to relieve ourselves of unemployment, poor schools, dilapidated housing, and unhealthy food. Calling upon the black community to unify, he prodded black leaders to forget their petty organizational differences and antagonisms. Anticipating the question of white support, he stated that while blacks could accept ideas and financial support from whites, they ought not let whites join their civil rights organizations, for there could be no black-white unity until there was black unity.[7]

In the final few months of his life, from June 1964 to February 1965, Malcolm X was greatly influenced by his trips to Africa and the Middle East. During that time, he shifted from the idea of a black revolution that focused solely on fighting racial injustice in the United States to one in which black Americans joined with Third World peoples. Together they would conquer racial bigotry, which he believed was mainly perpetrated by American and European powers.[8] From this perspective, he saw the human rights battle as one designed to encompass global human liberation. He broadened his definition of brotherhood by specifying that even white radicals could be allowed to join in the black revolution, as long as they were truly revolutionary and were willing to do whatever was called for in the fight for freedom. But he was adamant that they must follow the leadership of American black people.

The last phase of the black revolution would consist of true black unity throughout the world. This final goal would require the alliance of black Americans and the peoples of Africa, Asia, and Latin America. Thus Malcolm X's endgame in the war against racism was very similar to Fanon's. Whether they were colonized or not, most black people throughout the world were oppressed. Like Fanon, Malcolm X defined the superordinate goal of the black revolution as the liberation of all humanity.

At the University of Oklahoma, we learned to make sense of Malcolm X's initial repudiation of white people and his later shift to building alliances with some of them. A few of us were already doing that. It became evident to me that racial separatism might not be beneficial even at historically black colleges and universities. It certainly would not serve blacks well in places like the University of Oklahoma. For those reasons, I helped establish black-white coalitions in the University. We applied Malcolm's concepts of self-determination and self-pride within our own black enclaves, with an ultimate goal of leveraging our human resources to achieve racial equality.

When I lived in Detroit, I became friends with several Black Muslims, including Malcolm X. They tried to convince me to join their movement. Malcolm was more direct: "If we are to have a successful black revolution, we must have the black intellectuals with us." He was absolutely correct, but I had already cast my lot with Martin Luther King, Jr. For better, and sometimes worse, I embraced racial integration. It seemed like a good idea at the time. In another life or another time, I might have been a Black Muslim.

As a compromise, I told Malcolm that I would never do anything to hurt him. He looked into my eyes and said, "Fair enough, Brother Henderson. I won't have to watch my back when I'm around you." Nor did I have to watch my back when I was around him and other Black Muslims.

When the black students at the University of Oklahoma reached out to get a few white allies, it was not a contentious issue among most of them. Both Dr. King and Malcolm X advocated it. Especially during tough times, when the black students closed ranks, it was logical for them — with encouragement from crossover people like me — to reach out to potential white allies for support.

Martin Luther King, Jr., made eloquent arguments for racial integration, but he presented very few carefully thought-out plans or guidelines. Conversely, Malcolm X outlined a logical course for survival within all-black communities, but he did not focus on black-white coalitions. Although most of us wanted racial integration, only a few of us were able to achieve it. Sadly, from my perspective, segregation was not just an intermediate step for most blacks and whites at our university; it was the only viable step available to them.

Mohandas K. (Mahatma) Gandhi

Although Gandhi's principle of constructive conflict was symbolic in its purpose, he believed that it could become fully actualized in practice. Over a long period of time he used the revolutionary techniques of confrontation — strikes, boycotts, fasts, and other forms of civil disobedience — to bring about change in South Africa and India. With regard to social change, writers who identify Gandhi's nonviolent movement use two terms: "satyagraha" (soul force) and "passive resistance."[9] He preferred "satyagraha," but "passive resistance" became the widely accepted term.

Jesus' life provided an example for Gandhi to follow. He said several times that the New Testament had "awakened him to the rightness and value of Passive Resistance."[10] The dominant theme in his life became "Overcome evil with good," or, stated another way, "Turn the other cheek," or, yet another, "Love your enemy." He came to believe that the use of force was incompatible with love. As C. F. Andrews, a close friend of Gandhi's, put it, "The secret of Gandhi was this: he was the first to organize corporate moral resistance, and to obtain . . . through rigid discipline, a firmly united community ready to go to any lengths of suffering as a body for the sake of conscience."[11]

The means of achieving an end became the all-important thing to Gandhi. He did not want to use the wrong means to get the right ends, for he believed that the means preexist and determine the ends. He taught his followers to combat injustice and ruthless people through propaganda and constructive work. He also encouraged them to appeal to potential allies' concern for justice and their own welfare rather than to their fears, greed, or hatred. In his view, propaganda ought to be designed to arouse and maintain resistance to cruelty, and to confront our oppressors with the relative truths on which our demands are based. Propaganda was therefore an essential aspect of satyagraha.

Several students and I culled from Gandhi's life and teachings the principles that gave us the determination to challenge our adversaries. Just reading his philosophy of satyagraha gave us a greater appreciation of how words can empower people. His concept of "soul force" drew us together like a core magnet. It was as though we were peeking at our own history by reviewing Gandhi's. We then understood what Martin Luther King, Jr., meant when he said that "suffering is redemptive." Those of us who endured cruel rejections at the University of Oklahoma learned to see them as pain that could not only toughen us but could also spiritually enrich us. The little man from India was in many ways our soul mate too.

People at the University who doubted the lasting impact of the "feel good, suffer a lot" approach advocated by Gandhi saw the results in the black students who graduated with their dignity intact and their minds free of racial bitterness. It was those students who forestalled campus unrest. In the process, they learned the dysfunctional aspects of nonviolence, which caused culturally sheltered individuals to miscalculate the extent of racism on our campus. Except for a few handfuls of malcontents, the University was relatively peaceful, and that gave the false impression that the black and white members of the University were of one accord.

Martin Luther King, Jr.

Martin Luther King, Jr.'s college experiences awakened him to a wide range of philosophical and political conflict resolution alternatives. He was simultaneously drawn to and repelled by Karl Marx, but Thoreau's essay on civil disobedience stirred him more deeply and permanently than any other educational encounter of the period. It was King's conviction that Thoreau's concepts should be coupled with Christian love. King believed that a nonviolent rebellion is not submission to evil power; rather, it is courageous confrontation of evil using the power of love. Thus King's belief that it is better to be the recipient of violence than the inflictor of it came into sharper focus.

Unlike Gandhi, King did not initially decide to use collective civil disobedience to achieve his goals. Instead, King's emphasis, like Thoreau's, was upon the individual's right and personal responsibility to break, ignore, and resist morally corrupt local laws — no matter what the personal consequences are.[12] Of the bus boycott in 1956, he said that the spirit of the Montgomery movement came from Jesus and the technique came from Gandhi.[13] King realized that individuals who decide to oppose and resist an unjust law behave in the same manner as groups acting collectively. In final analysis, the distinction between the two kinds of resistance became rather academic for King, since both allowed him to achieve the same end.

King's theory, if it can be termed that, was based in his "dream," as he called it. It was his ultimate dream for all peoples, a dream concerning the nature of truth. He stated his dream in his 1964 Nobel Prize acceptance speech: "I believe that unarmed truth and unconditional love will have the final word in reality. That is why right temporarily defeated is stronger than evil triumphant."[14]

From the beginning, King sought situations that would crystallize public opinion and direct it in such a manner that a thoughtful person could not help but recognize the hypocrisy of racial segregation and discrimination in America, land of the free. In communicating his dream, he sought unyielding commitment from his followers: "If tokenism were our goal, this administration [John F. Kennedy's] has adroitly moved us towards its accomplishment. But tokenism can now be seen not only as a useless goal, but a genuine menace. It is a palliative which relieves emotional distress, but leaves the disease and its ravages unaffected."[15]

Although he experienced many setbacks and cruel adversities, King did not lose faith in our nation or abandon hope for the eventual union of all Americans into a truly United States. In *Where Do We Go From Here: Chaos or Community?* he stated that the aims of the civil rights movement had transcended the old concept of integration, which consisted of one group losing its identity, and had moved to a pluralistic version. By this he meant that the races could come together, but not to inculcate only dominant-group values.

King's writings showed blacks at the University of Oklahoma the virtue of love that anchors physical restraint. There was little our adversaries could do, short of killing us, to stop those of us who bought into King's beliefs. In the war against racism, other philosophers and theorists also led by example, but it was King who captured our imaginations and commitment. Because he was a prolific writer, the black students and I learned the value of putting our own civil rights beliefs in written words for our friends and our enemies to see. It was his transparency that guided us. Yet many of the students did not see a connection between the philosophies of Martin Luther King, Jr., and Malcolm X. Both were necessary pieces of our civil rights puzzle, providing us with meaningful approaches to community, state, and national changes.

Drawing heavily on King's approach, most of the students and I believed that nonviolent reconciliation opened people at the University, including ourselves, in ways that sometimes defied explanation. The joy inherent in this kind of community change stopped us from using rebellious, destructive behavior. We exercised our free will to seek peaceful resolution of conflicts. In the process, we learned to hate destructive behavior and to like, if not love, hateful people. To me, resolving conflicts through peaceful means was a palatable way to move across racial borders that we could not yet erase.

King's stirring rhetoric nudged us toward nonviolence, but it was not a pain-free or an error-free strategy for change. Our nonviolent victories antagonized as many people as they pleased, and there was an empty feeling within some of our hearts when we crushed our foes. Not even our profuse apologies could smooth over the hurt. So even in nonviolent victories there was pain. Perhaps the toughest lesson we learned is that victories achieved through both nonviolence and violence, including nonphysical forms, can have unpleasant consequences, including guilt, distorted egos, and regrets. There were fewer of those feelings among people who adhered to King's values and beliefs.

Putting It Together

That the aforementioned philosophies, theories, strategies, and men appealed to so many people at the University of Oklahoma, not just blacks, says volumes about how similar in form and function racism had remained over the years. Indeed, the various forms of racism in 1967–71 were quite similar to racism before then. And there were no pristine victims among us. Depending on the particular ways in which some of our race relations experiences had unfolded, our individual beliefs with regard to culturally different people were skewed into negative, positive, or neutral mind-sets. Therefore arguments for violent or nonviolent strategies for abating racism could be equally convincing. The differences between these strategies were not absolute, even if the rhetoric was.

Whether we were aligned with Martin Luther King, Jr., or Malcolm X, no poetic mystery surrounded our discontent. We were often overlooked as relevant campus-wide decision makers, and the depth of our hurt feelings was conveyed in various declarations, sit-ins, workshops, and news stories. The writings of Alinsky, Gandhi, and King showed us how to become campus leaders — little wonder most of us couldn't get enough of them! Each of them was a wellspring of liberation knowledge. The students and I learned to trust ourselves to interpret the culturally relevant meanings of our mentors' tactics and strategies for change. When lumped together with the strategies of Fanon and Malcolm X, the result was a hodgepodge of approaches. But when carefully selected and adapted to specific situations, one way or another each of them provided us with clear and compelling road maps to community change.

To Be an Activist in Oklahoma

I believed that if I was going to be a successful community activist in Oklahoma, it would happen only if special circumstances arose and engendered a readiness in people to let me assume a role in their lives that transcended the mundane. I also believed it could happen to me in Oklahoma, and that if it did, I would be extremely fortunate. But it would not be easy. I would have to somehow adroitly juggle teaching and community advocacy. I knew from similar attempts in Detroit that doing both of those things well in Oklahoma would consist of part skill, part guile, part collaboration, part patience, and part luck. I would have to overcome numerous hurdles, and without assistance, I might fail. Even with assistance I might fail.

Weighing those things carefully, I imagined a best outcome for a University of Oklahoma race relations scenario: the unusual (i.e., integration) would become usual. Black people would emerge from their seemingly nonexistent campus lives and become full University participants. There would be naysayers of course, but I decided not to let those false pretenders of social justice discourage me. Nor would I ignore them when they belittled the black students' tortured academic lives.

My Personal Commitment

In practical terms, I would collaborate with other activists in order to neutralize people who were bent on perpetuating racial stereotypes and discrimination. It was long past the time for institutionalizing respect and equal opportunities. I intuited at the outset that the problems confronting me as an activist or a community advocate in Oklahoma were varied and difficult. A quick summary of the seemingly insurmountable and rapidly worsening interracial problems at the University of Oklahoma — with a large increase in individuals espousing racial segregation and violence — had all but immobilized many of my colleagues. Even though I, too, was shocked awake by the immensity of the problems, I did not believe that standing wide-eyed in horror was an adequate stance for me to assume.

If I was going to help other people improve their lives, I realized that I had to forsake my own posture of an untrained, traumatized innocent person. My options were clear: I could either wring my hands and hire out as a mourner or become actively involved in fostering racial integra-

"*I believe that education must be relevant to current social issues.*

I attempt to bridge the gaps between social theories and community practices.
I believe that students must feel free to question all concepts—including mine.

I seek to make my classes forums for open, objective dialogues as opposed to an atmosphere of dogma and defensiveness.

"*I believe that students often learn more from their classmates than they do from me.*
I frequently serve as an education broker, bringing together dispensors and recipients of new ideas.

"*I believe that a teacher must also be a learner.*
I am constantly learning from my students.
I believe that I am hooked on students.
If I kick the habit, I will stop teaching."

DR. GEORGE HENDERSON
Associate Professor, Sociology and Education

Montage of Henderson teaching, 1968, from University of Oklahoma 1969 yearbook. Western History Collections, University of Oklahoma Libraries.

tion. I decided to try to become the kind of realist about whom Malcolm Boyd wrote:

> Shallow activism must . . . be changed into a considerably deeper and more sophisticated sense of involvement. This calls for listening to people outside one's own ingrown and myopic clique as well as sober examination of self-righteousness in one's motives and actions. . . . A realist throws away rose-colored glasses, straightens his shoulders and looks freely about him in all directions. He wants to see whatever there is to see, in relation to other people and things as well as to himself. A realist alone comprehends hope. Optimism is as antithetical to authentic hope as pessimism. Hope is rooted in realism.[16]

My commitment to social change at the University of Oklahoma would be not for disorder but for a new order. I would not be detached or neutral, though. Instead, I would publicly acknowledge being committed to racial equality and thereby would become a teacher who was anything but a cipher. I would not hide my social beliefs beneath a feigned dispassionate academic veneer. No, I would not play the value-free game that many of my colleagues subscribed to. Also, given the right moments or circumstances, I would teach others to be agents for change.

My critics in Oklahoma would focus on my egalitarian values such as racial equality and integration. That was all right, though. It was not up to them to provide me what some of my colleagues seemed to have lost: the willingness to be honest about my social beliefs. I speculated that as my life at the University unfolded, the intractability of some of the hurtful situations I was bound to encounter would set in with depressing clarity. Therefore I would have to carefully analyze them before responding, because peoples' lives or careers might be in the balance.

With those thoughts in mind, I dived headlong into Oklahoma civil rights activities. Once it began, my professor-activist life existed on the cusp of uncertainty. Community activism is not an exact science. There are too many confounding variables to be sorted. Still, I tried to account for as many of them as possible. I intellectualized my approaches by drawing on several behavioral sciences theories.

Peter Berger suggested three possible autonomous responses to one's social environment: (1) transform it, (2) withdraw from it, or (3) manipulate it.[17] Transformation and manipulation became the most relevant alternatives for me. I liked Berger's theory that transformation of social structures is possible because society not only forms individuals but also is formed by them. The survival of racial discrimination at the University of Oklahoma, for example, required the acceptance of the general population. Ethnic minorities could not be forced to perform all of the cooperative acts required for a smoothly functioning segregated university — it was ensured only through mutual consent. I would not surrender the campus to bigots. Social change in the University and in the city of Norman had begun long before I arrived. Yet there was more to be done.

The Academic Battlefield

Fragments of the University community consisted of discomfited white students who were exposed to black students who prodded them into jagged interpersonal encounters. As an example, black students coaxed white students to talk about racism on campus and chided them for not abolishing racist practices. The situation perplexed some of the white students and angered others. Notwithstanding various sciences of human relations, immutable processes of positive social change defied airtight strategies. That's where luck — good or bad — came in. At times, parts of our community seemed to be improving more by chance than through careful planning. Without being prodded, some students sought out friends in other ethnic groups. Consequently, the term "unpredictable human relations" is an appropriate metaphor for the interactions that eluded certainty. On several occasions, a change in race relations brought with it draconian choices such as who had to give up what and how much. As I moved from race relations theories to practice and back again, what bothered me the most was that I was not always able to recommend a foolproof course of action that minimized collateral damage.

Over time — as my activism informed other parts of my life — my teaching, research, writing, and speeches became more imaginative. The sheer weight of being an outspoken ethnic-minority-group faculty member pulled down many of the restraints that I had. Whatever else could be said of me, I became bolder in my work. Frequently, like life itself, the boundaries of racism at the University seemed endless to me, though they were finite. Time and time again I observed how little dignity accrued to anyone who was oppressed. Chunks of their self-esteem were torn away. Furthermore, neither the oppressors nor their victims were able to find peace. Both parties suspiciously watched each other so as not to be taken for granted. As a campus activist, I tried to add value to oppressed peoples' lives (and my own life) by helping them to survive with their dignity intact. But in my estimation, that was never a full solution.

Periodically, the intensity of African American students' rage broke the surface of their restraint and rushed out with a force that I could not calm with speeches or platitudes. In those instances, the aggrieved individuals wanted me to accept their anger and to offer solutions to whatever triggered it. That was not always easy for me to do. Once the aggressive beasts in them were unleashed, the students charged into the fray of battle without carefully thought-out plans. As might be expected, their adversaries responded with heightened rejections. Countless students got hurt physically that way. What's more, the spectators often got hurt too.

In the beginning, my initial reaction in such situations was to suggest nonviolence to the students, even though it was absurd for me to judge them on whether they were violent or nonviolent. I knew better. "It's easy for you to talk about nonviolence to us in this classroom," a black student once chided during my first semester at the University. "What would you have done if you was with my buddy and me in a Norman bar this past weekend? Two big ugly white guys told us to get on our knees and crawl out of there barking like dogs. I told them to go to hell as we tried to walk past them. That's when the fight started. My buddy and me got our asses kicked, but we didn't crawl or bark. A black guy walking past the bar got his ass kicked, too. If you was my age and my buddy, would you have crawled out of the bar?"

I was once like these students, and I knew that desperate people will sometimes use desperate means to survive, including violence. I said something vague like "Maybe I could have found another solution," but we both knew that I probably would not have crawled out of the bar, and I certainly would not have barked. Black males who grew up in communities like ours were conditioned to fight when their manhood was in the balance. Yes, if I were his age, I would have fought. So would most males in other ethnic minority groups — especially those who grew up in low-income communities. Learning to communicate effectively with those students was very much like becoming a successful singer. I had to compress words, hold them inside me, and release the right ones at the appropriate times.

Among the most creative students I tried to help were individuals who attempted to manipulate bureaucratic institutions by using caustic confrontational tactics that did not require skill. These students did not waste their time, as I often did, on theoretical debates centering on whether they should work within or outside established formal grievance procedures. Besides, most of them had been unable to win even when they did follow the established University procedures for resolving disputes. Generally, though, their inability to succeed was more the result of lacking an understanding of the appropriate procedures than their tactics. Campus politics was foreign territory for them, so they were just muddling through.

Other professors, including many of those mentioned in this book, and I became these students' allies. We filled in their knowledge gaps. A major problem black students had had in previous years was a lack of networking. They needed as many allies as they could get. As one of their mentors, I helped them garner more allies. Only when the students — regardless of the tactics they chose — had enough knowledge, emotional and faculty support, guile, and opportunities were they able to cross over into institutional influence. Slowly, as I worked with these students, I was putting the tactical pieces together in my own mind.

Making Sense of It

I found significance in the article "Bureaucracy and the Lower Class," written by Gordon Sjoberg, Richard Brymer, and Buford Farris. The authors discussed the inability of the lower-class clients in their study to manipulate social welfare institutions. Middle-class clients generally learned how to get special concessions through backstage maneuvers, but lower-class clients tended to be intimidated by bureaucracies and usually were unaware of their rights and of the institutional procedures for enforcing them. Because lower-class clients lacked knowledge of how organizations work, they were unable to manipulate social welfare institutions to fit their own needs or to access the programs that were available to them. The authors could have just as easily been describing most University of Oklahoma students and, in particular, ethnic minority students.

The disillusionment and hopelessness that characterized most Uni-

versity of Oklahoma black students shielded white students from whole-
sale confrontations with them. A mixture of caution and fear of academic
failure kept the black students in an anxious state. But the white students
did not get a free pass either. They were apprehensive about living among
blacks, particularly those who they thought were on the verge of violence.
It is not an exaggeration to say that interracial tensions were high in
situations where the disparate groups were in contact continuously. An
upside to this situation, however, created a novel twist. Black students'
anxieties resonated with socially and academically marginal white students whose own downward spiral of mobility was a real possibility. Consequently, black students often got unexpected help from other students
who themselves were at risk of becoming campus outcasts, including
antiwar protesters and hippies.

    With or without support, there was no lessening of the stigma at-
tached to being black. Any overreaching for equal opportunities by black
Americans typically drew swift rebuke from angry white people. This is not
to say that no black students gained equality in the campus community. A
few of them did. But throughout the University, racial discrimination was
unabated. It embarrassed and angered both blacks and fair-minded white
people. Still, before 1967 no provocative or powerful campus civil rights
moments at the University coalesced into deliberately orchestrated mass
protests. I had my work cut out for me if I was going to collaborate with
other people to help the black students.

    I found solace in Neil Gilbert's description of the dilemmas faced by
agency activists in antipoverty programs.[18] He noted that agency employees frequently tried to play a politically neutral role as "middlemen"
between the "distributors" and the "consumers" of social services. This
was a difficult role to maintain, because the interests of the poor frequently did not coincide with those of the welfare system. The dilemma
for practitioners was clear. On the one hand, if they attempted to avoid
overloading the system by placing a lid on consumer demands, they ran
the risk of being perceived by their clients as lackeys. On the other hand,
if they chose to support their clients' demands for better service, their
agency administrators called them "agitators." My community activism
in Oklahoma mirrored that of the antipoverty program professionals. At
various times I got crosswise with both black and white students as well as
with my colleagues and administrators.

Given that the establishment is never eager to finance its own destruc-
tion, or even significant alterations, one possible option was for me to
resign my teaching position and become an independent organizer or an
organizer for an antiestablishment agency. That is basically the approach
that was used by the radical labor union leaders of the 1930s and 1940s.
According to Alan McSurely, establishment-oriented professionals (1)
maintain objectivity and view their clients as "cases," (2) give their primary loyalty to their employer, (3) use one-way, downward communication links with their clients, (4) cater to the wishes of the existing dominant political forces within their organizations, and (5) develop new
programs mostly to placate the clients.[19] Antiestablishment activists,
whom McSurely favored, (1) treat their clients as people rather than as
cases, (2) give their complete personal commitment to the clients, (3)
have honest two-way communication with their coworkers, (4) try to build
strong new leadership and independent political forces within their clients' community organizations, and (5) empower clients to be critical
consumers of information about new programs that affect their lives.

Paul Bullock cogently described some of the problems encountered
by McSurely's antiestablishment organizers.[20] One is the difficulty in developing client organizations, which represent most of an entire community. It is rare for more than a small percentage of community residents to
become actively involved in an organization. For that reason, the indigenous people whose views are heard are usually those who are inclined to
speak out about their own problems. In the University, for example, students who gravitated toward leadership positions in campus organizations tended to be upwardly aspiring individuals who became fairly sophisticated about using available opportunities to accomplish their own
personal goals.

Another problem faced by antiestablishment activists is the defeatist,
cynical attitudes prevalent in low-status communities where little in life
nurtures either hope or the cooperative spirit required for successful
community organizations. When outsider community activists arrive,
they are viewed with suspicion. The residents assume that they are patsies
to be exploited by residents, or they think that the organizers have come
to take advantage of the residents. The immediate interest of community
activists ought to be to gain their clients' acceptance, not to subvert their

power. Those things considered, I decided that in order to be an op-
timally helpful activist, I would encourage students to create their own
organizations and to use me as a resource, even their voice, but not as
their leader.

One thing was evident: working out in the open and using public confrontation tactics in Oklahoma made me very visible, very vulnerable, and
very alone. I could, and did at times, get hurt that way. Life would have
been so much easier and less hectic for me if I had not gotten involved in
civil rights projects. At least that's what one of my white friends told me.

"Why do you think that you ought to try to shake up or alter the
University?" Bob Ohm, dean of the College of Education asked me. "Do
you have an academic death wish? Why won't you just overlook more
things?"

I bristled at the questions even though I thought he was playing
devil's advocate.

"Maybe I do have an academic death wish. Or maybe I would be this
university's Don Quixote," I replied curtly, sounding like a professor-
gone-wild. "Yes, I would be Quixote!"

Bob's demeanor turned serious, "Watch out for the people who are
hiding in our windmills. They will try to destroy you and your reputation."

It was good advice, especially for someone like me who was interfer-
ing with what many people believed was the natural or divine order of
things.

A Few Basic Strategies

A community activist can opt to work within the system, as most of them
do. The question for me was how effectively could I work for social change
within the existing University framework? Obviously the answer depended
on my analysis of the existing framework. I found guidance in Jack Minnis's observations: "Those who control the economy of the nation are the
only ones who have the power to change things. . . . I am now convinced that
the nature of power in this society is such that it is a dangerous delusion to
suppose those who wield it can be pressured to use it in ways they do not
choose to and that, inevitably, they will choose to use it to the detriment of
the people."[21] Following Minnis's lead, I chose my battles carefully, and I

encouraged students to do likewise. We had to decide how to deal most effectively with recalcitrant administrators and professors, some of who were complacent in their jobs.

C. Wright Mills probably would have not agreed with our strategy to go after University administrators.[22] Much of his work was based on the assumption that power in this country was centralized in the hands of a few. He described the liberal image of the American system of power as a moving balance of competing interests, and he dismissed the gutter fights of American politics as methods used by contestants on the middle level of power. The real decision makers, he concluded, were above and beyond it all.

In a similar vein, Floyd Hunter saw the top decision makers as puppeteers who operated behind the public scene. In his book *Community Power Structure: A Study of Decision Makers*, generally regarded as the classic documentation of elitist power structures operating on local levels,[23] Hunter identified a number of power pyramids but described the major economic interests as being overwhelmingly represented in the policy-making elite.[23] He believed that business leaders make up the power elite, operating as puppeteers behind the public scene.

Because neither I nor the black students at the University were likely to interact regularly with the kind of power brokers Mills and Hunter researched, we deemed it prudent to deal with the brokers' highest intermediaries: presidents, vice presidents, deans, and department chairpersons. There were certainly enough of them for us to grab hold of, and occasionally a lucky few of us were able to gain favors from some of them.

An elitist military-industrialist interpretation of social systems was a convenient explanation for people who believed that things were in a mess but who did not want to blame a system as a whole. The black students and I were not those people. We did indeed hold the entire University community, including ourselves, accountable for its bigotry. At this juncture of the analysis process, we concluded that University resources that could be used to improve the lives of all University members were most often unequally distributed, and they were widely dispersed so that no one group had all of them. In the 1960s and 1970s, for example, the personnel who had control over their own resources used them sparingly for blacks or not at all. It was just old-fashioned racial bigotry.

A few individuals outside the president's staff, mainly those in the Athletics Department, were powerful in all or even most of the significant areas of their students' academic life. The general pattern was for various individuals and groups within an academic unit to make decisions affecting different issue areas. That structure hindered our search for areas to target in order to gain more rights and privileges for black students. During a conversation that I had in December 1967 with several black students, I made what later turned out to be fortuitous conjecture, "Scholarship athletes, especially football players, are the poster people of the University. And winning football games is everything. What kind of effect do you think black athletes could have on our efforts to achieve equal opportunities if black athletes protested racist conditions at OU?"

Howard Johnson, a black athlete said, "You got to be kidding, Doc. Black athletes are on a very short, very tight leash. They're like the three monkeys: hear no racism, see no racism, and don't talk about racism in public."

Although we all thought that the athletes would not risk their scholarships to fight racism on our campus, we also thought that they could shake up the University in ways that the rest of us could not. We could easily imagine the outcome — this was not the first time that the students had run up against an idea pertaining to race relations in the University that smacked of wishful thinking. When Howard left the meeting, he shook his head and laughed at me. Once again I had engaged him in idle chatter about an outlandish tactic. Little did we know that all of us at the meeting would soon be proven wrong about the readiness of the University's black athletes to challenge institutional racism.

In addition to Minnis, Mills, and Hunter, I also found relevance in an article by Edward Banfield and James Wilson that described bureaucratic autonomy. [24] They pointed out that the top officials in local governmental hierarchies usually make policy decisions that are essentially political in nature. Therefore most agency administrators are essentially politicians. That was certainly true at the University of Oklahoma, where the academic departments and colleges had become rogue empires that independently denied students rights and privileges promised to them by the president and the Regents. Most academic units were controlled by rules and regulations decided at their local level, and those decisions were largely unmonitored.

Much of my work as an activist required me to be politically savvy. Before I could become an effective adviser, sponsor, mentor, or whatever the students needed from me, I had to learn how to function effectively as a University politician. I was mindful of Gordon Tullock's advice: "The successful organization politician must be trusted by other persons, particularly by his superiors. . . . If he should develop a deviant personality, he would be unlikely to inspire much confidence in others. The rational politician will, therefore, make every effort to conform to the image of the 'proper' person that is held by the membership of the organization man. He must become an 'organization man.' "[25]

I did not want to become a University of Oklahoma politician or organization man, but I did. There was nothing inherently wrong with being either of them, though, if I could maintain my integrity. I could have played this role cynically and merely put on an act, but I chose sincerity. Erving Goffman used the term "sincere" to describe people who believe in the roles they perform.[26] My belief in the individuals and groups I tried to help was sincere by that definition. I was not trying to manipulate others for my own personal ends — my job as a professor was my professional end. In short, I did not want to be a Machiavelli, undermining my faculty colleagues so that they would not rise above me. As for the students, I wanted them to achieve more in their college experiences than I did in mine.

CHAPTER THREE

Creation of the Afro-American Student Union

The late 1960s through the early 1970s was a period of black conscious-ness-raising and student demands for racial equality at historically white colleges and universities. The revolt was seeded by national events, including racial unrest in several American cities, the black power move ment, the urging of black students to organize by Floyd McKissick of the Congress of Racial Equality, and the formation of the first black student union, at San Francisco State College (now San Francisco State Univer-sity) in 1966. San Francisco State already had a black social organization that was called the Negro Student Association. By changing its name to Black Student Union, the students there signaled the demise of Negroes and the birth of active blacks. Malcolm X was one of the foremost spokes-persons in the shift from Negro to black. He led the way in the 1950s by dis-carding his Anglo-American surname, Little, and his Anglo-American ethnic group descriptor, Negro. Although the word "black" initially had negative connotations among most Americans, Malcolm and other "radi-cals" turned it inside out for most African Americans: black is beautiful; black is power. Within a year, dozens of similar black organizations had been founded on historically white campuses around the country. The University of Oklahoma's Afro-American Student Union is one of them and, like the others, has its own touchingly sad, hopeful, and memorable history.

OU Black Students Unite

From 1948, when George McLaurin became the first black student enrolled at the University of Oklahoma, until the late 1960s, black students at
the University wished year after year that goodness would prevail and they
would be treated as people of equal worth to whites. But it seldom happened. They held on to that unfulfilled dream too long. In one of his
poems, "Harlem: A Dream Deferred," Langston Hughes asked, "What
happens to a dream deferred? Does it dry up like a raisin in the sun? . . . Or
does it explode?" At the University of Oklahoma, the dream exploded on
November 12, 1967, during an exploratory meeting of concerned black
students who were enrolled at the Norman campus. The organizing meeting was convened to answer the question "Do we need an organization
that will represent all of the University's African American students?" The
conveners selected the term "Afro-American" in order to make a distinction between themselves, descendants of slaves, and other black students
enrolled at the University. Approximately ninety black students and the
three African American faculty members—Melvin Tolson, Lennie Marie
Muse-Tolliver, and I—packed the small basement auditorium in the Student Union.

From my vantage point at the rear of the room, I observed with great
interest the general seating patterns: students from the same high schools
sat together; roommates sat together, athletes clustered by sports, graduate students sat together, and unaffiliated students sat wherever they could
find a seat. There were many acquaintances but relatively few close friends.
This was an opportunity for all of us to become friends with more black
people.

The question about the need for a new organization opened a flood-
gate of emotions and pushed the audience into a free fall of recollections. Before they began to share their stories, three ground rules were
set: (1) Discourteous conduct would not be tolerated. (2) Personal things
said in the meeting were confidential and could be disclosed to others
only with permission. (3) All people present, including the faculty members, had the right to express their opinions. It is unclear to me who
initiated the rules, but they worked. They bemoaned the harshness of
their college lives that most often rested on the margins of acceptance by
white people. Leaving little to interpretation, they expressed with pin-

point accuracy their unhappiness with continuing racial segregation and discrimination at the University, despite its supposed outlawing in 1950. They knew what bothered them and they were relieved to tell it. But before they shared their stories, the students agreed to a straightforward process for conducting the meeting: First, there would be an informal, unstructured sharing of their race-relations experiences at the University; next, there would be recommendations and voting on them within the procedural parameters of Robert's Rules of Order; and finally, at the end of the meeting, a decision would be made about the next steps, if any, for the group to take. The unstructured portion began with gusto.

As in most unstructured meetings, a few individuals did most of the talking initially. Still, everyone had standing and could speak for himself or herself and, with permission, on behalf of other black students who were present. Amiable individuals welcomed the chance to connect with other black people. For the first half hour or so, the room was alive with students introducing themselves to others who were outside their own cliques and clubs. An undergraduate female sitting in the row in front of me said hi to a youngish-looking male and added, "We're in the same intro psychology class." Then she formally introduced herself — name, hometown, major, and the place of her University residence. There were only three blacks in the course, but until now they had not taken the time to get acquainted.

For the first time, the University did not seem to be a socially cold, restrictive place to some of the students. Also for the first time, black students were the majority group at a large campus gathering. Tense bodies relaxed, scrunched-up faces gave way to smiles, and the students began to bask in their temporary emancipated state. Loud jive talkers mixed with their socially reserved peers. It was as though they had found a safe place in which to take off their minority-group masks. Most important, they felt like members of a scattered family that was now being reassembled; they wanted to share some family stories and recount their arcane details.

During the larger meeting, the students talked about white people who called them uncomplimentary names, ridiculed or ignored them in classes, disappeared as roommates, denied them campus opportunities, and otherwise treated them like unwanted siblings. Everyone had a story to tell, but only a few of them had found willing white listeners or, more to the point, someone in authority to be their champion. Graduate students and seniors were the most compelling storytellers. They recounted their long-suffering abuses—on campus and off. Their emotionally painful stories, augmented with precisely remembered details, suggested a certain amount of sadistic behavior by their oppressors, who consisted of a small number of white people. New students and old ones alike chimed in. They did not like being called derogatory names by strangers while walking on campus or in Norman, and they did not like seeing white students in black face mimicking black people at Halloween or during homecoming week celebrations. Their sorrows and fears were portable and but not easy to carry. Worse yet, misery tagged along, uninvited, semester by semester.

Earlier in the semester, I had made a special mental note of the body language of two of the students who were at the meeting. When walking across the campus, they kept their heads and eyes down as if to defer the upcoming sights to students whose positive self-images gave them the right to see all that was available for them to see. Meanwhile these two less confident students seemed to laboriously drag their bodies from one destination to the next. What little energy they had was reserved for withstanding the indignities awaiting them in classrooms and laboratories. When they looked up, it was with what I described to a colleague as whale eyes—eyes that stared into space but did not display excitement about the images before them. Antsy and vulnerable, they seemed to shuffle through college as lost persons.

Now, at the organization meeting, they said it was impossible for them to begin a school day emotionally unencumbered. Their feelings of hopelessness and powerlessness were obvious, yet by hook or by crook they managed to survive. Their numerous academic problems came together incident by incident into a single conundrum of unfulfilled aspirations as they described them that day. Their persistent efforts to earn the highest grades possible based on their performance but falling short so many times were classic cases of frustration. They wished for respect, not pity; for acceptance, not rejection. Simply stated, they wished to be treated with dignity. That wish was urgent in the same way their slave ancestors' lives had been urgent: urgently needing to go beyond mere survival.

Listening to the students reminded me that their minority-group status was an assault on their personhood. Indeed, their academic jeopardy as members of an ethnic minority group was due to a betrayal of something pretending to be an equal quality of education. The faceless professors, whom several of the scholastically marginal students called "those people," had dogged their survival. Pessimists listening to the students might have questioned the value of rescuing them — to do what? But that wasn't how I felt. I did not have those dilemmas. It was evident to me that it was not the students' minority-group designation that disadvantaged them but the unfair treatment they received. Obviously, college was not a cabaret for them. They certainly needed to be rescued in order to become integral members of the campus community. Except for interactions with their friends, they had little pertaining to the University to sing and dance about. While this had always been true, it seemed even more so now, when their grievances were aired so openly.

I heard a common message. It was about educational goals falling apart one after another. There were no greater soul-wrenching truths of the caste-like conditions of the black students than the incidents I heard about at the meeting. A senior complained that, despite her efforts to be friendly, only three of her white classmates had ever interacted with her. Because she did not have friends in many of her classes, she was left out of informal study groups, and she could seldom get copies of class notes when she was absent. In short, like most of the other black students, she had very little, if any, peer support in her classes. Several of the speakers were more disappointed than angry. According to them, there appeared to be no end to the indignities they had to endure. The students said that several of their professors talked down to them. They also said that white students frequently ridiculed them during classroom discussions, and some white students and all of the professors initially assumed that none of the black students in their classes were merit scholars. Some of the students wanted to give up and leave the University, but they were too proud to admit it. All of them were determined to earn higher grades than their critics believed possible. So they plodded on to their destinies. Why not? A college degree was thought to be the best ticket to good jobs and, ultimately, a better quality of life than almost all of their non-college educated friends had. I detected emotions that teetered between despair and optimism. Their sorrowful tales were somewhat assuaged by occasional hopeful ones.

Self-pity — or at least its overt display — did not preoccupy many of the students. Instead of wallowing in despair, they chose to focus on surviving. That was especially true for individuals who had been honor students in high school. Despite having been victims of so many acts of bigotry in college, they still managed to joke about their plight. Nevertheless, their overall demeanor was unmistakably guarded. Life kept throwing racial abuses at them. Still, more of them than the odds makers would have predicted were excelling as students. Indeed, for these individuals dreams of academic success did not die, even though discrimination against them was excessively spelled out, excessively felt, and excessively demeaning. Surely, I mused, Dante's hell was less torturous. Although black students were not the only oppressed people in the University, at this moment, at this meeting, they were the only ones who mattered. A few of the marginal students, conditioned to their plight, came across as pathetic without knowing it. It was as though they were sleepwalking through college.

It was evident to most of us in the room that overt bigotry at the University had not receded — it was alive and well. It was more complicated and more painful than a headache or a toothache, and it lasted much longer. A consensus quickly formed: the students needed an organization that would unite them so that they might, as a single group, greatly improve their campus situations. After nearly two hours of talking, they appointed a representative group to draft bylaws and a constitution for what would be called the Afro-American Student Union (ASU). A few days later, on November 19, 1967, the bylaws and constitution for the organization were adopted. The various subgroups of students had finally merged and morphed into an inclusive membership.

On November 28 the first official meeting of the ASU began with the election of the organization's first officers: Harold L. Andrews, president; Bruce N. Robinson, vice president; Zelbert L. Moore, general secretary; and Winston C. Fouche, treasurer. After the members considered amendments to the constitution, they collected dues. Financially lean individuals groaned a bit, but they paid their share. Some of the students then left to study or to attend other activities. Twenty-five students, Melvin Tolson, and I stayed for the *Sooner Yearbook* photo to be taken. It was the first of many group pictures that would insert black faces into the media images of University students. The inclusion of more African Americans in positive news stories was good for the University's public image.

Afro-American Student Union (ASU) membership in November 1967, from University of Oklahoma 1968 yearbook. Henderson is at the far left in the top row. Western History Collections, University of Oklahoma Libraries.

Great Aspirations

The stakes were higher than some of the students thought. My admonition to them — "Don't be surprised when your enemies fight back; there will be casualties" — seemed at the time to have an exaggerated ring to it. There were valid reasons to argue for or against creating an organization "by Afro-American students at OU, for Afro-American students at OU, and of Afro-American students at OU of a common cultural heritage." This was uncharted territory. We had no comparative history to guide us. Several different outcomes were possible: it could empower the students; it could expose them to charges of separatism or militancy; it could create a much-needed sense of a united black community; or it could in later years fracture the students into competing organizational pieces, largely the ASU versus the black Greek organizations. So what else could happen? Time would tell.

When someone called for a binding vote, the students had one final opportunity to rescind their decision to create the ASU. Again the decision was made to adopt the constitution and to seek formal approval to function as a University-approved organization. The students had bonded and made a sincere commitment to help each other. They would no longer be isolated soloists decrying racism. Instead they would become the equivalent of a loud, well-rehearsed choir. Melvin Tolson, Lennie Marie Muse-Tolliver, and I agreed to support them in every way possible. Melvin became the official sponsor of the organization, with an understanding that he and I would function as co-sponsors.

Most of the students correctly surmised that proactive, rather than reactive, activities would be their best conflict-leveling approach. The next-to-the-last question before the remaining members disbanded was "What should we do as an organization?" They decided to begin by initiating programs to educate themselves on black history and otherwise find ways to maintain positive self-images; next, they would sponsor public speakers to enlighten others about African Americans. It was important to have allies who were truly empathetic rather than pseudo allies who feigned sympathy for the cause. With the help of sincere allies, the students envisioned that they would expand the University's curriculums to include black history. The rationale for black history was quite simple: blacks and whites alike tend to be more honest with each other when they take unblinking looks at each other historically, warts and all. That goal seemed modest, but it was really quite difficult to achieve. If the ASU succeeded, as we all hoped that it would, the social status acrophobia that had been passed on from one generation to the next might end.

Previously, each new generation of black students had generally set its sights on achieving little more than those who had preceded them. Thus they often set their sights too low. That kind of goal setting was unacceptable to the ASU members. They vowed to excel and to challenge teachers who gave them unfair grades. In previous years, defensive University personnel had refuted claims of racial discrimination in grading. They usually prevailed, but their arguments did not lessen the sting of bigotry. To think otherwise was a delusion. Obviously something more than individual complaints was needed to correct the situation. That something, most of us believed, was a cohesive organization like the Afro-American Student Union in which we could support one another.

Earlier attempts by black students to create academically potent organizations at historically white institutions in Oklahoma had failed. There were many reasons for the earlier failures, but this time there was the right mixture of graduate and undergraduate students and faculty support. We were poised to be the state's flagship institution in something other than football and selected academics—the black students and faculty at the University of Oklahoma were ready to harness their individual human resources into a new organization.

I detected a sense of rekindled optimism in the room. Sprinkled with healthy doses of realism, the attitude was not Pollyannaish. We agreed that the new organization would focus on practical issues and not spend the members' time intellectualizing or pontificating about things beyond their educational needs. Prudent people, we decided, must be cautious about which injustices they try to abate or prevent. The key then was to find the best ways to improve the quality of their lives as students. "The operative word is 'best.' That means 'well thought out,'" I said. "To do less would likely result in debacles that might set back black people at the University of Oklahoma for several more years." The students nodded. Several of them shook their fists. The synergy was almost breathtaking, and it took me over.

I looked across the room and caught Melvin's eyes. We smiled at each other. It wasn't just the stories or the enthusiasm that sent chills throughout my body. It was also the mutual agreement about our common situation and our overwhelming desire to change it. I began to believe that something very special was unfolding before my eyes. Prior to this second meeting, I was wishful that it would not be a waste of my time. Now, after it was well under way, I was sure that this was where I ought to be. It was like going to a movie and watching the good guys figure out how to get out of a deplorable situation their captives believed was escape-proof. But I wasn't watching a movie. I was an actor in one. Although a lot of things still had to be done, I imagined either a happy ending or a glorious academic death trying to achieve it. So, too, did the other people in the room. Yes, a momentous drama was developing as we spoke.

We would figure out later what changes should be made, and by whom. Some things would have to be done with black people and white people together; others we would need to do independently. Whether the ASU programs were good or bad, there would probably be times when most of the members would be only minimally involved. When that happened, the ASU leaders would have to figure out how to engage as many of the members as possible. The leaders would have to become consummate diplomats or incur the wrath of the active members.

A few minutes before adjourning, a student asked the last question: "What will we do if the white people think we're a bunch of Black Panthers?"

It was a good question.

"I don't care what they think," a booming voice responded, followed by laughter and cheers throughout the room. They were not fanatics or fools, but they were ready for the challenge.

The most thoughtful and prophetic answer was given by Sterlin Adams: "Whenever more than a handful of us get together on this campus, some white people think we're planning a riot. We shouldn't worry about what they think. We have to get ourselves stronger mentally and educationally. This organization will do that. When the time comes for us to silence our critics, we will do it. First, we have to take care of our own business."

Sterlin quickly grew into the role of a campus leader. Just one year later he would try to publicly silence our critics. On November 19, 1968, in an *Oklahoma Daily* article titled "Afro-American Students Plan Black Heritage Week," written by Sue Russell, Sterlin Adams, the new ASU president, was quoted as saying: "We are not a separatist organization. We are an organization where black students can fully identify," he said. "We have homogeneous problems and backgrounds. We are not a group of black militants. The American system taught us that we are black. Black power is the ability to do one's will. It is human dignity. We will take the best of black power and make it a realization." Sterlin also informed the writer that the ASU did not deny membership to any regularly enrolled students of other ethnic groups as long as they were in good academic and disciplinary standing, as determined by the University's dean of students, and they were willing to abide by the organization's constitution and bylaws. Of course, they also had to be willing to support the organization's fundamental goal: to promote a communal bond among students of African descent.[1]

Sterlin was an articulate, no-nonsense, task-oriented leader with considerable commitment and fortitude. When he spoke, he exuded confidence by conveying the students' indignation and resolve in just the right proportions. In the old days it had hardly mattered to most University administrators what black students said, but these were new days, and what black student leaders said did matter. The decision to create the organization meant that its members would tangle with the University's heavyweight champions — president, vice presidents, deans, chairpersons, and the other brokers of institutional power.

The Privilege of Helping the Students

Contrary to common rumors, the ASU was not conceived by Melvin Tolson or me. To suggest that it was discounts the students' creativity and independence. On their own initiative, with our encouragement, the graduates and undergraduates came together to create the University's first inclusive all-black organization, with more than one-fourth of the school's enrolled black students as active members. Melvin and I participated in the discussions, gave the students our advice when it was requested, and otherwise supported them.

Lennie Marie had tenure, but Melvin and I did not. By supporting the ASU, he and I were putting our careers at the University of Oklahoma on the line. If enough senior faculty members in our respective academic units believed the ASU was an undesirable organization, Melvin and I could have lost our jobs. Of course that was not something we wanted to happen. As things would turn out, most of our colleagues not only applauded us for sponsoring the ASU but also lent their support to it.

After that first official meeting of the ASU, while we were walking to our cars, Melvin said to me, "There's no turning back now, George. We are going to be in for some very interesting and difficult times. This begins a new day in race relations on this campus." It certainly did.

The ASU meetings became the classrooms in which we all — students and faculty members — taught and learned change strategies, solidarity, humility after victories, and strength after defeat. The meetings were where Melvin and I grew closer together. He became the brother I never had. He was a teacher extraordinaire and an insightful person. Our friendship was important to the students as well because the two of us had to be of one accord in order to provide consistent guidance to them. Lennie Marie lived in Oklahoma City and was less involved with the students and less known to them than were Melvin and I. We both imagined that we could emerge from the rubble of racial discord and various kinds of discrimination and teach a few of our best lessons. We also believed that the results of our involvement with the students might not always be grand, but they could always be more than satisfying for us.

Furthermore, we agreed that ASU program setbacks would not dull our enthusiasm for assisting the students. Together, as their mentors and advocates, we would try to find effective ways to present the ASU case to our colleagues in order to shore up the list of supporters. We guessed that a few positive program results would firm up any tepid student members' commitment to staying on what was surely going to be a long and trying journey. The challenges ahead of all of us were momentous. We wanted to feel good about ourselves, and we wanted to do good things for ourselves and for the University. But we were under no illusion that the ASU would be a permanent fix for all, or even most, of our racial problems. Unanticipated consequences abounded. Still, we thought that the ASU would be a helpful organization. Equally important, it probably was the best chance the black students had ever had to create a united presence in the University.

Summary

It is sad when bigotry comes to any town or school, and it is frightening and tragic when it is rampant in one's own. Decades of pent-up emotions were simmering near the edge of the students' restraint. It would have taken people far more forgiving than those students to shove the racial slights they were subjected to into corners of their minds reserved for trivial things. To them, nothing about racial segregation and discrimination was trivial. In the absence of strong leadership before 1967, the students who fought racism at the University of Oklahoma had muddled through as best they could, but they were not garden-variety students. As a whole, they were well-read, mature, and talented. The only thing missing was a comprehensive organization in which their latent abilities could be nurtured and applied.

Melvin and I thought that the Afro-American Student Union had the potential to become a principal countervailing civil rights force in the University. It was clear to me exactly why the ASU was created. The students belonged to separate and competing black fraternities, sororities, cliques, and clubs that did not achieve equal opportunities for most them in the University, so they had wisely decided to unite. They were finally ready for an umbrella organization that could cement them into a community of interdependent relationships.

Within the ASU, the black students would read and share theoretical perspectives, try out leadership roles, and take turns being loyal followers. If done correctly, I speculated, all of those things could make the University an intellectually fertile place for black students unmatched by any other college or university in Oklahoma, except perhaps Langston University. What mattered most to the students was the opportunity to be full citizens in the University community, as measured by the quality and fairness of the instruction they received. Beyond our animated discussions of strategies and tactics was the real world of resistance to change. Each new encounter with keepers of the status quo, I thought, would flush out the pseudo believers in this new organization. Those who remained active in the ASU would be its hard-core members — full-time rebels like Sterlin Adams.

Sterlin Adams Remembers the Beginning of the ASU

My wife, Norish, and I made contact with the University of Oklahoma and the city of Norman, Oklahoma, for the first time during the summer of 1964. My memory of that first experience is quite vivid. As we drove from Nashville, Tennessee, to Norman, we were unable to use public facilities and accommodations such as restaurants, hotels, and, in numerous instances, public restrooms at gasoline stations. They were reserved for white people only. While in Norman, as was customary for black people at the time, we endured the uncertainty of how we would be received by the OU students, staff, faculty, administrators, and other white people who lived there. The reception we received was mixed. But we were cordially and graciously received by some of the faculty members in the Department of Mathematics. That softened the impact of the campus environment, which tended to convey to us that we were summer school appendages and not truly desired students.

We were particularly struck by the near absence of black University employees. In addition to not seeing blacks as faculty and administrators, we noticed that there appeared to be no blacks employed as support staff in maintenance, security, grounds keeping, clerical positions, and so forth. There seemed to be a conscious effort to exclude blacks from all visible aspects of the University, including the art on the walls of buildings. The symbol of black life—individual black endeavors, contributions, and achievements—that we saw was contained within a large mural on the walls of a hall in the College of Business building. It depicted blacks in a field picking cotton. We did not have an opportunity to visit the athletics buildings to ascertain the type of representation of black participation that existed there.

Our contact with other black students was very limited. We saw and met only a handful of black graduate students. In conversation with them, we were told that the University had one black faculty member at its main campus in Norman. While pursuing coursework that summer, we were very relieved when President Lyndon B. Johnson signed the 1964 Civil Rights Act on July 2. The news enhanced our enjoyment of Independence Day, and it made our return trip back to Tennessee much less stressful. The comparison between the trip to Norman and the trip from Norman highlighted to us in a very clear and significant way the tremendous amount of stress that we black Americans had to endure as we navigated life from day to day.

Sterlin and Norish Adams at the Afro-American Ball, University of Oklahoma, February 15, 1969. Sterlin Adams collection.

Full-Time Students and National Events

Norish and I returned to OU for full-time study in the fall of 1966 as graduate students in the mathematics program. Norish was working toward a master's degree, and I was working toward a Ph.D. I observed no change in the near invisibleness of black faculty and staff members. And the cotton field mural in the College of Business building was still (to the best of my knowledge) the only visual depiction of black endeavors, achievements, or even existence at the University that was on display in a non-athletics building on the campus. Significant activities and changes had taken place elsewhere in the two intervening years since our first visit to the campus. Malcolm X had been assassinated, and the Student Nonviolent Coordinating Committee had developed much greater strength, power, and aggressiveness successfully expanding student-driven operations and activities.

Martin Luther King, Jr.'s march from Selma to Montgomery, Alabama, highlighted the widespread southern practices of using poll taxes and tests to screen out potential black voters. Also, a series of riots had taken place in major American cities—Cleveland, Los Angeles, New York, Philadelphia, and San Francisco—as black Americans protested brutal, oppressive force used by police; denial of voting rights; discrimination in hiring; discrimination in education resources in city schools; denial of access to historically white universities operating with public funds; and chronically high black unemployment and low income rates.

In the broader society, civil rights activities and black protests escalated at a rapid pace. As our 1966–67 academic year started, graduate students in particular began to get together for social and political conversations. Always at the center of those discussions was the paucity of blacks employed by the University, the small enrollment of black students, the lack of services to address our basic grooming needs, the glaring omission of cultural and social activities for blacks that were planned and sponsored by the University, and the belief that black students were not thought to be an integral part of campus life. Our informal black student network continued to grow, spurred by the tumultuous efforts and activities that were taking place throughout the country to address racism and the disenfranchisement of black Americans.

We were isolated socially. In many ways we were racial and cultural outcasts who had marginal acceptance and were given little regard in the mainstream academic enterprise of OU. Fortunately a modest number of people of goodwill and sensitivity openly sought to make black students feel as though they were welcome as full participants in University activities. I believe that all of the black students appreciated and valued those humane expressions and efforts extended to them. Despite that, the dynamics of the issues, incidents, and outcomes pertaining to the broader societal issues of race, civil rights, and injustice were so exceptionally frequent and intense and had such a great impact that the shortcomings of the University pertaining to racial integration were magnified.

Networking

As we continued to network and get together, our informal meetings became more frequent and the number of participants grew larger and larger. The growth was fueled in great part by the incidents and activities that were occurring with increasing frequency in the growing black revolt in America. In addition to the continuing national fight for civil rights led by Dr. King, the intensified battle for black political representation at local and state levels, and the black power movement for economic uplift and community control, were making headline news. There was a dramatic surge among blacks for positive self-identity and abolishment of institutionalized racism. Cultural awareness was enormously heightened among us at the University of Oklahoma and similar universities, and it culminated in the creation and maintenance of Afro-centric organizations.

Through our networking and group dialogues, we shared a greater knowledge of the barriers that impeded blacks' full participation on campus and statewide in education programs. Together we learned the history of the University's racial segregation policies and practices. Those barriers and history were generally unknown to the University community, and the institution showed no willingness to educate students, faculty, and staff about its historically negative responses to legal challenges pertaining to systemic conditions of racial segregation and discrimination. The University of Oklahoma had a long history of behaving unfairly and inequitably toward blacks who sought equal access and equal opportunities in its educational programs and jobs.

In our study groups, we learned of two of the most important events and court decisions pertaining to the behavior and commitment of the University to the education of blacks. The first of the two occurred in 1946 when Ada Lois Sipuel applied for admission to the law school and was denied it because of her race. After she was finally admitted on June 18, 1949, the University assigned her to a restricted area in the classroom; her chair was marked "Colored" and roped off from the rest of the class. Further, she was required to eat her lunch in a separate chained-off guarded area of the law school cafeteria. The second case was the federal court decree that ordered the University to admit George W. McLaurin, a black applicant, to the Graduate School. The College of Education required him to sit at a designated desk in an anteroom attached to the classroom where his fellow students sat; to use only a designated space in the mezzanine of the library; and to eat at a different time from that of his fellow students in the University's cafeteria, sitting at a designated table with a sign overhead that read "Reserved for Colored Only." In both instances, several white students tore down the barriers and removed the offensive signs.

The civil rights initiatives, protests, and outcomes in the broader society greatly affected my fellow black students and me. The aggressive, proactive, and organized push for an end to the oppressive and demeaning treatment of African Americans resonated with us. As we pursued our studies, we were bombarded with the daily news of efforts by blacks elsewhere to facilitate needed community and institutional changes for the betterment of all black Americans. Many of our black brothers and sisters were making the ultimate sacrifice—they lost their lives. We watched with great emotion and understanding as Bobby Seale and Huey P. Newton founded and launched the operations of the Black Panther Party; as Maulana Karenga developed the organization Us and originated the first Kwanzaa celebration; and as student protests escalated against the United States' involvement in the Vietnam War. Our consciousness was heightened about the unfairness in the way the draft and armed services assignments led to proportionately higher casualty rates for black GIs than for whites. We became incensed that black soldiers were fighting to maintain a free South Vietnamese society while our own nation abused us, denied us equal opportunities, and limited our access to those aspects of American society that represented high qualities of life.

As we carried on our academic activities and tried to master the knowledge of our chosen fields, we were emotionally absorbed in the swirling events throughout our nation in which black men and women were acting to gain equality for all of us. We had significant dialogues among ourselves when Martin Luther King, Jr., first spoke out against the Vietnam War and called the U.S. government "the greatest purveyor of violence in the world." We were spellbound as he attacked U.S. sales of weapons to foreign countries, encouraged draft evasion, and proposed a merger between the antiwar and civil rights movements. With a sharpened conscience, we watched heavyweight champion Muhammad Ali refuse induction into the U.S. Army and undergo arrest after being denied conscientious objector status. We were emotionally distraught when Mississippi police officers fired on a women's dormitory at the historically black Jackson State University when several students staged a protest demonstration. Two black male students were killed, a dozen other students were wounded, and no action was taken against the police officers. When the U.S. Supreme Court overturned the antimiscegenation marriage laws of the state of Virginia and fifteen other states, it served as a strong reminder to us of the massive systemic legal-based reasons why many white people still thought blacks were inferior to themselves.

Most searing and heart wrenching to us, as we sought to focus on our academic endeavors, was the loss of black American lives in late 1960s race

riots that stemmed from resistance to and rebellion against racial segregation and discrimination. We read about the 127 U.S. cities where that resistance left a toll of more than 75 dead black Americans and 4,000 injured.
Atlanta, Boston, Buffalo, Cincinnati, and Tampa had riots in June 1967. In
July there were riots in Birmingham, Chicago, New York, Milwaukee, Min-
neapolis, New Britain (Connecticut), Plainfield (New Jersey), and Rochester
(New York). The worst incidents occurred in Newark and Detroit. The beating of a black man after a traffic arrest on July 12 sparked the riots in
Newark that continued for five days. Police and National Guardsmen shot
indiscriminately at blacks. They killed 24 and injured more than 1,500. Riots
occurred in Detroit from July 23 to 30; federal troops were called in. Of the
43 people who were killed, 36 were blacks. More than 2,000 people were
injured, the police arrested 5,000, and another 5,000 were left homeless. H.
"Rap" Brown and Stokely Carmichael urged blacks to arm themselves for
an all-out revolution. Martin Luther King, Jr., called for a campaign of massive disobedience to bring pressure on the federal government to meet
black demands for racial equality and social justice. We felt a strong need to
do something noteworthy at the University of Oklahoma.

A Critical Mass of Black Students Come Together

Initially we were mainly graduate students networking to reinforce one
another as we attempted to meet rigorous academic benchmarks. But with
the perceived handicap of being defined by our teachers and fellow white
classmates as individuals who belonged to a disenfranchised minority racial group, we discussed ways to induce changes that would allow us to
succeed as scholars. We had lofty goals and an abundance of energy. Soon,
though, it became clear to us that we ought to seek out undergraduates
whose needs and ambitions coincided with our own. Together we could
possibly explore issues that affected us and identify strategies, tactics, and
resources that could help us bring about the changes we believed would
result in desirable outcomes for us. We all generally agreed that in order to
successfully navigate academic programs at the University of Oklahoma,
the institution ideally ought to have a commitment to friendliness to black
student life, reflected in a culturally inclusive learning environment that
encouraged and supported black involvement on every level, instead of
leaving blacks out of almost all "open" organizations. We did not believe
that our best performances were forthcoming in the current environment,

where at almost every juncture all indices suggested that more academic accommodations for us were not going to happen without our action.

The feeling of isolation in a cold and unwelcoming environment caused the black students to look outward to Oklahoma City's black community to find most of the services that we wanted. This included social, religious, and emotional support as well as recreational activities. The most obvious indication of the University's insensitivity to our needs was the absence of adequate financial, academic, social, and emotional services for us. Except for the black student athletes, who were somewhat embraced and insulated by special housing, academic tutors, and team membership identity, the black students were adrift on the campus. Incidental social abrasiveness, lack of University-sponsored social and cultural events that appealed to ethnic minorities, and inconvenient access to personal care and hair grooming services were a set of shared common experiences of black students.

There was a dearth of black faculty at the University of Oklahoma in 1966. When the black students began networking and reacting to the energy of the emerging black uprising of the late sixties, we were aware of only one black faculty member, Dr. Melvin Tolson, Jr., on the Norman campus. He was a very understanding, encouraging, and supportive person who in informal discussions with individual black students softened the harshness of the OU black student experience. He inspired many of the black students, and that inspiration enabled some of them to persevere and achieve their educational goals.

In 1967 Dr. George Henderson became the second black faculty member that I was aware of on the Norman campus. He joined the faculty at a time when black students at OU were coalescing toward the formation of a formal black student organization. There was a realization among us that the issues we wanted the University to confront and address could be resolved only if black students spoke with a common voice. Only through an organization with an ongoing life within the University could there be the continual prodding required to help steer and change it into an institution that exemplified excellence in its services to black students. Only then would there be parity by race in the distribution of benefits, social justice, and other indices of fairness and integrity in decisions that affect the conditions of all people at the University.

The kinship between the two black faculty members and the black students was extraordinary. George Henderson, with his great eloquence of expression, distinguished himself with his oratory and became a voice from the black faculty that echoed the heartbeat of our student struggle. For many black students, his home and family became the essential elements of inclusion that made the University a bit more tolerable. To the black students, most of whom felt fenced out of campus and Norman's community activities, his doors were always open. And behind those doors for all of us was a wealth of understanding. His identification with our needs and our struggle to get those needs met was always apparent. In addition, his participation with students in their efforts to facilitate change was exemplary as he gave his voice to communicate broadly the appropriateness of black student involvement in the promotion of change at the University.

The formation of the Afro-American Student Union was done carefully, with the understanding that there would be a great deal of concern within the University if someone organized a formal group to advocate for changes to transform the institution into an entity that was sensitive and responsive to the needs of African American students. First, we formed an Afro-American student study group that consisted of thirty-two graduate and undergraduate students. During the next three months of the fall semester of the 1967–68 academic year, we established a plan of communications and organization to inform and encourage all black students at the University—and other students who were interested—to participate in an open organizational meeting.

On Sunday, November 12, 1967, we discussed the elements, framework, and details of a constitution and by-laws for the organization and delegated to a constitutional committee the task of writing a document reflective of the input from the study group. A draft of the constitution was immediately forthcoming from the committee, and it was widely circulated on November 16. On November 19 the student senate approved the Afro-American Student Union as an official University student organization, with Dr. Tolson as the faculty adviser. Because Dr. Henderson signed the constitution, he could not be an official faculty adviser, but in every other way, he was indeed an adviser. Thus a vibrant, effective organization was established. Norish and I were proud to be founding members, and we committed ourselves to the struggle for the realization of the organization's goals and objectives.[2]

CHAPTER FOUR

Seeds of a Rebellion

L ong before the black students at the University of Oklahoma created
the Afro-American Student Union, there was an undeniable bub-
bling of discontent among them about problems that centered on racial
segregation and discrimination. Also there were sporadic interracial public discussions that some people interpreted as solving problems. In fact,
most of those discussions were shallow debates about racism that seldom
amounted to anything more than intellectual donnybrooks. Consequently, the results were more exasperating than ameliorating. Equally
important was that there were no ultimate winners — only callous discussants. It would be a mistake to say that nothing positive came out of those
interactions, but unfortunately, conciliatory results were too few. So the
race relations pot just kept boiling.

The Pot Boils Over

On February 1, 1968, Sue Cummings wrote in her *Oklahoma Daily* column, "Expanding," a terse indictment of white fraternities and sororities: "The annual George Wallace Separate-But-Equal Award goes to
those brotherly and sisterly societies for their contributions to the field of
intolerance. (Where would discrimination, prejudice, oppression, and
Campus Corner be without them?)" Rebuttals from irate white Greeks

came immediately. A trickle of lukewarm complaints gave way to a torrent of acidic defensiveness. The editorial opened to public debate decades of questions that were inherent in parallel Greek and non-Greek university communities. The swiftness and caustic nature of the responses laid bare a divide that extended beyond Greek societies. All aspects of the issue — excluding the reasons for the continued existence of racially segregated fraternities and sororities in an allegedly desegregated school — were passionately discussed in several letters to the editor of the *Oklahoma Daily* and in other formal and less formal dialogues. Few people wanted to admit that racially segregated Greek organizations were a problem.

In cooperation with the University Christian Movement and the University's Union Activities Board committees, the Afro-American Student Union held the first annual Oklahoma Conference for Black Collegians on February 16, 1968. The theme "Where Do We Go from Here?" was taken from the title of Dr. Martin Luther King, Jr.'s recent book. Sterlin Adams, the president of the ASU, was the conference chairperson, and black representatives from most of the Oklahoma colleges and universities attended. Ron Karenga, chair of the black national cultural organization Us, was the featured speaker. His presentation was emotionally engulfing. One minute we were laughing; the next, we were grimacing. The overall effect was consciousness-raising. He challenged each of us to accept responsibility for preventing or abating racial abuse — or for perpetuating it. Mostly, though, he relieved us of our complacency. He urged the blacks in the audience to close ranks and foster black self-pride, self-determination, and, if necessary, self-defense. Guest speakers who presented separatist ideologies always made it difficult for the black students to retain their moderate supporters. But they attracted fringe supporters, particularly those who believed that racial integration was a cruel hoax foisted on blacks to pacify them.

Eight black students presented workshops at the conference: John Coleman, Zelbert Moore, Norish and Sterlin Adams, Willie Wilson, Bruce Robinson, and Preston Dinkins, all graduate students, and Guinnevere Hodges, a junior. In addition, three faculty members — Melvin Tolson, psychiatry professor Chester M. Pierce, and I — were presenters. As the final conference speaker, I suggested that we ought to move from talk to action centering on the overarching goal of fostering racially inclusive and less hostile colleges and universities for black people. Several of the other presenters had made the same points. Even so, our respective campuses held numerous reminders of the difficulty in taking such actions.

Two days later, Richard E. Young, chairman of the Metro Denver (Colorado) Fair Housing Center, delivered a campus presentation that exposed yet another fissure in black-white relations at the University of Oklahoma. His speech focused on housing ("Open Housing — Is a Law Necessary?"), but it etched itself deep into the minds of individuals who feared violence from blacks. The nation had experienced several race riots from 1965 to 1967, and a consequence was rampant fear among countless white people, including many at our university, who thought that desegregated dormitories and Greek houses would put white students at unnecessary risk of being hurt by black students. During the question-and-answer period that followed Young's speech, a white coed asked him about violence.

Before Young could respond, Bruce Robinson said, "Based on a survey conducted by the Afro-American Student Union during Black History Week [February 11–17], few — less than 10 percent — of the 500 respondents believed that violence was a good way to counter racism. That's probably true nationally, too." Still, neither the coed nor her sorority sisters who were present at the meeting were convinced. It never dawned on them that blacks might abhor violence too.

That same week, one of several black students eating lunch with me in the Student Union asked me what I thought about the Loyal Knights of Old Trusty. He was asking about the College of Engineering honor students who donned black robes and black hoods with holes for the eyes. They fired a cannon to symbolically protect their college from marauding law school students, and also during Engineer Week, when their identities were revealed. Created in 1920, this campus ritual apparently had no racial purpose, at least at this time. The Loyal Knights of Old Trusty was the only Oklahoma-approved state organization that wore hoods, however.

I said, "Maybe they're the sons or grandsons of members of the White Knights of the Ku Klux Klan."

We laughed, but it wasn't a comforting laugh.

One of the students said, "That's a scary thought." Indeed it was.

Were we being paranoid about the Loyal Knights of Old Trusty?

Loyal Knights of Old Trusty (LKOT), 1968. Western History Collections, University of Oklahoma Libraries.

Probably. Our perception of the Loyal Knights was grounded in history. For most black people there was nothing funny or cute pertaining to white people dressed in up in sheets and wearing hoods like the Ku Klux Klan. So, yes, we took the Loyal Knights out of context. From time to time we turned innocent people or events inside out in our minds. That's what oppressed people often do. If that was paranoia, then so be it. We chose to err on the side of being cautious. Too many of our ancestors had been fooled into accepting supposedly well-meaning white people who in reality hurt them.

"What should we do about those hooded guys?" another student asked me.

This is a teachable moment, I thought, as I responded, "What do you think Saul Alinsky would do?"

Two of the students, almost in unison, suggested, "Turn a negative situation into a positive one."

That is exactly what I had in mind. Pleased with their response, I said, "Yes, I agree with you. Let's talk about how we might do that. For the sake of our discussion, let's say that members of the Loyal Knights, the highest student engineering honor society, are anything but positive role models for black people. Still, they could be worse. Under other circumstances, they could be running around at night wearing sheets of any color with color-coordinated hoods and doing something far more harmful than firing a cannon on campus. They could be out at night looking for you and me to beat up or lynch. So how can we turn the concept of the Loyal Knights inside out?"

I expected them to pick up on my train of thought. Instead the student who had started the conversation surprised me by mixing a bit of my own philosophizing with Alinsky's tactic. "The Loyal Knights is a concept," he argued. "If this concept isn't doing anything to hurt black people, let's do what you call 'mind over mattering them.' We don't mind them being on campus where we can see what they're doing; and they don't matter to us as long as they aren't harming us. The black hoods look menacing, but looks can't kill us."

Another student had a different approach: "I find the Knights offensive in the same way that I find the Rebel flag offensive. And I don't want white people on our campus wearing black hoods. I think we ought to express our disgust about the Loyal Knights and request that they cease to exist on this campus as a University-recognized club or group." The consensus among the group was to follow this student's strategy. He had picked a target, frozen it, personalized it, and devised a strategy to destroy it. Alinsky would have been proud of him.

I wrapped up the discussion with "Enough said," making a note to myself to file an official complaint with University president-designate J. Herbert Hollomon. I followed through the next week. That didn't put the Loyal Knights out of business, but the groundwork had been laid.

In working with students, I learned to let them give new life to old strategies, based on their unique life experiences. Indeed, I opened myself to truly seeing how the students made sense of the University from the perspective of their own needs. In all instances, I wanted them not merely to read the words of various theorists but also to absorb their meanings. Equally important, I wanted them to be open to alternative approaches to applying the theories. Whenever I offhandedly rejected their points of view, a rigid barrier sprung up between us. Perhaps the most painful lesson I learned was that no matter how well read or prepared the students and I were, situations always arose that defied happy endings for us. Sometimes when that happened, my emotions clouded my judgment, as it did on the day after Dr. King was assassinated.

April 4, 1968, was a memorable day. I was driving to the University to pick up a report that required more revisions. When I approached an outer edge of the campus, a subdued voice on the radio interrupted the music with a news report: "Martin Luther King was shot and killed in Memphis." I wondered why someone would kill Dr. King's father. The voice continued, "The world has been shaken by the death of one of its most respected civil rights leaders."

Then I realized that the unthinkable was true. Martin Luther King, Jr., was dead. When I thought Dr. King's father was dead, I was upset; Dr. King's death emotionally pulverized me. I screamed, "No! Damn it, no!" I turned the car around and drove home. Barbara and four of our daughters were sitting motionless in the living room, crying and staring at television coverage of Dr. King's assassination. She and I gathered the girls into our interlocking arms and drew them close to us. In her typical calming voice, Barbara assured them they would be safe. Then she looked at me and mouthed, "You better be safe." Later that day, when our other children came home, she and I talked to them about the importance of honoring Dr. King's memory through nonviolent behavior when seeking racial equality.

Around 10 P.M. Maggie Gover, president-designate Hollomon's administrative assistant, called and asked me to join Hollomon and Bruce Robinson, president of the Afro-American Student Union, as speakers at a noon memorial service the next day, honoring Dr. King. Although Hollomon would not become president until July 1, he wanted the University community know his beliefs about race relations in general and about Dr. King in particular. President Cross and Hollomon had already issued a joint public statement condemning Dr. King's assassination as a depraved act. The ceremony would give Hollomon an opportunity to elaborate on the statement. After I agreed to be a speaker, I realized I would not be able to say everything I wanted to in the fifteen minutes allocated to me. I stayed up the remainder of the night writing and rewriting my speech.

On April 5 about 1,500 people gathered on the South Oval, many of them openly weeping as they slowly staked out places to sit and hear the speakers. As I made my way through the sea of silent, somber faces of various ethnic groups and ages, I saw fifty or so black students sitting together, away from the main body of spectators. They were crying, hugging, and otherwise consoling each other, as though a member of their family had been killed. Culturally, that is exactly what had happened. When I reached the platform and took my seat, I began sobbing. It took all the self-control that I could muster to regain my composure. Hollomon was sitting next to me. He reached over and put his right hand on my back, giving me a gentle pat. Then he then got up and delivered a compassionate message of sorrow, and he promised to make Dr. King's dream real at our school.

I thought about the group of grieving black students. They had come to the memorial to hear my voice speak for them. I hoped that I would be able to adequately express our collective grief and anger. In other venues throughout the United States, those same emotions had fueled riots. My body was in Norman, but my mind was in a black inner city far away. Unfortunately, I ceased to be a spokesperson for all of the people present and instead became an angry black man whose hero had been murdered. It was hard for me to speak. I deviated from my written speech and uttered these words in anger: "We black Americans are losing our zest for

Henderson speaks at Martin Luther King, Jr., ceremony, South Oval, University of Oklahoma, 1968. *Norman Transcript*; reprinted with permission.

the so-called 'American dream.' A portion of that dream died with Martin Luther King. . . . [He] was a nonviolent man, and you [white Americans] killed him."

I wish those words had not been spoken — and certainly not by me. I had accused innocent people of committing a heinous crime. Some of them were my allies. I had done what I deplored: I generalized and stereotyped people. "Shame on you," someone rightly wrote to me a week later in an anonymous note. All of the hours I had spent encouraging students and others to respect and accept each other were thrown into question during that brief fit of rage. Some of those I'd accused were also ardent civil rights advocates, committed to the movement for religious or moral reasons. They were the kind of white people Malcolm X encouraged blacks to form coalitions with. This incident was a painful reminder to choose my words judiciously. Words matter because they have consequences.

A few days later, on April 10, Herbert Inhaber wrote this in an *Oklahoma Daily* column: "In general, there is far less bias against foreign students in housing than against Negroes. Yet if color is a criterion, many foreign students are darker than many Negroes. Could it be that landlords know that foreign students will return home, and that Negroes might want to stay in Norman? So much for housing. It seems that the good burghers of Norman may be less pleasant than they seem at first."

Inhaber had spoken the truth. Safe havens from racism for blacks at the University of Oklahoma or in the city of Norman were few. To the extent that I was able to decipher the black students' muffled emotions that grew out of being discriminated against when seeking housing, they included anger, disgust, and sadness. Not all of the black students were silent. A very small number of them, whose anger had mutated and multiplied, became physically combative. They preferred retribution of any kind instead of rapprochement. I told those who sought my counsel to refrain from fighting and to protest nonviolently. When they repeated their grievances to me, I had difficulty convincing myself that they ought to turn the other cheek, so to speak, especially when they had no unbruised cheek to turn. All things considered, I knew from my own experiences that whenever black peoples' anger, even in words, was publicly turned outward to white people, it usually led to retaliation. White vengeance or rejection, instead of either justice or acceptance, was a likely outcome. It was a lesson that several black athletes would also learn.

Unhappy Black Athletes

On May 2, 1968, Benjamin Hart II, commonly known as Ben Hart, engaged in what most Oklahoma football fans defined as the ultimate betrayal. His *Oklahoma Daily* interview ("Ben Hart Discusses SEE [Students for Equal Employment], Race Relations, Football") by student journalist David Wise was the first volley in several allegations of systemic racism in the University's most prized and publicly visible asset: the football team. Ben, a former football star and now a graduate student, said that black athletes, more than white athletes, were exploited, discriminated against, and thrown away when they could no longer perform. If he was correct, and I believed that he was, then as the messenger he was in harm's way. No amount of damage control by the Athletics Department's news spin-

Ben Hart, 1968. Western
History Collections, University
of Oklahoma Libraries.

ners could put the genie's message back in its once tightly sealed public
relations bottle. Nor would ignoring the allegations make them go away.

On May 3, Ben came to my office to get my opinion about the interview. "What do you think, Doc? Did I tell it like it is?"

He was obviously feeling good about the interview. I wasn't sure that
he would like my answer: "What you said needed to be said by an athlete
of your status. But some people will say that you should have said something while you were playing football. And there will be the question of
your timing. Perhaps it's better late than never for you to have had the
interview. But I bet that thousands of OU football fans would have preferred that you never gave it. Why did you wait so long?"

He had anticipated my question. Almost before I could finish the
sentence, he responded, "When I was playing ball and getting the honors, I was only concerned about me. I didn't want to rock the boat. I
bought into the team concept of not ratting on my coaches and teammates. Whatever happened on the field and within the team stayed there.

Then you came to this school and started talking about using our popularity to help other people. You and my other professors in the College of Education challenged me to speak out when I see abusive conditions. It's way past time for me to set the race relations situation straight in football at this school."

He was relieved to get those words out. It was as if he had lifted several years of guilt off his back. He straightened his shoulders, tilted his head up, and said, "Whew!" Yet he and I were reasonably certain that the worst was yet to come. We guessed correctly. The public reaction to him would be like none he had ever experienced before. His long career with its many accolades became tarnished in the minds of an indignant public that worshipped the University of Oklahoma football team and its players — but only if they were loyal. Ben was no longer a star, and his allegations of racial discrimination in the football program took away his team player aura. The ripple of disgust over the newspaper interview spread quickly throughout the University and the state.

On the next day, Oklahoma radio talk shows were flooded with scurrilous opinions about Ben's exposé. The mean-spirited nature of the tirades made me thankful that we were not living in an 1800s Wild West community where lynch mob justice sometimes settled bitter disputes. Symbolically, though, Ben's critics substituted words for a rope, and he swung mercilessly from the end of their sarcastic comments such as "an ex-jock who didn't complain when he was feeding out of the scholarship trough" and "an egomaniac who will do anything to see his name in the papers again" and "a misguided person duped into spouting civil rights trash."

Whether callers agreed or disagreed with Ben, none of them were impartial. A few — largely blacks — supported him, but most callers said that his allegations were a bunch of nonsense. One caller said that the story was a smear planted by an Oklahoma State University fan. The general sentiment, on and off the campus, was that Ben was way out of bounds for, as they saw it, trying to pander to black civil rights leaders. Rightly or wrongly, Ben had become the University's Benedict Arnold. I was infuriated by the crassness of most of the critics who lined up to take a verbal shot at him. The cheaper the shot, the more it resonated with other critics. Battered by public opinion and crestfallen, a distraught Ben Hart came to my office to garner my support, which he already had. Then

I asked him a question we both knew the answer to: "Why is there so much anger about your interview?"

He looked at the floor, as if a more profound reply were hidden in the dust on my carpet. Then he looked up at me and said, "I broke an OU Athletics Department commandment: speak no evil of the Athletics Department, its coaches or players."

A week after the interview, appalled and frustrated by the general public's mostly derisive comments about him, Ben convened a meeting with a dozen University of Oklahoma black athletes in an apartment on the University campus, and he asked me to attend. I was pleased to oblige him. The small living room was filled with some of our most highly celebrated black athletes in football, basketball, track and field, gymnastics, and wrestling—past, present, and future. They had already discussed several issues before I arrived, and their mood was somber. I was asked to formulate a strategy that would help abolish what a couple of the young men referred to as "rampant racist behaviors." I agreed to facilitate the discussion but under no circumstances would I devise their strategy. And I was emphatic that unless at least the majority of the athletes who were present, as well as those absent, could agree on a strategy, support it, and not denounce it after it was executed, we were all wasting our time at the meeting. They agreed with me.

"So where are you in the decision-making process?" I asked them.

Ben answered, "We've made a list of problems that impact black athletes in OU sports. Some of the guys want to wait until the semester ends before pursuing solutions."

"Would that be the best time? How many of you will be here after the semester ends," I probed. Only three hands were raised.

Willie Wilson, a basketball player, said that it would be a cop-out to wait because by then almost all of the men in the room would be long gone. "We have to do this thing before the semester ends if we're going to do it at all." I agreed with him, and so did most of the other men in the room.

"Is timing the only other issue that needs to be aired?" I continued the discussion.

Another basketball player, Garfield Heard, spoke up. "No, it isn't just about timing," he said. "The big thing is reprisals. Some of the guys in this meeting are afraid of reprisals. What we are about to do could cost several of us big time in terms of our life after we leave here. The football and basketball players might be labeled as troublemakers, and that could cost us big bucks if we got a pro contract."

I could not believe what was happening. The unspoken fear had been spoken. That opened the door for me to give my "sacrifice" speech: "Anything worth doing that goes against established norms will have risks. Each of you will have to decide how much you are willing to risk losing." Then I said rather forcefully, "A lot of people risked their careers, jobs, and lives so that all of you could be at this school. If this protest is too great a risk for you to take, I encourage you to leave now." I told them that not every black athlete had to have been discriminated against for the charge of institutional racism to be valid.

They looked at each other. No one said a word, and nobody got up to leave.

Granville "Granny" Liggins spoke for the first time. "We've got to do something for the young bucks that will be coming to this school," he noted. "And for those who still have playing time left. This is not for me or Ben or Willie."

They all nodded. Anxiety spread slowly across their faces, betraying their bravado. The lucid, thoughtful discussion that took place, if video-taped, would have dispelled any notion of dumb black athletes. The young men in the room were as skillful at presenting their arguments as they were at performing in their sports. Finally, they reached a unanimous decision about their strategy. Representatives of the group would present their grievances to the athletics director; if he did not respond in a positive way, they would give him a formal list of grievances, with signatures from all of the athletes who were present in the apartment and most of those who were not. But the reality of doing that was not that simple. They were going to tell things that they did not feel comfortable telling the public. As they filed out of the apartment, I thought I saw tears in the eyes of a few of the men who were fearless in their sports. But now they were afraid that they were going to put their pro careers in jeopardy in order to do battle with a very strong foe: racism. Win or lose, they agreed to be a team of black brothers.

After meeting with representatives of the group, Gomer Jones, the athletics director, failed to grant them even one concession. At the annual "O" Club banquet on May 8, graduate students Ben Hart (football) and Willie Wilson (basketball), senior Granville Liggins (football and wrestling), junior San Tol DeBose (football), and sophomores Garfield Heard and Charles Shiver (wrestling) gave him a formal list of 27 grievances, and then they and several other black athletes walked out. Never before had black athletes en masse boycotted an Athletics Department activity or any other University activity to protest racial discrimination. That got the Athletics Department's attention, as well as widespread radio and newspaper coverage. The boycott, however distasteful, was just what the University and the public needed in order to be awakened to the pervasiveness of the black students' unrest. The uproar wasn't over a list of grievances drawn up by a mere six athletes, however. Thirteen other black athletes signed the list of grievances too. The football, basketball, wrestling, gymnastics, and track and field programs were each a source of the grievances — all of the OU sports that had black scholarship athletes. The University needed those athletes, and that inconvenient fact stuck in the craw of most of the coaches.

Among the grievances, the following ones stood out: (1) No black coaches, counselors, trainers, secretaries, or other personnel were employed in the Athletics Department. (2) Black athletes were not allowed to have mustaches, beards, or long hair. (3) Coaches talked down to their black athletes but seldom to their white athletes. (4) Interracial dating, specifically between black athletes and white females, was discouraged by the coaches. (5) Black athletes were assigned black roommates or had their own room if no other blacks were available. (6) There were no black athletes on the baseball, tennis, golf, and swimming teams. (7) Black athletes competed with each other for the same team positions, thereby leaving most of the positions exclusively for white athletes. (8) There were no black quarterbacks, and none had been recruited. (9) Black athletes were seldom told about or referred to summer jobs; unlike most white athletes, they and their spouses had to find their own jobs.

When challenged, most specifically, about the legitimacy of the allegations and the solidarity of the black athletes, Charlie Shiver, careful to not overstate the problem of racism, gave an eloquent reply to Larry Chilnick, managing editor of the *Oklahoma Daily*, on May 16, 1968: "I knew from the start that in committing myself that whatever the result, good or bad, we would be held responsible as a group and not as individuals. Whether we were wrong or right in presenting the complaints is beyond the point. Each and every individual is entitled to his or her personal opinion about the grievances that we presented. Regardless as to how I feel and whether or not I was affected by those grievances, my support is still with the group of athletes."

Numerous public comments poked fun at the black athletes, and an onslaught of unsettling newspaper and radio comments about them ensued. Several of the athletes were mocked as being deceitful or, worse yet, outright liars. But they did not break ranks. On May 10, track and field's Wayne and Glen Long and Gregory Graham were publicly criticized in the *Oklahoma Daily* by their white teammates. Shortly thereafter, the black runners were dismissed from the track team for missing a practice. What could have resulted in a hardening of polar positions was resolved in a pleasant manner. After a series of reconciliation sessions, Coach J. D. Martin reinstated Wayne, Glen, and Gregory, and the track team was unified for the first time. It was a good outcome.

The black basketball players had the most contentious and long-running feud with their coach, John MacLeod. They vehemently objected to several of his rules and his punitive behavior, including his "clean shaven and short hair" requirement, his verbally and physically abusive style of coaching, harsher rules for blacks than whites, unequal meal funds, dismissal from the athletics dorm without providing for alternative housing and meals, and a generally condescending attitude toward the black players. The hair restrictions negatively affected only the black athletes, whose cultural norms associated Afros and beards with black males' manhood and dignity. The grooming codes of the white athletes fostered clean-shaven faces and cropped hair. Although both the black and the white athletes resented MacLeod's verbal and physical coaching style, only the black players complained about it publicly. The grievances of all of the athletes would be echoed seven months later in a news conference called by the Afro-American Student Union. Thus, the "O" Club boycott was a seminal moment in what would later crystallize into a black student revolt at the University of Oklahoma.

Closer to Home

In August 1968 two important but generally unnoticed appointments were made in the College of Fine Arts: Thomas Carey and Carol Brice

Carey were hired as visiting professors of music. Their appointments increased the number of black faculty to five, and they were the second black homeowners in Norman. Their prior concert performance commitments greatly limited the time they spent at the University in 1968–69, but in subsequent years these internationally famous singers would put their own unique mark on the University of Oklahoma by recruiting and training black singers and founding the Cimarron Circuit Opera Company (1975) and the Jazz in June program in Norman (1984). Equally important, they became two of Barbara's and my most treasured friends..

During the spring 1968 semester, I made a passing remark in my social problems class. Specifically, I said that most apartments in Norman were racially segregated, and the University was complicit in it. A skeptical student challenged my remarks, "What facts do you have to back up those outrageous claims?" She knew of several places where black students lived, including in her eastside apartment complex. The six black students and half of the thirty-two white students in the class sided with me. For many of the white students, the most troubling aspect of my comments was the allegation that the University contributed to the problem. I had not planned to focus on housing discrimination, but my off-the-cuff remarks opened the door.

I decided to let the students check the veracity of my allegations. They would use a common open housing test used by a civil rights agency. I divided the students into teams of two: fifteen all-white teams, two racially mixed teams, and two all-black teams. Each team had one of its members go to the University housing office and get a list of approved apartments for rent that was updated weekly. The property representatives on the list had declared that their apartments were available for all applicants who could afford them. In essence, the University served as an unpaid broker. The students then divided the listings among them. Every apartment would be checked to see if it was still available for renting to the all-white, mixed-race, and all-black teams.

One week later, as I approached the classroom, I could hear the students talking loudly. They were furious. The results of their test verified my allegation of racial discrimination. The all-white student teams were offered every rental on the list. The mixed-race and all-black teams were offered apartments only in the complexes that already had black renters. All of those apartments were on the east side of Norman. To

President George L. Cross explains University housing policies to students, 1968. Western History Collections, University of Oklahoma Libraries.

make matters worse, in every instance where the mixed or all-black teams were denied apartments, it was because they supposedly had already been rented. But when the all-white teams inquired shortly after the other teams had been turned down, they were offered the apartments, with the assurance that no blacks would be allowed to live there.

I asked the furious students, "What can we do about this situation?"

"Burn them down," someone volunteered.

Another student said, "Picket them."

They almost immediately lost the desire to commit arson or to form picket lines. But a consensus formed to tell the University housing office about the discriminatory practices the students had uncovered. Several of the students also called the president's office and complained. President Cross met with approximately one hundred demonstrators on the North Oval outside the administration building and assured the students, many of whom were enrolled in my classes, that the University did not in any way

Dick Gregory gives a public speech at the University of Oklahoma Field House, 1968, from University of Oklahoma 1969 yearbook.

condone racial discrimination in housing — on or off campus. Over the weekend, the University stopped providing students with lists of vacant apartments. Although that put an end to the campus listing service, it did not stop or even mildly curtail the discriminatory act of denying black people access to certain apartments. Even so, it was an important accomplishment for the students.

On September 20 civil rights activist Dick Gregory gave a public lecture at the University field house to a packed house of more than three thousand people. The mood of the audience alternated between glee, sadness, anger, and shame. Plying his skills as a comedian, orator, and outraged citizen, Gregory stimulated our emotions by explaining how a wide range of topics — politics, war, crime, racism, and justice — intersected. I took mental note of his ability to jab at our guilt, pull back with calculated humor, and ease in again with burning questions. Gregory's extemporaneous bursts of excitement reached out and pulled me in with him. It was a teaching technique that I adopted with startling results. I

became a better teacher and a better community speaker. The day before
his speech, Gregory was a guest at my house. My older children were
pleasantly surprised by his playful nature and concern about their school
grades. Barbara was equally surprised by his love for her sweet potato pie,
which he ate in large bites. He was a delightful houseguest.

The Ohm Committee

On December 6, 1968, in a letter to the *Oklahoma Daily*, the Afro-American
Student Union demanded that basketball coach John MacLeod be fired
for discriminating against his black players. Reacting quickly, the Athletics
Council established a committee on December 9 to investigate the allegation and make recommendations to the council. The full Athletics Council in turn would forward a final report, along with recommendations, to
President Hollomon. The committee was chaired by College of Education
dean Robert E. Ohm. Also on the committee was Zelbert Moore, assistant
to David Burr (vice president for the University Community) and a member of the Afro-American Student Union. All of the Ohm Committee
members except Zelbert were also members of the Athletics Council.
Shortly after his appointment, Zelbert and I discussed the committee. I
asked him how thorough and objective he thought it would be.

"I'm on it. Don't you trust me, Dr. Henderson?"

"Of course I trust you, Zelbert. But it seems to me that a committee
loaded with members of the Athletics Council would not find it to be in
their best interest to say that John MacLeod was guilty. That would be an
admission of their negligence in overseeing the basketball program. Also,
those conclusions, if true, would be a public relations nightmare for the
University. It would provide fodder for anti-OU talking points that basketball coaches could use when recruiting the same athletes as us."

"Then are you saying that I'm wasting my time?"

"No, I'm suggesting that you ought to give serious thought to what
helpful information you can insert in the report that will allow those who
read it to better understand the gravity of race relations problems at OU."

We stood on the South Oval for close to thirty minutes discussing,
debating, arguing, and finally agreeing that Zelbert had a rare opportunity to educate naïve people about minority cultures and social equality in athletics and in the University. Like many of the young men and

women in the ASU, Zelbert was well-read, articulate, and a fantastic debater, and his philosophy courses gave him a splendid edge. He would hold his own, I thought as we parted. Even if he was outvoted, he would represent blacks at the University of Oklahoma exceptionally well.

The Ohm Committee completed its deliberations around the first week in February, and the Athletics Council submitted its own report and the Ohm Committee Report to President Hollomon on February 13, 1969. David Burr submitted a separate report to him. One member of the Ohm Committee signed an exception to its report. I didn't have to ask Zelbert if it was he who signed the exception. He told me. The two reports plus David Burr's cleared Coach MacLeod of the racial discrimination charges. However, all three of the reports cited his racial insensitivity, inconsistent team rules, informal team policies, and overall University deficiencies in human relations skills. Most of the so-called errors in judgment, which were typical nationally among coaches in all sports, were moot points because supposedly they had been rectified. I saw Zelbert a few days after President Hollomon's exoneration of Coach MacLeod.

"You were right, Doc. I was outvoted before we formally voted — "

"But you were able to have the racial insensitivity statements inserted, weren't you?"

I was proud of him.

It was at most a shallow victory for the black students. In reality, it was a bitter defeat for the members of the ASU, which had demanded MacLeod's termination. Sterlin Adams's reaction to the exoneration gave little hope that the ASU would utilize the human relations committee that David Burr recommended in his addendum to the Ohm Committee Report. The committee would investigate charges of discrimination. Sterlin said that the ASU was not in a mood to trust another Hollomon committee: "We considered this a test case of the new administration to see how fair and thorough it would be in matters of this type. . . . We went through what they call 'proper channels.' We played our role as they say we should. Now we may have no choice except to go outside those channels."[1] The ASU was not ready to abandon the black athletes' grievances. Those grievances would soon be brought forward again.

A few days later, Professor Fred Silberstein came into my office, visibly shaken. He was holding in his right hand a sheet of paper that was meant for me, but someone had mistakenly put it in his mailbox. It contained

Henderson addresses a "teach-in" audience at the University of Oklahoma, 1968. Western History Collections, University of Oklahoma Libraries.

vile words, and a crude hangman's noose was drawn at the bottom of the page. Gaining his composure, Fred asked me, "Are you going to report this to the police?"

"Which ones should I report it to?" I asked him. "The OU police, who can't catch the creeps who are scribbling anti-black messages on the campus sidewalks, or the Norman police, who periodically harass blacks for being in certain neighborhoods, stores, and restaurants?"

"It wouldn't do much good to report it," he said apologetically. Fred had done nothing wrong, but he bore shame for those who had.

When I told some of my white students about several of the blatant acts of racism that many black people in Norman and the University had to endure, I felt like a science fiction traveler, picking up tales of abuse on one planet and sharing them with unsuspecting race relations novices on another one. At first they had difficulty making sense of what seemed to them to be fabricated tales of a university that bore no resemblance to their reality. After they talked with other black people, however, many of the anti-black incidents at the University formed so precisely in their minds that they ceased to be novices. They became enraged. My ongoing conversation with the students about racial discrimination was as therapeutic for me as it was disconcerting for most of them. I found out that when my concerns pertaining to racial abuses were fused with other people's empathy, the result was a soothing emotional balm. It mattered very much to me that Fred Silberstein, other faculty colleagues, and many of my students cared about me and the other human targets of bigots on our campus. On November 5, I told over 250 students at a "Day On" teach-in lecture about racial issues, especially segregation. It was an excellent way for me to spend a "holiday."

Calm before the Storm

In 1969, Black History Week fell on February 9–16, and its celebration on campus was the calm before the activist storm. The Afro-American Student Union sponsored public appearances by authors Louis E. Lomax and Arna Bontemps and saxophonist Julian "Cannonball" Adderley. These three deeply touched the students' inner resolve to do more than spout cute phrases such as "Black is beautiful" and "Power to the people!" The visitors also stirred timely slivers of hope within the students. Lomax asked them to decide with certainty what price they were willing to pay for gaining their equal rights, Bontemps asked them what history they would make, and Adderley told them to sing songs of freedom. Suddenly the black students' campus lives seemed unbearably meager when compared with the lives of their white classmates. Lomax, Bontemps, and Adderley were added to a long list of black celebrities whom Barbara and I would have as our dinner guests during their brief visits to the University of Oklahoma.

On the cool, muggy night of February 9, Louis Lomax, three students, and I sat in his Howard Johnson Inn room, staring at a half-empty fifth of bourbon. We had gone there after his public presentation so that he could wind down. After the students left, I poured two equal shots and gave him one. We were silent for a long time, waiting for the alcohol to take effect. We had already reminisced for more than two hours about the civil rights movement and our dreams, victories, setbacks, and fears. Then, as if speaking to himself, Louis said in a soft voice, "You know,

Left to right: Sterlin Adams, Louis Lomax, and Melvin Tolson, 1969. Sterlin Adams collection.

George, we have spent the better part of our lives trying to gain our freedom so that our children can come to an almost all-white place like this and say, 'I don't want to live here or even go to school here.' I can't blame them. I'm tired of trying to live in communities like Norman too."

I smiled a faint smile and said, "It's about the right for them, and not some bigot, to make that decision, isn't it?"

Louis didn't answer me. He didn't have to. We laughed and embraced briefly, as friends often did in those days before saying good-bye. I left him with his thoughts and the rest of the whiskey. The night air felt cooler than usual to me as I walked to my car, my mind drifting to thoughts of the challenges ahead for the ASU.

The black students were at the crossroads of desegregation and segregation. I felt both happy and sad — happy because they had a choice, but sad because they might, from my perspective, make the wrong one. Right or wrong, I would not second-guess them. Nor would I desert them. Only one question really needed to be answered: how could we collectively move forward with our equal-opportunity agenda? A year earlier, the black athletes had shown us a possible way when they publicly complained about discrimination within their sports and the Athletics Department.

Now What?

How did we get to this unhappy situation? Actually, to a great extent, University president J. Herbert Hollomon was responsible for much of the angst. He had often, and in several venues, encouraged the students during his president-designate year to assume their fair share of responsibility for restructuring the University into a racially safe and nurturing place. Months earlier, during his inauguration speech on the North Oval on October 18, 1968, Hollomon had inspired the audience with compassionate eloquence that was hardly typical of most University of Oklahoma administrators. To some members of the audience, his speech was compelling theater and several of his statements were deemed inflammatory. The black students disagreed with that assessment. They believed that with these words Hollomon encouraged them to lock horns with him and challenge his administration:

> Nations in their domestic and international affairs share the same problem. How can a nation assure the critics on the left and right and the minorities that they are a legitimate part of the political process? And how can the temptation be resisted to look to the President as Deity responsible for failing to remedy all the particular injustices of each citizen and each group? The nation must be large and just enough to have compassion for dissent and a process for its expression. . . .
>
> Is it possible for us to accept the fact that conflict does and will continue to exist within our universities and in society? Under these conditions perhaps a sharing of values will come about only through a ritualistic battle, not a real one, within new forms where the confrontation can be made explicit, open, and nonviolent and the resolution understood and accepted peacefully.

The black students left the inauguration believing that their new president had given them verbal permission to demand an immediate end to racism at the University. Later they felt betrayed. Their anger rested squarely at the intersection between what they had hoped to get from Hollomon and what they actually got. The unraveling of the relationship began with an implied promise of racial equality that was not quickly achieved. Hollomon spoke of long-term gains; the students expected immediate gratification. It was a serious misunderstanding.

On February 28, 1969, Guinnevere Hodges brought me a copy of a declaration that the ASU was going to deliver to President Hollomon and local newspaper reporters the following week. They had been writing it for several days.

Anticipating my uninvited critique, she said, "We know there are spelling and grammatical errors in it. We'll try to correct them and give you a revised copy. But you know how difficult it is for groups of people to write a clean report."

"What do you and the other students want from me?"

"We want what we've always wanted from you — your support."

"I told you when you began writing this declaration that I would support you. I also told all of you that we must support each other. This document will unleash the wrath of people we know and those we don't know. It's going to get ugly around here."

She said, "Things have always been ugly around here."

CHAPTER FIVE

A Black Declaration and a Response

S everal members of the Afro-American Student Union met with Dr. Hollomon four or five times shortly after he became president of the University. After most of the meetings, they came away thinking that he had agreed to something that he later denied when he met with other people. Conversely, he asserted that he had extracted from the ASU a commitment to draft specific suggestions for better ways to recruit and retain black students and that they had not done it. So both parties were disappointed with the results of their meetings. On March 4, 1969, believing that President Hollomon had betrayed them, members of the ASU decided to make their confrontation with him explicit, public, and non-violent. They wanted so badly to be understood by him. Their campus presence was utterly and instantly transformed on March 6 when four students, representing a total of 175 students, delivered the following declaration to him.[1]

The Black Declaration of Independence

The events of the past few weeks indicate that black students at the University of Oklahoma can expect little progress toward the elimination of *institutionalized racism* inherent in its creation,

105

government, and administration. The Afro-American Student Union has used every approach possible to awaken the administration, faculty, and student body to the injustices rendered black students through obvious deficiencies and discriminatory mechanisms in the operation of the University as well as the subtle and concealed discriminatory components. We have worked with student organizations, the constitutional convention, and the old student senate, but find their minds completely closed when confronted with the idea of self-determination and full inclusion of blacks into the University program.

We have met with the illustrious president, J. Herbert Hollomon, on several occasions and have found him to be deceitful and insincere in his statements and plans. Several shining examples are his opinions concerning a program for black studies, the Ohm report concerning discrimination in the athletics program, dismissal of Coach John MacLeod, and the student constitution. He has told black students in private that he plans and supports a school of black studies. In Tulsa, during a speech, he stated that he opposed a black studies program. He told black students he would deal fairly with the MacLeod issue and even made statements to the effect that he was aware of MacLeod's shortcomings. He then shafted us with the treachery of which only a politically motivated expert is capable. He has continually expressed his non-involvement with the student constitution, but has recently voiced opinion in the direction of the proposed document. The greatest treachery and deceit lies in his establishing an ominous police force with thousands of dollars spent in this direction to intimidate OU students (especially blacks) and suppress their expressions against the oppressive segments of the University program. Meanwhile, he continually denies there is enough money to attract black professors to campus.

We have also talked with faculty groups and committees. When the facts are presented they openly confess their lack of power to effect the changes they agree are desirable. We say, we've had it! Blacks have been screwed enough and we are not interested in anymore philosophical rhetoric and bullshit. The white students are getting theirs, so we are going to get ours. If Judas

Herbert Hollomon, faculty, and students expect blacks at OU to sit idly by while a government is being formed which will deny them adequate representation, and make them objects of suppression, then check this out: "Take the foul document and rule yourselves ridiculously with it. Black students hereby declare themselves independent of any document to which we do not consent."

We reserve the right to govern ourselves by whatever document we consider relevant to us and to our well being at OU. We also make the following demands which are rational, moral, and just:

1. *Black Vice President of Black Student Affairs.* There shall be established a Department of Black Student Affairs. A black individual shall administer this department with the title vice president of Black Student Affairs. The department shall handle all the areas of University life affecting black students, especially— counseling, employment, cultural activities, community relations, public information, recruiting, and housing. The vice president of this department will assume primary responsibility for the implementation of programs and duties associated with such department. He shall be directly responsible to the president of the University and black students, with rank equivalent to that of the other ten (10) vice presidents at the University, and have a salary commensurate with that position.

The services and courses offered on this campus are geared to whites who talk, identify, and feel comfortable around other whites. The University has ten (10) white vice presidents, from the vice president of operations to the vice president of University projects. The black student has no such services, administrators or programs. Justification and finances can be found for everything from a study of Munich to a college for computer science. The black student is trampled, kicked, and literally knocked into invisibility by such institutionalized racism. Oklahoma University has failed to include blacks for consideration in top administrative positions. Moreover, the obvious insensitivity of the University to problems of black students and the inclusion of blacks into the University programs can only be solved by creation of an arm of the University empowered to do exactly this.

The black vice president of Black Student Affairs shall be hired no later than September 1969. Black students feel that the University should find this individual, and that blacks at OU have the right to accept or reject any candidate and to make the final choice based on the aforementioned criteria.

There is no negotiable position less [than] the exception and immediate establishment of the post of a black vice president of Black Student Affairs.

2. *Black Dean of Admissions.* There shall be established a position for a black dean of admissions for the purpose of evaluating, interviewing, accepting or rejecting black applicants to the University of Oklahoma. The acceptance and rejection shall be based on standards of admission for black students, determined by black students. There shall be personnel for the administration of this office who are *responsive* to the backgrounds, educational environments, and college potential of black applicants. The office of dean of admissions of black students shall be commensurate with the other fifteen (15) deans, and equal in rank and salary to the present white dean of admissions. Realizing the vastly different cultural, environmental, and educational factors found in the black students entering OU, there should be a person who is sensitive to their needs and can relate to them as individuals on a fair and equal basis—especially, a person who is capable of identifying and understanding the problems of black students. Someone who can evaluate them, not on the basis of white middle-class standards that he has never had any contact or opportunity to learn, but on black standards that he has gotten in the hand-me-down textbooks, roof-leaking high schools, and page-torn library books. The dean of admissions for black students should be an individual who is responsive to choosing black students who will be able to bear up under the repressive, apathetic, and deeply ingrained racist OU community.

The office of the Black Dean of Admissions shall be established not later than June 1, 1969. The president of the university shall appoint, or a designated committee shall hire, said individual subject to the right of black students to recommend, interview, and evaluate the candidates for this position. Final approval shall be at the discretion of black students.

There is no negotiable compromise less than that mentioned above.

3. *Change in Entrance Requirements for Black Students.* Entrance requirements should allow any black student who has a bona fide high school diploma to be eligible for enrollment at the University of Oklahoma at the beginning of any regular enrollment term.

Entrance requirements at Oklahoma University are inherently discriminatory. Blacks and other minorities are judged by their performance on culturally and environmentally biased examinations. Blacks are selected from a society in which they have had unequal opportunities and the University subjects them to the same entrance requirements as the well-educated white students. This is systematic elimination of blacks from this university. Energetic recruiting of black students is lacking, and the ability of University personnel to communicate with prospective students is hampered by severe racial, social and cultural barriers. Only the freedom of choice and realistic avenues to gain admission to the University in light of these conditions can help the black student embark on a college career.

All means and methods shall be used to implement this demand as soon as possible.

This is negotiable only with the approval of the black dean of admissions' signature, and that of the Afro-American Student Union.

4. *Black Studies Program with Master of Arts and Doctor of Philosophy Degrees.* Black Studies Program is here taken to mean a comprehensive program with curriculum relevant to black people, black nations, and black involvement in world affairs. This encompasses African studies, black literature, art, music, history, economics, sociology, and political science. It requires the establishment of an undergraduate major in the area, along with masters and doctoral programs in this field. Included in this demand is a black chairman with ample staffing of black professors along with any others who may meet established qualifications.

The African continent, or the Third World as it is called in political circles, is increasingly becoming more important and significant in world affairs. The world is finally becoming interested in Africa's 240 million blacks and its unlimited wealth and resources. Notwithstanding the fact that anthropologists and archeologists have long realized the importance of Africa as being the continent of the origin and early development of Man, himself, white societies in general have attempted to ignore Africa, which is a sleeping giant preparing to awaken.

Universities and colleges throughout the nation are beginning to initiate black studies programs but the pace is exceedingly slow. Most schools have programs in Asian and Latin American Studies, but few have begun to develop African studies programs. The role of a university is to give its students the best education possible and to offer them as broad a range of study as possible. The University of Oklahoma is lacking in this respect, especially in the area of concern for the black student and the black peoples of the world. Only one course is offered at the University in black studies, and this is a black history course in which there is only one section and the enrollment is limited. If the University of Oklahoma is interested in progress and the welfare of its students, especially its black students, it will waste no time in initiating a Black Studies Program, complete with B.A., M.A., and Ph.D. degrees offered.

This program should be implemented no later than September 1970 on the undergraduate level. The master's and doctoral degree programs should be initiated by September 1972 and September 1974, respectively.

The Black Studies Program is non-negotiable, but the target dates may take into account the problems of staffing and planning.

5. *Black Head Basketball Coach (or head coach in a major sport).* The hiring of a black head basketball coach (or head coach in a major sport) who will have control over the sport for which he is hired, as the head coaches in the other major sports have at that time. Salary should be commensurate with previous record and position.

The athletics staff is almost void of blacks. The buddy system of contact for jobs in the coaching profession is not geared toward the impartial employment of blacks. The discriminatory nature of white universities across the country is revealed by the fact that after years of excellent competition on predominantly white university campuses on the part of blacks in all major collegiate sports, there are practically no black assistant coaches, nor head coaches in the predominantly white university.

Evidently a black has no opportunity to move into a head coaching position through the buddy-recommendation system. Therefore we black students realize that the cycle of discrimination in this area can only be stopped by appointing a head coach. Since the position of head basketball coach should be open at the end of this year, we feel that all efforts should be made to replace the present coach with a black one. In essence we believe that the actions and record of John MacLeod cannot be cleared.

There is no negotiable coaching position less than the appointment of a black head coach in a major University sport.

6. *A Dormitory Facility Designated for Black Students with Black Counselors and House Personnel.* This demand requires the designation of a suitable dormitory facility for black students attending the University of Oklahoma. A facility where black students know, when they enroll, that the housing accommodations afforded them will be one in which the black students are in the majority. "Black counselors for the black dormitory" is self-explanatory. Black personnel include "any persons associated with the maintenance and upkeep of the facility."

The transfer of an individual from one society to another is quite a difficult task, especially if it is from a predominantly black one to one that is nearly totally white. In order to create an atmosphere more conducive to pursuing the interest, both academic and social, of the black students on this campus, we feel the definite need for community housing accommodations for black students at OU.

This need, created by offensive stimuli, has manifested itself in various ways. An issue, which frequently reoccurs, is that of "who is going to live with the black student." It is rarely the case that the black individual has a choice, for he is at the disposal of the white establishment who decides with whom he shall live. The black student is left to face the psychologically damaging occurrence of a white declining to room with him, within hours after he reaches this campus for the first time. For matters of alleviating this and similar conditions, we deem it necessary for a type of housing to be established which will enable black students to carry out projects that will be constructive and relevant to them as students at the "Citadel of Intellectuality." Another vitally important factor is the cultural difference between blacks and whites. Our history, our music, our manner of dress, our general uniqueness is enough to warrant some type of a safeguard in carrying on our tradition. We think it is important to give white students a chance to improve themselves culturally by staying with a majority of black occupants. Whites have the option of living with a white majority; blacks do not have the option of living with a black majority. Black students are at present forced to live in majority white occupied dormitories, with no escape from the pressures of alienation found in their daily lives.

This demand should be met by July 1, 1969.

We are willing to discuss other lines of thought concerning this demand.

7. *A Constitution for the Student Body Acceptable to Black Students or the Right for Black Students to Function Independently Under Their Own Constitution.* This calls for a document, which will allow for adequate representation of black students and other minority groups on campus. Also, this document will clearly define the role of the student government in affecting University policy. The alternative described is for the University administration to recognize, fund through usual channels, and include a constitution for black students at this university in the University constitution.

Blacks have been discriminated against and oppressed through their lack of adequate representation in government here at the University and in the outside society. A familiar line the establishment feeds the black populace is that the role of blacks will be changed through their involvement in politics and education. The University negates this basic assumption by denying — through the methods of selecting student government representatives — blacks the right to gain experience in government at the university level. If blacks are to become politically sophisticated to the extent that politics will be a strong arm in their progress in this racist dominated society, it is fundamental that the college-educated blacks have full participation and voice in the student government. A contrast between communism and institutional racism can be established by saying communism is your fight, institutional racism is ours.

This controversy is happening over the entire country. Black students want a voice and we want it now. Self-governing wouldn't be titled as a separate power. This is the white point of view. On the other hand, it would be significant to the incoming black students. The only way blacks can identify and function independently is to have black representation or an independent constitution drawn up specifically designed for black students. We've had it with white opposition. We've told you how we feel about your constitution. Your constitution was not accepted by the blacks.

It is time for us to uphold our awareness and create a constructive environment for ourselves. Halting our progress and limiting our power will only bring about future dissention.

Implementation of this demand must be made before acceptance of a constitution for student government by the administration.

This demand is non-negotiable.

8a. *The Right for Black Students to Have the Determining Voice in the Hiring of Personnel Indicated.*

8b. *The Right of Black Students to Review the Records and Attitudes of Current Personnel, Both Black and White, with Regard to Their Relationships with Black Students and Their Problems.*

Black students must have veto power in the appointments of vice president of Black Student Affairs, black dean of admissions, black coach, and dormitory personnel. This demand encompasses the right of black students, with the Afro-American Student Union as their official agent, to interview, review records, and sample the opinions of suggested personnel and to suggest personnel for these positions. Included also is the right for black students to review the records of all personnel in the University, to investigate actions and policies affecting black students and programs of their concern.

In all positions created by actions of black students at the University, the administration has exploited the efforts of the students by hiring persons who place the security of their position ahead of the interests of the black students who, in reality, created those positions. These persons, who have been forced into the University program, are then used as tools by the administration to combat black students' struggle for full participation, and as showpieces for federal and private agencies. If black students expect their movement to have continuity, it is imperative that they have the power to identify abnormal behavior in this hired personnel due to the tremendous pressures exerted on them by the establishment. With personnel currently employed at the University and future employees, black students have no reason for enthusiasm. There are employees at the University whose racially biased actions remain unchecked by the University. Racial discrimination is a problem too essential to the psychological well being of black students to leave the review and investigation of such cases to a historically biased establishment. Blacks must be given the responsibility to initiate, complete, and reveal their findings to the University community with the assurance that the fair and equal implementation is carried out by the University.

The only negotiable position is that of immediate action taken in the direction of this demand, implemented by the administration and black students.

This demand is negotiable only with regard to the review of records and study of attitudes of personnel.

9. *Full Five-Year Scholarships for Black Athletes.* Five-year scholarships should be given to black athletes if, at the end of their four years of eligibility, they have not been able to complete the academic requirements for graduation through normal progress under existing circumstances.

It takes many athletes five years to complete their academic requirements for graduation. This is particularly true for the black athlete, who like the black student, has entered this university with educational, emotional, and social handicaps that have been inflicted by years of exposure to an inferior educational background, and lived under the pressures of constant subtle and overt discrimination. The black athlete, who usually comes from an economically deprived family, is often completely dependent on his athletic scholarship to remain in school. Thus it is often the case that he must drop out of school after four years of eligibility because of a lack of sufficient funds. The result is a black athlete who has given the University a name but who does not have a degree.

This program should be initiated by September 1969 in consultation with, and approval of black students, black athletes, and the Athletics Department. This demand shall be retroactive for black athletes whose eligibility ended in June 1969.

This demand is not negotiable short of the above mentioned requirements.

10. *Scheduled Competition with Black Schools in All Major Sports.* No clarification needed for this demand.

The myth perpetuated by the University in its athletic programs is that black schools are inferior and not worthy of consideration for competition with this university. This is an extension of the myth that the University fosters in general. Blacks and black institutions are considered legitimate if, and only if, they are controlled in an obvious manner directly by this institution. This has caused an insensitivity on the part of white students to predominantly black institutions, their contributions and excellence as well as precipitating mental anguish and a lowering of self-esteem and pride among blacks. The University has scheduled many white schools that discriminate openly against black athletes with no regard to the black athlete it exploits for the sake of athletic prowess. It consistently schedules schools that have no more to offer from a competitive standpoint than black schools except they are white. Competition with black schools will increase the interest in athletic activities by black students. It will act as a channel of communication between OU and black schools and it will remove misconceptions and broaden the sphere of knowledge within the community about black people and their institutions. Finally, it will eliminate one of the visible stamps of racism at this university.

Implementation of this demand shall apply to the following sports as designated: Track — black schools should be scheduled for this season approaching. Basketball and baseball — black schools should be scheduled for the 1969–70 seasons. Football — black schools should be scheduled for the 1972 season.

This demand is non-negotiable, and, if necessary, scheduled appearances should be cancelled in football, basketball, etc. to meet this demand.

11. *Faculty Exchange Program with Black Schools.* A program should be initiated which would permit the exchange of OU faculty members with faculty members from black schools on a semester or yearly basis.

At the present time OU has only three full-time black instructors. The black students on this campus feel that not only blacks, but also the entire OU student body, is being short-changed by not being exposed to black instructors and their different views and ideas. Since many of OU's white students harbor erroneous myths and prejudices against black people, it would be enlightening to them to have academic contact with a black professor. We feel that we are not getting an accurate overall concept of the principles of learning from a lily-white faculty which delivers a one-sided (lily-white) view.

This program should be initiated by September 1970 or before.

We will consider negotiations within substitution of comparable programs which may accomplish the same goals.

12. *Student Year Abroad Program for Black Students at Universities in Black Countries.* A program should be set up to encourage and stimulate interest by black students to spend a year abroad at a black university in a black country. This program should be glamorized for its educational and cultural benefits as are the programs urging white students to attend white universities in white countries. Special consideration should be given the fact that the average black student is usually less prepared financially to help to finance a trip abroad than is the average white student.

It should be understood now by intelligent and informed persons that black students in America must no longer be denied knowledge of the role that black countries play in the affairs of the world. This university has been extremely negligent in exposing the student body in general, and the black student in particular, to the contributions that are developing. Black countries have played and are now playing a more active role in shaping the affairs and opinions of the world. The University has clearly indicated its lack of concern and respect for black countries (and thus black students) by only establishing programs geared to sending whites, or pseudo-whites, to white countries. It should be realized that a visit abroad at a white university in a white country has little appeal to the black students who are now desperately trying to establish their identity as a citizen of the world.

Black students would profit educationally and culturally from first-hand experiences in black countries, just as white students profit from their experiences in white universities in white countries.

This demand shall be implemented into the University programs no later than the school term of 1970–71.

This is a non-negotiable demand, except for operational procedures.

13. *The Attainment by 1973 of a Student Body That Is 20 Percent Black.* No clarification needed.

We feel that with this percentage we are assured of the minimum representation, based on the national population, and regions from which OU draws most of its students. Our numbers would be sufficient to effect constructive change as far as our welfare is concerned. We fully realize that our cultural background will not be perpetuated nor our unique needs fulfilled until the number of black students on OU's campus is sufficiently large. The black dean of admissions would determine the speed at which we should approach the attainment of at least 20 percent black student enrollment by 1973.

Black students feel that this demand is negotiable to the extent that the recruitment of black students is stepped up and the above-mentioned administrators hired. The black dean of admissions for black students shall determine the explicit procedure of attainment of said number.

14. *A Review of the Records with Intent to Reinstate Black Students Who Have Failed Under the Stress of Academic Racism.* By "academic racism" it is meant the sum total of the effects of the University's environment upon black students that adversely affects classroom performance. Included are improper advising; racially prejudiced instructors, administrators, and staff; lack of adequate counsel and guidance; general attitudes of fellow students; white-oriented system that negates his existence; and the lack of choice of quarters in which to seek an escape from the overall abnormal pressure.

Racism is found universally on this campus, just as it is in the society from which we all come. It manifests itself in many ways. It can be found to be both overt and subtle forms of behavior. The overt forms are much more discernable than the subtle forms. In this sense, they are easier to attack and correct than the subtle forms. Subtle institutionalized academic racism has to be the most insidious form of racism in American society. This is primarily because of the blatant incongruity of the University purpose to dispensing the highest form of education, while at the same time subjecting black students to forces of racism from which they have no redress. The fact that most black students come from inferior secondary educational backgrounds is overshadowed by the fact that when they attend class or perform any kind of academic function they by and large feel that they are representing the entire black race. The University has no mechanisms designed for relating to black students with regard to the effect of the environment on their academic life. This type of psychological pressure caused by the lack of such mechanisms is astronomical in its effects. This is witnessed by the hideous dropout rate of black students who have come to this institution.

Action should begin immediately upon the appointment of the black dean of admissions for black students who will head a committee to review these records.

This demand is fully negotiable, subject to the approval of black students.

IF THESE DEMANDS ARE NOT MET WE WILL HAVE TO TAKE THE ONLY ACTION DEEMED JUSTIFIABLE.

Significance of the Document

In the absence of other formal requests for redress of abhorrent conditions of racism at the University of Oklahoma, written protest was the students' medium and message — a valid starting point for a long-overdue dialogue that would hopefully result in positive actions. It was also a clear indication that members of the Afro-American Student Union were tired of being academically marginal people adrift on a fast track to continued disillusionment with the University. The role of trust was difficult to disentangle from the threads of deceit. So it was not easy for the students to factor in the veracity of Hollomon's comments. Many things had to be accepted on faith. The declaration was an audacious move. It could have backfired, but instead it opened for discussion previously ignored issues. It also obscured the source of some of the students' anger: that they had not done as much as they could have to abate or prevent hateful University conditions. President Hollomon responded quickly, in the form of the following press release on March 6, 1969.

Four black students at the University of Oklahoma met Thursday afternoon with OU President J. Herbert Hollomon and heard his answers to the 14 demands contained in the Black Declaration of Independence which they submitted to him.

"The students were courteous, thoughtful and friendly in presenting their requests," Hollomon reported after the hour-long session.

Meeting with the president were Ronald Lee King, Oklahoma City freshman; Guinnevere A. Hodges, Norman senior; Gary S. Fowlks, Metuchen, N.J., freshman; and Eddie Parker, Tulsa freshman. The document was signed by Miss Hodges, King, Sterlin Adams, graduate student from Memphis, Tenn., and Theopal Tyner, Duncan senior, who identified themselves as "representatives for 175 Black Students."

After Hollomon commented that he would accept the document as one prepared by four people, because it was signed by four people, the students offered to provide him with the full list of 175 persons they said submitted the declaration.

The president asked for time to read the 12-page document, then gave his response to each of the 14 points.

"I told the students that I realize there is a very real problem with communication between black students and the rest of the University community," Hollomon stated after the meeting. "I suggested that an appropriate number of people — perhaps 10 to 15 — be selected by the black students to meet with me and other members of the administration under conditions of good faith, so that we could discuss with them not the demands, but the problems that underlie these demands. They suggested that meetings be arranged in the president's conference room. We would discuss matters of substance, not demands.

"I told the students we could not make progress in helping minority students if their requests are presented in the form of non-negotiable demands. This technique only leads to confrontation and polarization of the attitudes of even the most well-meaning people. This technique is clearly not even in the best interests of the black students. I have no intention of discussing these demands except to indicate what steps were under way or could be undertaken to solve the underlying substantive problems which the demands represented."

Hollomon added that only a few of the demands presented by the students had been discussed previously with him.

Concerning the students' charge of "institutionalized racism" at the University, Hollomon said that any such charges should be documented and presented to a committee which will be formed within the next few days. Plans for formation of a University-wide committee to investigate charges of discrimination were announced at the time the Ohm Committee Report on black athletes was released.

Following the private meeting with students, Hollomon summarized his replies to the students' 14 demands.

1. *Black Vice President of Black Student Affairs.* "We have a vice president for the University Community to handle housing, counseling and similar matters. I have no intention of dividing the University Community into separate parts, dealing with different student groups, and I will make no recommendation to the OU Board of Regents relative to a black vice president. I do realize there may be certain problems among the black students that need attention, and I will discuss this matter with black students to see what can be done to aid them."

2. *Black Dean of Admissions.* "We have a dean of admissions. In addition to black students, we have students of other minority groups and international students. I will not consider the recommendation that we have a black dean of admissions to deal with black students."

3. *Change in Entrance Requirements for Black Students.* "I grant we may need to work together with black students and those from other minority groups to determine if we should look at admissions policies differently. The policies are set by the Oklahoma State Regents for Higher Education, and I couldn't change them if I wanted to. But perhaps we could have more summer programs which would help prepare disadvantaged students to succeed at the university."

4. *Black Studies Program with Master of Arts and Doctor of Philosophy Degrees.* "We are looking at the possibility of further offerings having to do with black studies. We have certain courses now that deal with black history and literature. Dr. Pete Kyle McCarter, vice president for academic affairs, is evaluating all courses at the University to see if the black point of view in such things as history is considered appropriately. The plan for the future of the University contains recommendations on international area programs, and one may be for African studies, but no decision has been made. We are not considering establishing a department of black studies. When and how degrees would be granted must be determined by our faculty and ultimately the state regents."

5. *Black Head Basketball Coach (or head coach in a major sport).* "We try to hire coaches on capability and merit. I consider the matter of Coach John MacLeod's past performances settled. We should seek to employ members of minority groups not only in athletics but also on the staff and on the faculty. Coaches will be selected on merit when vacancies occur. We cannot guarantee that a black head coach of a major sport will be hired. The Athletics Department is attempting to hire members of minority groups when possible."

6. *A Dormitory Facility Designated for Black Students with Black Counselors and House Personnel.* "A committee headed by Dr. J. R. Morris, dean of the University College, is responsible for looking into residential matters. I will make certain that the committee considers or has considered the desirability of a residential unit for black students. I cannot commit the committee to meet any demand, including the demand in this document that a black dormitory be established by July 1, 1969."

7. *A Constitution for the Student Body Acceptable to Black Students or the Right for Black Students to Function Independently Under Their Own Constitution.* "Within a week the committee will be appointed to write the constitution for the University. The University constitution will guarantee rights of minorities. We could not tolerate two student constitutions. I believe that student minority groups should work through the appropriate student government."

8a. *The Right for Black Students to Have the Determining Voice in the Hiring of Personnel Indicated.* "The authority to hire people rests with the OU Regents and is delegated in part to the administration. Since students are only temporary residents, and the University lives on after they leave, the determining voice with respect to hiring must rest with the permanent officers and faculty."

8b. *The Right of Black Students to Review the Records and Attitudes of Current Personnel, Both Black and White, With Regard to Their Relationships with Black Students and Their Problems.* "The personnel records of employees as well as students should not be investigated by other students. Charges of discrimination may be investigated by the committee to be named in the next few days."

9. *Full 5-Year Scholarships for Black Athletes.* "I am informed this

is not possible under NCAA rules, which limit a student to four years of sports participation under an athletic scholarship. However, there may be cases in which a student, no matter what his race, may need a fifth year to complete his education and may not have money enough to do so. I will ask appropriate people to determine the seriousness of this problem, and, if necessary, we will take action within our means to see that such students are able to continue their studies."

10. *Scheduled Competition with Black Schools in All Major Sports.* "The Athletics Department is already investigating the possibility of competition with black schools of comparable athletic ability. It would be most unfortunate to schedule contests between teams that were not evenly matched. We will schedule events as soon as possible, but we do not intend to cancel any existing contractual agreements."

11. *Faculty Exchange Program with Black Schools.* "I have discussed this with several heads of black colleges. A recent report in the *Chronicle of Higher Education* indicated that there is great reluctance on the part of black college administrators to enter into such a program, because black institutions might lose black faculty members and might be unable to replace them with white professors. We will continue to make every effort to recruit black faculty members. Recently an outstanding black professor was offered a position here, but he turned it down because of a better offer from the University of California at Los Angeles. The faculty is continuing to look for qualified black professors, but so is every other university in the country. There is no shortage of jobs for these people."

12. *Student Year Abroad Program for Black Students at Universities in Black Countries.* "A student year abroad program is recommended in the plan for the future of the University and is considered highly desirable. But it should not be just for black students. White students should also be able to go to Africa, and black students should be able to go to Europe."

13. *The Attainment by 1973 of a Student Body That Is 20 Percent Black.* "I could not accept any such specific goal. Black students must decide if they want to come here. I realize that many stu-

dents who come here are poorly prepared, and it is the responsibility of the University to help correct this condition in any way
it can. We need to work with the high schools, and we need more
programs such as Project Threshold to prepare disadvantaged
students to compete in the University Community. Five months
ago I asked the Afro-American Student Union to develop a program for informing and assisting black high school students and
for providing better communication between black students and
the rest of the University community, but no program has been
presented."

14. *A Review of the Records with Intent to Reinstate Black Students
Who Have Failed Under the Stress of Academic Racism.* "The academic
performance of students is determined by individual decisions of
the faculty, and if there is any discrimination, it can be brought to
the appropriate body. It would not be proper for students, black
or white, to investigate the records of other students."

In reply to the last statement in the document, which reads:
"If these demands are not met we will have to take the only action
deemed justifiable," Hollomon stated, "I am rather disturbed
that the students would not specify what action they consider
justifiable. Our position is clear. The University administration
intends to take whatever steps are necessary to insure fairness,
freedom and order on the University campus."

Significance of Hollomon's Response

President Hollomon's response to the declaration was carefully crafted —
probably by his assistant Gordon Christenson — to appeal to two broad
groups: the black students who initiated the demands and the rest of the
University community who wanted to know the parameters within which
he would allow dissent. For most bystanders, Hollomon was tough enough
to say no to demands for change and yet flexible enough to handle pressure for radical transformation of the University of Oklahoma. Clearly, he
would bend but not bow to external pressure. At least that was his public
persona as implied through his response to the black students' demands.

To the black students, however, the president's response contained
enough qualifiers to cause them to believe that backstage, away from

public scrutiny, he might indeed bow to portions of their demands. To them it appeared that the negotiation game was not over. Publicly, Hollomon might have scored the first point, but the students believed they would get other opportunities to score. The changes President Hollomon proposed were microscopic in contrast to the remaining problems. Therefore his response did not satisfy the black students, who were well aware of their relative academic deprivation. Both parties knew that the hard work was ahead of them. They would have to find ways to overcome communication dead-ends and strategic wrong turns, and they would have to learn to trust each other again. The declaration and the response to it made it publicly clear that all of them had made some mistakes, but they might need some help from other people to overcome them. I volunteered to be one of those persons.

CHAPTER SIX

Public Fallout and the ASU Push Back

B ecause he was an astute negotiator, President Hollomon was not upset with the black students who issued their declaration of independence. He understood precisely what the document conveyed in addition to a litany of historical and current grievances and rigid demands. Unlike the general public, he interpreted it as an invitation to enter into a meaningful dialogue with them. Even after a groundswell of critics had begun to soundly denounce the document, his empathy for the black students did not waiver. He thought of himself as a racially sensitive person, and he was. But he was first and foremost a politician. From that vantage point, he did not believe it was politically wise for him to cave in to any student group's demands — public or private.

Impasse

A week after President Hollomon issued his response to the ASU demands, he telephoned me. "The declaration reminds me of two lovers probing each other for the most sensitive spots," he said. "However, when they made their demands public, the Afro-American Student Union ticked me off. I will meet with them again, but not soon. I don't like to be blindsided, especially in a public announcement to the press. I thought we were making progress, but their demands say otherwise."

I told the ASU leaders what Hollomon had said. They were pleased to hear that he would follow through with other meetings, but they were disappointed that he would not set the date for the next meeting until sometime in the distant future. That left them in limbo. Still, the delay gave all of them time to cool off. As the ASU members plotted their endgame, an alarming truth came to several of them: time was on his side, not theirs.

Within less than three months, the spring 1969 semester would be over and the campus would be empty of all but a few students. Therefore a very long delay probably meant that the Black Declaration of Independence would lose its media attention, and Hollomon would have something else to deal with, such as another group's rebellion. The students' fate was where it had always been — resting precariously in Hollomon's hands. In the meantime, Hollomon appointed Guinnevere Hodges to a committee that would draft a student government constitution, and he appointed Jafus P. Cavil, Jr., to a committee that would draft a revised University constitution. Campus life was slowly ebbing and flowing away from exclusively black civil rights issues.

Obviously, an indefinite delay for a follow-up meeting was not ideal for the black students. They had become victims of their own strategy. The declaration had certainly gotten Hollomon's attention, but going public with it temporarily stalled the initiative. A few of the ASU members wanted to escalate their activities to include picketing Hollomon's office or sitting in it until he convened a second meeting. One student suggested bringing in outside agitators to "really shake up this place." Sterlin Adams, Melvin Tolson, and I defused those strategies by warning the students not to start anything that might put them and other people in harm's way. They seemed relieved that we intervened before their anger could spiral out of control. Thus, almost as suddenly as the escalation talk had started, it ended. Still, the major question of what to do next remained unanswered.

When the ASU members issued their declaration of independence, their mood was almost giddy, with an overabundance of optimism about the rebellion. The first draft of the declaration was less grandiose than the final version, but after an extensive discussion, they decided to go for broke and ask for far-reaching changes. That was a proven labor union tactic. If successful, the negotiations would result in more and better conditions and opportunities for blacks than they currently had. By design, the narratives explaining the demands were more culturally illuminating than conciliatory. The grievances cited in the document had not been obvious to or understood by most of the people who read them, but the narratives expressed the black students' feelings of frustration and despair.

As the solidarity of the black students began to wane, Melvin Tolson reminded them that their strength resided in unity, not in splintered groups. He told them to be patient; it was unrealistic to expect Hollomon to meet with them eagerly so that they could collaboratively devise ways to undo seven decades of University traditions grounded in racial segregation and discrimination. Tempers calmed among the ASU members, but they flared at other students. Despite a trickling of support, the general sentiment on campus was anti-ASU. People who had never heard of them before the declaration was issued labeled the ASU members as troublemakers. There was a kernel of truth in the accusation. The declaration had indeed stirred up trouble, but that trouble was not of the ASU's making. The declaration was an outgrowth of blatant discrimination.

The ASU members were accused of being childish spoilsports who wanted to be University of Oklahoma students only on their own terms and who would segregate themselves from the other students if their demands were not met. Parroting the ASU, letters to the editor of the *Oklahoma Daily* demanded separate governments or special privileges and personnel for a wide array of student groups, including students with disabilities, fat students, and language majors. Also ridiculing the ASU, French students demanded "French maids in the dormitories; Swedish students demanded masseuses[;] and so on until the black demands were lost in laughter."[1] It was simply mean-spirited for the critics to minimize the significance of the black students' declaration. The critics believed what they wanted to believe and not what the truth offered them.

Numerous campus debates about the ASU demands took place. One of the most rancorous ones occurred in a sociology class taught by Fred Silberstein, who invited me to present my perspective of the uproar to his class. Instead of spending time explaining the black demands point by

Henderson explains "black unrest" in a University of Oklahoma sociology class, 1968. Western History Collections, University of Oklahoma Libraries.

point, I asked the students for their questions about them. A dozen hands shot up.

A white male asked the first question: "What do they [the ASU members] really want?"

After making it clear that I was giving my perceptions only, I said, "They want to be treated like you and their other white peers. They want equal opportunities to fail or succeed as students based on their own merit, not their race."

Someone in the back of the room shouted out, "Then why don't they act like the rest of us and stop demanding special treatment?"

A smattering of catcalls followed. Two of the black students urged the white student to sit down and shut up. Although my instinct told me to let it go, I turned to one of the black students and asked him, "If you were white, wouldn't you ask the same questions or slightly different ones?"

He did not back down. "Maybe I would," he said, "but as you can see, I'm not white. As a black man enrolled at this white university, I've thought about doing something far more violent than issuing a list of demands."

"Such as what?" I nibbled at his bait.

"Such as punching out some white faces with my black fists and making those faces shut up and treat me like the man that I am." I was startled by his frankness.

"You got to bring your butt to get mine," a white male sitting in the front of the room said. He stood up, turned to the black student, and snarled, "Where do you want to do it? In here or outside?"

The second black student stood up and motioned for the white male to come to him.

This was not what Fred had in mind when he invited me to speak, and it certainly wasn't what I thought would happen. The room exploded into loud, angry clusters of white and black students arguing the merits of the ASU demands. Fred called for an end to the squabbling. Then he said in a disgusted voice, "I believe that members of the Afro-American Student Union have the right to express their opinions. I also believe that members of this class have the right to make fools of themselves — on their own time, not in this classroom."

A silence came over the students. Their facial expressions registered embarrassment. Without further comment, only thirty minutes after the class had started, Fred waved his hands and shooed the students out of the room. He had had enough excitement for the day, and so had most of the rest of us.

As on several other nights during the past two and a half years, I sat alone in the dark and thought about some of the events of the day. Memories of Fred's class received most of my attention. I wondered what I could have done better. According to a couple of my friends, the racial brinkmanship I had witnessed was occurring in more than a few classes. My friends and I were beginning to feel like volunteer firefighters standing by in case violence erupted. If it did, we had only our words to throw at it. Would they be enough? The self-doubt lasted only a few minutes. There would be other opportunities for us to become more proficient as race relations firefighters.

Disinformation about blacks at the University gained considerable traction among people who wanted to believe it. Critics of the ASU demanded detailed, concrete reasons for the allegation of institutional racism in the University. At the same time, their rebuttals to our explanations were less than factual. It was a silly symmetry that perpetuated circular arguments and demonstrated how difficult it was going to be for the campus community to move from the status quo to even a slight restructuring of privileges and power. As ridicule of the ASU grew louder, the black students' solidarity grew stronger. Whatever ideological differences existed among ASU members were insignificant when compared with their need to be vindicated. As the racial tension grew higher, the black students and their allies refused to give up. At best, it was a standoff; at worst, a debacle. Channels of communication broke down before the conflicting groups had even fully explored the nooks and crannies of their own respective beliefs.

In mid-March 1969, President Hollomon asked me to serve on a soon-to-be-announced committee that would receive complaints of discrimination and recommend appropriate actions to him. I agreed to be a member of the committee on the condition that he follow through with his promise to meet again privately with some of the students who signed the Black Declaration of Independence. With that understanding, my name was added to the list of the other individuals who would make up the University of Oklahoma's Human Relations Committee: E. Kenneth Feaver, chair and minister of Norman's First Presbyterian Church; Charlyce K. King, program analyst and extension specialist at the University;

Jerome C. Weber, associate professor of physical education; Jack Stout, assistant vice president for the University Community; and students Amy Amette Tiger, a junior, and Gregory Watts, a freshman.

The time was right, I thought, to put additional pressure on Hollomon to meet with the ASU representatives. On March 25 the *Oklahoma Daily* published a letter to the editor from me:

> I would imagine that both Dr. Hollomon and members of the Afro-American Student Union have received many letters and other communications supporting "get tough" and "no negotiations" positions. It is time that both parties receive communications from those of us who want them to meet and seek solutions to the problems that gave rise to the "demands."
>
> The advantages of being able to use words are not without negative repercussions. In many crisis situations, we become similar to Alice in Lewis Carroll's *Through the Looking-Glass*:
>
> > "When I use a word," Humpty Dumpty said, in rather a scornful tone, "it means what I choose it to mean — neither more nor less."[2]
> >
> > "The question is," said Humpty Dumpty, "which is to be master — that's all."
>
> Now that the vital social issues have been raised by members of the ASU, I hope that neither they nor Dr. Hollomon will get bogged down in semantical differences. In short, which is to be master — the words or the humans who create and respond to the words? This is not the kind of contest in which if one party wins, the other loses. Either both win or both lose.

The Human Relations Committee was officially appointed on March 26. Just as I had told Hollomon earlier, the ASU had no interest in dealing with another of his committees. On March 28 the *Oklahoma Daily* published an open letter urging President Hollomon to meet with the black students and resolve their differences. Eleven Norman residents were the signatories. That night President Hollomon telephoned me at my house.

"George," he began in an irked voice. Then he paused for about a minute, sighed, and said, "With troublemakers like you and your Norman friends, I need a friend. I agree with your letters. Next month I'll meet with some of the students, and I want you there so that you'll stop writing those damn letters to the editor." I started to reply, but he continued: "Let's have the meeting on April 12."

The overall campus responses to the declaration had not been satisfying for the black students and their allies, but at least the public volleys of disdain had pushed the racial discord to the front page of the *Oklahoma Daily*. Soon, I hoped, at least some of the issues would be resolved, but for now I just wanted an end to the vicious charges and countercharges that had followed the publication of the declaration. Perhaps they would stop once Hollomon met privately with members of the ASU again.

The Crossroads

During the interim before the meeting with Hollomon, a time some of the black students derisively called "a period of nothingness," critics of the black students resorted to every means possible to discredit them. It was a perfect opportunity for the ASU members to score public relations points by not overreacting. In our lucid moments, we knew that most of the people who tried to denigrate us had merely denigrated themselves. Also, we believed that civility was appropriate. Still, it was tempting to be uncivil, and a few ASU members did succumb to the temptation.

Maybe it was inevitable that some of the black students' optimism would give way to pessimism — mine did too. We were not impervious to public criticism. Engaging in wishful thinking about the realities for black students rather than citing facts, our critics were consistently sarcastic each time we tried to explain our allegation of racism. The lag time between issuing the students' demands and waiting for the next meeting with President Hollomon was nerve-racking, but we decided to wait him out. The students had not been aggressive up to this point, to be sure, so why didn't they become more aggressive now? Although some of the ASU members' violent protests were not only prudent but moral imperatives in some situations, this was not one of them. Nonviolent diplomacy had to be brokered, for a very obvious reason.

A year earlier, in 1968, Curtis L. Lawson, a black Oklahoma legislator, had been appointed to chair a committee charged with studying the race relations climate in the state. The committee concluded that three major cities — Oklahoma City, Tulsa, and Lawton — were ripe for riots. Meanwhile, the state House and Senate passed a riot control bill that gave Governor Dewey Bartlett broad new powers to curtail riots by using any means he deemed necessary. During that same year, the House passed a bill to give Oklahomans the right to carry guns. The bill was killed in the Senate, but the message was clear: blacks who participated in riots could expect swift, violent retaliation. That the University could become a site of carnage if students demonstrated was a grim possibility. Ideally, that danger could be lessened through diplomacy.

While we waited for our meeting with Hollomon, however, viable options for reconciliation seemed to disappear. It stood to reason that we were irritated, and it seemed to me that only conflict resolution magicians — of which I was not one — would be able to conjure a quick breakthrough. Short of magic, I decided to redouble my efforts to resolve the conflict, and I enlisted Sterlin Adams in that endeavor. Sterlin had been the glue that kept us united when no tangible progress was being made. Even though a few of the ASU members and their friends were almost too mercurial to wait patiently for a meeting with Hollomon, they were loyal enough to Sterlin to hold back until he met with Hollomon. Within that context, my role, as I conveyed it to Sterlin, was to be his moral, emotional, and academic supporter. I promised him that I would do all I could to be his guardian within the University's hierarchy. In reality, though, I could not protect him from his critics there, especially those who found no academic value in his campus activism.

A Symbolic Meeting

John Herbert Hollomon, Jr., generally known as J. Herbert Hollomon, was the University of Oklahoma's eighth president, and one of its most misunderstood. During his two-year tenure, I observed that everything engineering and manufacturing innovator Donald N. Frey had said in a 1992 memorial tribute to Hollomon rang true:

> Hollomon tore through life, leaving in his wake myriad expanded minds, changed lives, and reformed institutions. Combative, controversial, often ahead of his time, and always pushing those around him to do more and do better, he was a colorful and

complex man. He touched those around him in a tense and personal way. . . . He could be provocative in the extreme, could take outrageous positions to see what would happen, but always made you think — and he was very often right in his views.[3]

When negotiating or simply arguing with others, Hollomon would draw extensively from the insights he had gained through his administrative experiences at the General Electric Company and the U.S. Department of Commerce. Students at the University of Oklahoma could not have had a better teacher of conflict resolution. But his blunt, straightforward style initially alienated most of them, especially if they had been told by their parents to be truthful with elders during formal arguments but not confrontational or disrespectful toward them. In any case, Hollomon seemed to delight in pushing students, faculty, and staff to the edge of their restraint. The engineer in him required of other people — and himself — accuracy and precision of thought. Those who knew him well were aware that, despite his blustering, he truly cared about his colleagues and students. In order to sharpen the students' public presentation skills, in particular, he would present the arguments of their foes, allies, and bystanders — sometimes all in the same conversation.

"Why are we here?" President Hollomon asked the four students at the April 12 meeting. Before they could answer, he continued, "Surely there is more than your declaration to justify this meeting. Why are we here?"

Stunned, irritated, and more anxious than he wanted to show, Bruce Robinson said, "Maybe we shouldn't be here if you, our president, don't understand racism and don't know that this is a racist university."

True to form, Hollomon showed no emotions. He took out his pipe, lit it, and scowled. "I'm not a racist," he said.

Ronald King accused him of "messing with our minds for no reason." Hollomon was not doing that. Rather, as an accomplished provocateur, not a trifler, he set out to uncover the multiple levels of the issues at hand. By asking his question, he set the agenda and forestalled their questions about his responsibility as president. It was a ploy.

"Nobody in this room has accused you of being a racist, Dr. Hollomon," I intervened. "I think we can all agree that racism does exist — even at the University of Oklahoma. And I believe that we all agree that it should not — "

"Let the students talk, George," he said, cutting me off. "You and I can argue anytime."

"We'll talk, but you should let Dr. Henderson finish what he was saying," Bruce said in my defense.

Hollomon smiled for the first time. Looking at the students, not me, he yielded the conversation back to me: "Go ahead, George, but keep it short."

The sudden shift back to me temporarily unnerved me. I had attracted unwanted attention to myself; I preferred it to be on the students. I gave a brief recitation of common oppressive conditions the black students endured. It was not new information. My speech trailed off and turned to silence as I returned the conversation to the students.

Guinnevere Hodges was the next to speak. In her usual soft, carefully measured but stern manner, she said, "We are not here because we don't have anything else to do [such as homework assignments or washing clothes]. We're not doing those other things because we want to know what you intend to do about the plight of black students at this school. And, no, I'm not going to threaten to use violence. Nowhere in our demands did we mention violence."

Hollomon's body relaxed, and he slumped back in his chair. Although his approval was barely noticeable, there was no mistaking the slightly upturned corners of his lips.

Guinnevere continued, "We care very much about this school. But I'm not sure the feeling is mutual. In a nutshell, we are tired of being treated like field hands on a plantation. We work hard without getting many rewards. We understand your response to our demands. What we need to know now is what else we can expect from you." It was a masterstroke that instantly raised the conversation beyond personal attacks.

Ronald, Bruce, and Theopal Tyner nodded. Guinnevere had made a powerful statement, and it created a mesmerizing moment. The game playing was over. All of us were now ready to move to the next level of discourse. It felt good to relax.

At his savvy best, President Hollomon became a master teacher. He shared with the students his perceptions of the strengths and weaknesses of their declaration. Then he summarized the bind that he was in: whatever he did for black students within the next year or so was likely to be considered too little by them and too much by their adversaries. Even so, he admitted that he admired the ASU members who were trying to change a basically hostile and discriminatory university into a more egalitarian one. In a sentimental but not pandering voice, he said, "If I were black, I would be an ASU member."

I watched the cagey fox go from trying to emotionally devour us to pledging his support for our survival. He had tested us and we had passed. All of us had overcome the rocky beginning and were much closer to a smoother ending, or, more correctly, a beginning. The major thing missing was confirmation of the actual programs that his administration was undertaking or planning. He rattled off a list of projects he would implement within a year or less to improve the lives of black students. Specifically, he would ask the Student Congress and the Faculty Senate to study the extent of racial discrimination on the University's Norman campus and to recommend changes; have Dean J. R. Morris convene a committee to review all programs that affected disadvantaged students and to recommend changes; request federal funding for Project Threshold to provide academic advisement, registration assistance, and tutorial assistance to low-achieving students, with an emphasis on minority students; hire more minorities, including someone in the president's office to provide oversight of minority affairs; encourage the sponsors of student clubs and honor societies to seek out and induct more minorities; and meet weekly with ASU representatives to assess progress toward achieving those things.

"I need you and your organization to support me with your patience, understanding, and vigilance," he pleaded. "There will be programs and personnel appointments that I hope you will interpret to your members as progress."

As the meeting drew to a close, he told us that whenever there were conflicts between him and us, he would negotiate faithfully for a fair resolution on behalf of the entire University community, and that meant we might not get exactly what we wanted. "But if you maintain your focus and critical reasoning abilities," he added, "there will be instances when you will get all that you bargain for." He was quite convincing, but realistically it would be difficult for him to do all that he had promised. A large number of student groups were already competing for the same campus funds for their own pet projects. He would have to satisfy one or another.

The meeting ended with nothing implemented, but with a lot of hope — hardly enough for the ASU representatives to quell the unrest simmering within their own ranks. The students were suspicious of administrators who promised sweeping remedies to discriminatory practices. They would have been foolish not to be suspicious. Countless promises had been made to them in the past, but few had been kept. Even so, I did not think that the projects Hollomon cited were bogus initiatives presented merely to pacify the students. At the very least, the frozen conflict was beginning to thaw. But a lot of goodwill would be squandered if he did not quickly deliver on some of the changes he had described. The score keeping had already started. I hoped that it wasn't too late for both the University and the black students to win.

Frustration, Anger, and Regrets

For most of the ASU members, including the officers, it seemed that they had expended a lot of energy but achieved few tangible results — and a lot of scorn from both black and white students. The frustration, which for most of them had accumulated over a lifetime, was becoming a heavy burden to bear. Any gains that would come from long-range activities were inadequate for the students who sorely needed immediate results, especially those who were graduating or otherwise leaving the University. The best example of that assumption was Sterlin Adams's prophetic speech at a University memorial service honoring Martin Luther King, Jr., on April 9, 1969:

> I come here a little bitter, as words are concerned, but not bitter toward the people gathered here. I think the people here have that distinct quality that makes possible men like Martin Luther King, Jr. We [ASU members] are convinced that you [whites] continue to manipulate and control black people as you do black students on this campus. . . . Why should we even gather here when we know that once a year we'll pray together, and the rest of the year we'll hardly even stay together. . . . Talk is the cheapest commodity on the world market. What we need is expensive action by the president of OU. If Martin Luther King can sacrifice his life, then Dr. Hollomon can sacrifice his job, and I can sacrifice my degree.[4]

Unflinching, Hollomon verbalized the University's commitment to embracing Dr. King's dream of racial equality for all Americans, particularly blacks: "If the time is now, the place is here. It is first in our hearts and then in our community [where] we . . . must make the University open to . . . black students."[5] Then he pledged to make the University reflective of all cultures, not just white cultures.

Hollomon was not the first University of Oklahoma president to be publicly emphatic about racial integration (George Lynn Cross was the first), nor would he be the last one. I gave what had become my signature plea for unity, civility, and compassion for one another. During my short time at the University, I had learned through trial and error that meaningful reconciliation between estranged racial groups was seldom achieved in public meetings. The real progress was almost always made in private ones. So the memorial program was mainly public posturing.

Nobody lost his or her job that day for talking, but some of the people there lost their commitment to the ASU after being lumped with the broad group of oppressors that Sterlin accused white Americans of being. Overall, the memorial service produced mixed results. That was not what David Wanser, a senior and the event's coordinator, had hoped would happen. Yet it could have been worse, if Sterlin had not said that he felt no ill will toward the approximately one thousand white people in the audience. Still, one man's frustration, mixed with residual anger, had culminated in a combustible speech, just as mine had a year earlier.

The spring 1969 semester ended with three noteworthy ASU activities: the Afro-American awards banquet, the installation of new ASU officers, and a regional conference. At the banquet on May 9, Guinnevere Hodges was given the top recognition, the Sterlin N. Adams Distinguished Service Award, and was also named the Outstanding Afro-American Student at the University of Oklahoma. Sterlin Adams received the Martin Luther King, Jr., Leadership Award; Ronald King, the George Henderson Human Relations Scholarship; and Gregory Watts, the Malcolm X Commitment Award. Theopal Tyner was given the W. E. B. Du Bois Scholastic Award; and Larry Eason, the Muhammad Ali Athletic Award. Public information assistant Mary Lyle Weeks was given the Black Award as a white University employee who gave service to blacks at the University beyond her official duties. All of the awards were well-deserved tokens of gratitude for notable contributions to the ASU.

The new ASU officers installed at the banquet were juniors Jafus Cavil, Jr., prime minister, and Steve Manning, chief of staff; sophomores Marye E. Dickson and Jacqueline Huey, ministers of communication; and freshman Glenn D. Hawkins, minister of finance. Also installed was a council of ministers that included sophomore Raymond F. Gray and freshmen Gregory Watts, Ray Velie, and Dwight D. Sanders. The organization's new leadership structure was similar to that of the Black Panthers. The new officers and their supporters had peeled themselves away from the moderate ASU members.

I was concerned that the new structure of the ASU would cause a decrease in its membership and a precipitous decline in its allies. The original structure was acceptable to both moderates and radicals, with an overwhelming majority of the leadership being moderates. A few days later, I shared my concerns with Jafus, not to attempt to alter the new structure but to give him an alert. He assured me that the members had discussed the implications of becoming more Black Panther–like than NAACP-like in structure. "This is what we new breed of students want," he said. Perhaps as a parting shot at the outgoing ASU officers, Melvin Tolson, and me, he said in a judgmental tone, "We tried it the Negro way. It hasn't worked. Now we'll try it the black way." His voice grew louder, and he looked away from me. The arrival of a new era was reflected in his expression too. There was a kind of arrogance and confidence in his demeanor that was both disconcerting and refreshing.

Sensing my reaction, he said that he wasn't talking about Melvin or me. He would come to us for advice, he promised. That seemed like a good note on which to end our exchange, but a sudden, sinking feeling of sorrow came over me. Perhaps it was my wounded ego that was crying out for moderation. I had told Jafus that whatever negative thoughts I might have about the organizational changes were not going to lessen my support of the students—that is, as long as they did not gravitate to violence.

As if my conversation with Jafus had not been stressful enough, my skills as a diplomatic community activist were again tested the next day during a meeting outside Norman. A community group in Durant had invited me to be the keynote speaker in a meeting about open housing. When I asked where Durant was located, I was told that it was in Little Dixie. This was another instance when my unfamiliarity with Oklahoma history did not serve me well. As I got deeper into the southeastern part of the state, I noticed that cars seemed to disappear and were replaced by pickup trucks with rifles strapped to the back window. It gradually dawned on me that I was entering cowboy or farmer country. The meeting was held in the basement of a funeral home, and the speaker's podium was set up in front of an open casket. I had a nagging feeling that I was way out of my usual element, and I wondered exactly what was it I had gotten myself into. Long after the meeting ended, certain things would remain vivid in my mind.

I gave one of my most impassioned speeches in favor of racially integrated neighborhoods. Except for the four people who had invited me to speak, the audience sat motionless and expressionless as I methodically interspersed humor with heart-tugging examples of reasons why housing ought to be integrated. During the question-and-answer portion of the program, an elderly white man with a frown that appeared to have been chiseled on his face by a hatred of black speakers, stood up. Pointing his right index finger at me, he snarled, "Boy, do you know what we do to carpetbaggers like you who come down here and try to rile up our good colored people?"

"Huh?" I responded in complete ignorance. After a pause, I opened my mouth again to say something else, but no words passed my lips.

Without waiting for an answer, he pulled back his jacket so that I could see a holstered revolver. His contempt for me was in full display. I was completely out of my comfort zone by then. The sweat on my brow had nothing to do with the temperature of the meeting room, which was probably ideal for both living and dead bodies. It was fear that had over-heated me. The remainder of the meeting became a blur. I couldn't take my eyes off the man who threatened me.

When the program ended, I rushed to my car and made one of the quickest exits in my life. My students would have said that I burned rubber to get out of there, narrowly missing a lamppost. The tree-lined, two-lane highway that led back to Norman was poorly lit. Shadows of trees seemed to reach out for my car. In my rearview mirror, I watched as a vehicle followed me for about half an hour. When my engine began to misfire, I thought about the man who had disrupted my sense of security. What if he was in the car behind me? As quickly as that horrible thought came to my mind, another one popped up and said that if death came for me that night, so be it. I was ready to die for my belief that housing ought to be racially integrated. The car behind me turned in another direction just before the Norman exit. When I got home, I told Barbara about the encounter and my mental acceptance of death, if need be. She closed her eyes, shuddered, and shook her head. We never spoke of it again.

The third major ASU activity of the semester was co-hosting the first Midwest Regional Conference on Black Student Collegians on April 18–20, 1969, coordinated by Guinnevere Hodges. The other co-hosts were the ASU chapters of Oklahoma State University, Central State College (now University of Central Oklahoma), Oklahoma Baptist University, and Oklahoma City University. Out-of-state participants came from the University of Kansas, Lawrence; Iowa State University, Ames; the University of Texas, Austin; Texas Southern University, Houston; the University of Houston; the College of the Ozarks, Clarksville, Arkansas; and the University of Missouri, St. Louis.

I addressed the 150 black collegians at the luncheon on the last day of the conference. In my speech, "Building Bridges, Saving People," I advised them never to lose their humanity and compassion: "We who have been objects of hate and distrust are capable of being hateful and distrustful. . . . We must be dedicated to equality for all black people, not just a select few. . . . And there must be no more fighting in public among us. No more derogatory remarks about our black brothers to our white friends." I stressed the importance of establishing coalitions with white people. In conclusion, I stated that racial bigotry was not complicated; it was an action of fools who believed they were wise. Although I was speaking to a general audience, my primary targets were the University of Oklahoma students who were present.

At the afternoon panel, during the question-and-answer session, one of the students said that the morning panelists and I, as the luncheon speaker, were too concerned with black-white coalitions. Clara Luper, one of the panelists, responded by saying that, to her knowledge, every successful black civil rights rebellion or movement had had white supporters. "Establish coalitions with the white man in order to meet the immediate needs of Negroes," she proffered. Suddenly, to that student at least and maybe to others, I wasn't an Uncle Tom after all. But I could not shake the feeling that the new University of Oklahoma ASU leaders thought I was too committed to racial integration. If that did indeed bother them, establishing a comfortable working relationship with them next fall was going to be difficult for both them and me.

Although Sterlin and a few other ASU leaders were constantly concerned with trying to resolve race relations problems, most black students were not, and neither were their white peers. Both groups probably spent only a small fraction of their time dealing with racial issues, although black students were much more negatively affected by racism than white students. Nevertheless, most of the black students managed to find time to be "normal" students. They fell in and out of love, agonized over what field of study to major in, joined cliques and clubs, competed for grades, partied, and cherished their friends. And they derived deep satisfaction when, through their academic accomplishments, they tilted university life in their favor. Sandra Rouce's recollections illustrate those points.

Sandra "Sandy" Rouce Remembers OU

When I graduated from Booker T. Washington High School (BTW) in Tulsa in 1966, I did not think much about racism or problems I might face attending the University of Oklahoma. In fact I did not think about OU at all. At that time, my sister was completing her junior year at Howard University in Washington, D.C. I thought that I too might attend Howard until my father told me that I could attend any school that I wanted to . . . in Oklahoma. The University of Oklahoma seemed to be the best option in terms of academic quality.

I loved my high school and all the activities it provided. I was captain of the majorettes, secretary of the student council, the worst gymnast on the gymnastics team, and a part-time art enthusiast. OU was a stark contrast. I graduated with the highest grade point average in my high school class of approximately three hundred and was a National Merit finalist, but I did not receive any scholarship offers or financial assistance from OU. My high school counselor never discussed applying for scholarships with me, and I just assumed that OU would offer one to me once the admissions office saw my academic record. They did not. The picture today is dramatically different, with OU aggressively recruiting minority students and offering them academic scholarships.

A Wonderfully Strange Beginning

In 1966 it seemed that the only black students wooed with OU scholarships were outstanding athletes. The number of black students at the University appeared to be less than a hundred. Our numbers were so small that most of us, with the exception of a few hefty athletes, could fit into one section of the Helm Restaurant in Norman, our unofficial weekend meeting place. I remember attending a party during my first week at OU and someone asked who the new freshmen were. We raised our hands, thinking that they were going to give us a special welcome. There were no special introductions, simply an announcement that half of us would not be around at the beginning of the next academic year. By my estimate they were wrong, but it was possibly the beginning of our junior year by the time that half of my black peers were gone. Those who remained became some of my closest and dearest friends.

I came to OU with my high school sweetheart, Theodric "Ricci" Hendrix. So, things did not appear terribly bleak for me, as they did for most other black freshmen. However, the large amount of social isolation that black students experienced at OU was reinforced by the fact that the small number of entering black female freshmen students were spread out among the several dorms of old Cate Center. Only two black girls were assigned to each dorm as roommates. I had already met the girl who would become my roommate, Wanda James, from Wewoka, Oklahoma. We met at a National Science Foundation Scholars Program at Florida A&M University during the summer of my sophomore year in high school. Wanda was a math major, and maybe it was my minor in math that made us a perfect match. I could not have had a better roommate.

Wanda had strict rules about studying. She set aside a certain amount of time each afternoon in our room for studying, with the radio, our only form of entertainment, turned-off. The black Oklahoma City radio station that we listened to was only on the air for a limited time in the afternoon and early evening. So this was a major sacrifice. Another ritual was the weekend bath. We took showers every day except for Saturday night. On that day we would take a bath after all the other girls had gone out on their dates. We were extremely fastidious and alternated being the first bather because that person had to scrub and disinfect the tub to our strict specifications.

Wanda and I were fiercely protective of each other; we knew that we always had each other's back. But we were also very competitive. We took the same math classes because she was a math major and I was a math minor. Although I got good grades, she always made higher scores on our math tests than I did. It wasn't until Wanda got married during the summer following our freshman year that I finally got higher math scores than she did. I remember that she would come to our evening class smelling of liver and onions or some other entrée that she had cooked for her husband. (Years later, when I became a busy wife and mother, I felt guilty that I had the nerve to be proud of beating that tremendously smart and resourceful nineteen-year-old young woman. Wanda Edwards graduated from OU and went on to earn a doctorate in mathematics.)

With curfew and classes, mealtimes at Cate Center were the only convenient times for us to congregate during the week. Dinner was my favorite meal because I could leisurely sit and converse with other black students, most of whom remain my close sisters/friends today. (Beth Mack Wilson, Gwendolyn Carey Fedrick, Rosita Brown Long, Pamela Cash Menzies, and I get together every year at Beth's house in Dallas for the OU-Texas weekend, rooting for OU even though we all now live in Texas, with the exception of Pam, who lives in Chicago.)

I pledged Alpha Kappa Alpha (AKA) Sorority in the spring of my freshman year, 1967, and after nearly a full year of pledging, I became a member that December. I pledged along with girls from three other universities: Oklahoma State University, Oklahoma City University, and Central State University. We gathered in Oklahoma City as pledges and then went to meet our big sisters from the various universities. My favorite big sister was Judy Eason McIntyre (now state senator McIntyre). She was available to harass—or, rather, encourage—me even when I was in Tulsa during holidays and summer vacations. While there were many memorable experiences as a new sorority member, the one that sticks most in my mind was the invitation we received for dinner at an OU white sorority house. We were excited because after several weeks of dorm food, the prospect of eating a meal at a table in a "home" was just too much. We fantasized about having roast turkey or maybe something with shrimp in it. We could not hide our disappointment when they brought out a platter of ham sandwiches and potato chips. I must admit, however, that those sandwiches had the freshest, crispiest lettuce that I had ever tasted.

Left to right: Pamela Cash, Gwendolyn Carey (president), Rosita Long, Sandra Rouce, and Doris Jackson make plans for Alpha Kappa Alpha's spring party, 1969, from University of Oklahoma 1970 yearbook. Western History Collections, University of Oklahoma Libraries.

Year Two

In my sophomore year, we all moved from Cate Center to other housing arrangements. I moved to an honors dorm in Walker Tower. I remember that there was a problem because I was the only black sophomore resident in the dorm. The other girls entered with an assigned roommate. Several days later, a Lutheran minister's daughter named Cheryl arrived at my dorm room. She told me that the housing officials made a special point of asking if she minded living with "a Negro." She didn't seem to mind, and we both learned a lot from each other. Our friendship started on shaky ground when, during our first week, a panty raid was staged by some of the boys on campus. Cheryl stood at our window waving her panties in the air. I was terrified. I often wondered how a minister's daughter knew so much about panty raids.

To me the University was like a city of twenty thousand people. And because I did not consider Norman my home, it really was like a city within a city. The only places that seemed to welcome black students in Norman were on Campus Corner, where we spent all of our allowance or earnings on shoes at our favorite store or shopped for special events clothes. At that time, special events were so limited that our clothes had names attached to the event. I distinctly remember that all of the black females had an "Aretha dress." The name was chosen for the long-anticipated Aretha Franklin concert on campus.

Our early years at OU were during a period of turmoil on national and local levels. We protested the war in Vietnam, cried over the deaths of Martin Luther King, Jr., and Robert Kennedy, and ushered in black activism on campus with the establishment of the Afro-American Student Union. Dick Gregory came to campus shortly before his hunger strike. He sat with us and discussed the policies and injustices of racism. He did so with little fanfare or pretense. He urged us to mind our conscience and be true to our black history and ourselves. We were full of promise for change, and indeed we watched changes occur on the OU campus.

Year Three

Until my junior year, I could not decide whether I wanted to be a psychology, math, or art major. So I took art classes along with math and psychology. My favorite class was a sculpture class. It amazed me that we were actually sculpting *nude* models, and nobody seemed embarrassed but me. The professor, who seemed around sixty-five years old, was hip and very liberal. He often sat in his office talking to the nude model, neither of whom seemed embarrassed that she did not have clothes on. He took a personal interest in me, especially when I asked to miss class to attend the retirement reception for my sixty-five-year-old father. I remember one class in which the model was not present. The teacher told us to pick someone in class to sculpt. After a few minutes, I looked up and every person was making a face with enormous nostrils and large lips. I thought to myself, "How strange . . . who could that funny-looking person be?" When they added large hoop earrings and an Afro, it finally dawned on me that they had all chosen me to sculpt.

By the time I reached my junior year, I received a little financial assistance from the University through the work-study program. The chairman of the Psychology Department, Dr. Lauren Wispe, hired me to work in the departmental office, but that was short-lived. I was so unaccustomed to office machinery that every time he received a phone call, I would get up from my desk and run to his office to tell him that someone was on the phone. I only spent a week in the office before he mercifully involved me in an Oklahoma City social psychology research project. I drove to Oklahoma City every weekend with a white male and white female student. The female student and I took turns dropping a bag of groceries in front of people on a sidewalk in order to measure differences in responses by people who passed by. The most interesting part of my day during that time was not the fact that I got helped less with my groceries than my white counterpart but the hostile reactions of individuals who saw me in the car with the white male graduate student who accompanied us. Many of them honked their car horns or called us names as we drove by.

Another memorable event was sitting in a psychology course when Arthur Jensen's theory of inferiority of blacks was discussed not as a theory but as a fact. I was the only black student in the class and the only one who questioned the validity of the contention. I remembered stories of Ada Lois Sipuel Fisher being roped off from the rest of the students as she sat in classes as the first postgraduate black law school student at the University of Oklahoma, and realized that we had not come that far. It was at that time that I decided psychology would be my major field of study.

Year Four

Dr. Wispe continued to be my mentor throughout the remainder of my years at OU. I tutored his daughter in math and acquiesced when he encouraged me to skip applying to a master's degree program in psychology and to apply directly to a doctoral program instead. My interest was child psychology, so two doctoral programs, one at the University of Illinois and the other at the University of Michigan, were selected. I was admitted to both programs and given scholarships to both of them. At the last minute, I learned that my fiancé had been admitted to medical school in Nashville, Tennessee. He encouraged me to apply to the psychology doctoral program at George Peabody College in Nashville, where I received my doctorate in clinical psychology in 1975.

My parents, aunts, and uncles earned college and advanced degrees during a time when graduation from high school was difficult for blacks. My father grew up in Hitchcock, Oklahoma, and he and his siblings were sent to Lawrence, Kansas, to attend high school because there was no black school in the area that they could attend. I remember my mother's story about a professor at Colorado State Teachers College who would not give her the A that she earned in his math course, because she was black. She had the grade point average to receive a college honor, but the dean of her college refused to give it to her during a public presentation. When the dean of students told her that she could come to his office to get the award, she told him to keep it.

I was always careful not to make my professors aware of my name or that I was black. Many of our classes were large and there was really no need to do so. In one large biology lecture class I remember that the teacher bragged that a student had made a perfect score on the latest test. I heard him spell out "R-o-u-c-e," then he asked Ms. Rouce to raise her hand so that he and the rest of the class could see the curve-setter. His jaw dropped when he saw my hand raised. He never acknowledged me again.

I graduated from OU in 1970 as apparently the University's first black Phi Beta Kappa honor society graduate. There were others before me who probably should have been given that honor but were not. Things were beginning to change at OU when I graduated. My neighbor Jocelyn Lee, who graduated from BTW in Tulsa and entered OU a year after me, was one of the first black students to receive an academic scholarship from OU. I did not get financial assistance other than work-study and employment as a dorm counselor; but the year that I graduated, the dean of women brought to the attention of two of my closest girlfriends and myself the American Association of University Women's Coretta Scott King Scholarship. We all got funded for varying amounts to complete graduate degrees. My scholarship helped me to go to any university that I chose, supplementing both tuition and living expenses.

Hindsight

My sister often brags about having a better undergraduate experience than I because she attended Howard University, a prestigious historically black university. I don't think that I could have made better or more long-lasting friendships than those I made at OU, nor could I have met a more successful group. I like opening my *Ebony* magazine and seeing Pamela Cash Menzies, vice president of multimedia resources, on its administrative page, or watching my friend Gwendolyn Carey Fedrick on public affairs television programs. My OU friends have given me an inside connection to mass media events. Also, I like living in Houston, where black people in barbershops talk about local entrepreneur and former pro football player Eddie Hinton, another of my Sooner friends. A few of my BTW classmates who live in Houston include musician Ronnie Wilson of the GAP Band, martial arts expert Larry Eason, and Chuck Cissel, CEO of the Oklahoma Jazz Hall of Fame. Although Senator Judy Eason McIntyre would be a friend regardless of my having attended OU, I know that she eased my transition there. She, with her strength and unflappable spirit as an early pioneer at OU, along with Shirley Ann Harris (B.A. and M.P.H.) and other strong black women, are wonderful role models. And I am proud when I display Rosita Brown Long's inspirational book in my home, knowing that she has served as my personal example and support, or when I name-drop and talk about my friend Beth Mack Wilson, J.D., an associate vice president at Southern Methodist University. Beth is the sharpest woman I know. I have stopped trying to defend my experience at OU, with its unique challenges, blessings, and friendships. Most of the time, I just nod and quietly say to my sister, "I think attending OU had its benefits too."[6]

CHAPTER SEVEN

The End of the Beginning

The year 1969 was a turning point both in black-white relations at the University of Oklahoma and in my professional career. The Black Declaration of Independence shook open opportunities for black students, faculty, and staff that had once been unthinkable. My appointment to an endowed professorship at the University—the first for a black professor in Oklahoma—was one of those opportunities. Overall, the year was bittersweet—although some of the numerous attempts to restructure the University and redefine its morality were successful, others were not. It was a time to be excited about what our institution might become and to be fearful of worst-case scenarios.

The Goldman Professorship

In April 1969, I told University officials and students that I intended to resign after the 1969–70 academic year. Several things prompted that decision, including my frustration at the slow pace of racial conciliation and the unabated hostility against black students, as well as my feeling of inadequacy as an agent of change. Working almost nonstop—ten to fifteen hours a day, six days a week—for the past two and a half years had taken a heavy toll on me. Although I felt as though I was burned out physically and emotionally, the decision to leave the University was heartwrenching. I had grown very fond of the people I worked with and for.

Still, it seemed to me that I ought to make room for someone else to move the equality agenda forward. When Barbara asked me a third time if I was sure that my leaving the University would be best for me and the University, I said, "I hope it will be." The announcement was prominently reported in the *Oklahoma Daily*, the *Norman Transcript*, and several other newspapers. I had already accepted a summer appointment at Langston University as a visiting professor of sociology, and I was weighing several job offers elsewhere. What I wasn't considering, however, was staying in Oklahoma. During the first week in May, I received a telephone call from President Hollomon.

"George, I have been informed by J. Clayton Feaver [David Ross Boyd Professor of Philosophy and chair of the Goldman Professor Search Committee] that you have not responded to his request for you to meet with the committee as one of the finalists. Why haven't you set a date?"

I was surprised to receive the call because I had made known my intention to leave the University. I answered him rather curtly, "Herb, my lack of response speaks for me. I am not a candidate. I don't want to waste the committee's time."

"Damn it, George," he said, bristling. "You ought to at least go to the interview out of courtesy to whoever the persons were who nominated you. Your participation would at least provide the committee the unique perspectives you have gained through your community activities."

"I don't want to waste my time — "

"You're going to spend your time doing something. So why not meet with the committee? I don't know who will be selected, but I want you to meet with them. Think of it as one of your community service projects."

I agreed to schedule a meeting with the committee. Then, for the first time, I read the information about the professorship that had been sent to me. The job description intrigued me. The Goldman Professorship was established in October 1968 through gifts from Sylvan N. Goldman of Oklahoma City and the Chapman Foundation of Tulsa, in the name of Leta M. Chapman. The professor would be responsible for creating and implementing a graduate-level program to train students to combat racial discrimination and other acts of bigotry as well as to assist organizations and communities throughout Oklahoma in the public school desegregation process. The job interview was stimulating and challenging, and I was delighted to be named the top applicant. On May

13, after discussing the appointment with Barbara and a few of my most trusted colleagues, I accepted Hollomon's offer to become the S. N. Goldman Professor of Human Relations. The appointment became effective July 1, 1969.

During the first week of June, John Ezell, dean of the College of Arts and Sciences, made me an offer. "I know that you won't immediately have a budget for faculty when you begin your new job," he said. "How would you like to have Vera Gatch as your first faculty member? She's an assistant professor of psychology, and I want to find another academic home for her. The faculty in the Psychology Department has had a bitter split between clinicians and experimental psychologists. She is a clinician — a very competent one, too. If both of you agree to the transfer, I will officially move her to your program once it is developed. . . . In the meantime she could help you to work out some of the details."

He arranged for Professor Gatch to meet with me at my house. She insisted that I call her "Vee." Within an hour of our conversation, I was convinced she would be good for the program. She was insightful, direct, and humane, plus she was available.

"I would like to join you," she decided. "You are my kind of person — a risk taker with the right values."

She then suggested that I meet with her and J. R. Morris to discuss possible steps and strategies for putting the program together. "J. R. is one of the smartest, nicest, and most academically and politically skillful persons I know," she said. That was how I perceived him too.

The three of us met at my house on a Saturday afternoon and discussed several things that Vera and I would have to address. In consultation with her, I would design a curriculum. In consultation with J. R., who spoke with incandescent clarity, Vera would find volunteers to teach in the program. It was the kind of meeting that I needed. Thanks to Vee and J. R., before the curriculum had even been designed, three adjunct professors had already volunteered to help me launch what would quickly become the largest and most ethnically diverse graduate degree program in the University: J. David Rambo, an eminent attorney and associate district judge; and two highly talented social workers, W. E. Duff and George Wheehunt.

Two Steps Forward, One Step Back

While the human relations degree program was being created, there were more than enough unfinished ASU projects to occupy my rapidly disappearing leisure time. Stung by the ASU allegation of housing discrimination in the University, the Student Action Committee (SAC) decided to conduct its own investigation. Thirty members formed an open housing task force that talked with students and examined the University's housing procedures. The committee corroborated the ASU claim of racial discrimination. Despite the absence of racial designations on the University housing applications, in almost all instances studied by the SAC committee, black applicants were paired with each other. The all-white housing administrators identified black applicants through their mailing addresses, high schools, and other race-specific clues. When no black roommates were available for them, the students were given private rooms. When the system occasionally misfired and white students were assigned black roommates, all of the white students who requested reassignments were accommodated.

Sally Gregory, a reporter for the *Oklahoma Daily*, stated that when David Burr, vice president for the University Community, received the SAC's final report in May 1969, he was greatly distressed and enraged that the discriminatory practices existed. He immediately notified all housing personnel that racial discrimination was an abhorrent practice in which neither he nor anyone who worked for him was to engage. On top of that, he inserted a clause in the *University Bulletin* that affirmed the University's commitment to complete racial equality. In September, Burr hired Wilbur P. Walker, Sr., to be the University's first black housing administrator. That was not the first black appointment Burr made, and it would not be his last. A year earlier, he had appointed Zelbert Moore as his administrative assistant. Few University administrators were as sensitive, kind, or morally correct as David Burr.

The Student Action Committee followed up with another important subcommittee study. It corroborated the ASU allegation of cultural insensitivity in University employment practices. The committee documented cases in which black and white male students who had mustaches, beards, sideburns, long hair, or Afros were denied jobs for which they were qualified. Most of the black applicants fit more than one of

J. R. Morris *(center)* and Steve Sutherland *(center right)* meet with Wilbur Walker *(bottom left)* and other housing directors, 1969. Western History Collections, University of Oklahoma Libraries.

those categories. In fact, almost all of the male student employees were white and clean-shaven, with short-cropped hair. No official dress code mandated this kind of grooming, but there were plenty of departmental biases for it. The report was given to the University employment office, but little came of it immediately. Unsurprisingly, the SAC's findings mirrored the citation of campus-wide cultural insensitivity in the 1968 Ohm Committee Report.

It would be untrue to say that nothing happened with regard to the workplace-grooming situation. The University culture was in fact undergoing changes in its norms — too slowly for most of us black people at the University, though. President Hollomon and his staff were beginning to address a very long list of human relations problems, including some related to employment practices. Because their efforts to alter formal and informal grooming codes were usually stopgap measures, it would take considerably more time for rules, regulations, and procedures that pro-

moted racial and cultural inclusion to be implemented. More committees and recommendations would follow, interspersed with a few quick
changes.

By the end of the spring 1969 semester, tirades against the black
students reached a crescendo. Racism had moved from predominantly
covert guises to largely overt manifestations. Hatred was scribbled on
sidewalks, toilet stalls, and bumper stickers. With nudging from President
Hollomon, the Student Congress and the Faculty Senate decided to study
racial discrimination at the University. On May 13 the Student Congress
established a committee to investigate institutionalized racism in student
affairs. Around the same time, the Faculty Senate appointed an ad hoc
committee to write an antidiscrimination report. The good intentions of
the student committee were not achieved, however. The semester ended
shortly after the members were impaneled, and after they left campus for
the summer break, nothing more came of the committee.

The Faculty Senate Committee, on the other hand, went right to
work. The committee, consisting of History Department chair and professor Donald Berthrong, modern languages associate professor John
Alley, zoology professor Paul David, Lennie Marie Muse-Tolliver, and
myself, completed its report in June. Cutting to the quick, the report
stated the obvious by concluding that racial discrimination did indeed
exist at the University of Oklahoma. Our recommendations called for
outreach activities to address several problems that impeded minority
faculty recruitment and contributed to lower minority student graduation rates. Hollomon called the report "generally acceptable."

Among the recommendations were these: (1) Qualified scholars
from minority groups should be sought out whenever the University had
vacant faculty positions. (2) A joint committee of students, faculty, and
administrators should be established to recruit and train University volunteers to serve as orientation aides for minority and low-income students during their freshman year. (3) Student volunteers should be used
as tutors to assist low-income students who were failing courses but could
not afford professional tutors. (4) Whenever possible, substandard student housing owned by the University should be eliminated. Also, students should pay different rates for housing based on the quality of their
housing units. In some instances, provision should be made for low-
income students to receive rent subsidies. (5) On-the-job training in

secretarial skills should be offered to unemployed wives of low-income students who were seeking jobs at the University. (6) Study-abroad and guided foreign tour opportunities should be available for every OU student who could profit from them. (7) Race relations seminars for University personnel should be conducted by the OU Southwest Center for Human Relations Studies.

The Faculty Senate Committee's report and the two Student Action Committee reports, along with articles written by the *Oklahoma Daily* staff, gave the administration sufficient documentation of racism in the University. An unexpected discovery by the faculty committee was the squalid living conditions in several of the University's rental apartments scattered near the campus. Dozens of black students and considerably more international students lived in decrepit units that reminded me of the slum dwellings I lived in when I was a child. Most of the faculty committee's recommendations were implemented in some form within several years.

I spent the remainder of the summer designing the human relations curriculum, and I also joined Bob Bibens and Dean Robert Ohm, members of the College of Education, and Raymond Lutz, professor of engineering, to create a desegregation plan for the Oklahoma City Public Schools. On August 1 it was approved by Chief U.S. District Judge Luther Bohanon. Known as the Cluster Plan, it was Oklahoma City's first comprehensive, federally approved desegregation plan. This endeavor was a welcome break from my University activism activities that had produced few totally gratifying results, but my excitement and pleasure over this success was short-lived. The extensive busing of the students was more emotionally disruptive than educationally rewarding, particularly for the black students. Fortunately, my gloom soon receded when good things began to happen at the University.

In August 1969, Walter Dillard was appointed assistant professor of zoology, becoming the University's fourth black full-time professor. (Thomas and Carol Carey had been appointed a year earlier, but they were visiting, not permanent, professors.) During that same month, the United Methodist Church rented its small house adjacent to its campus chapel on Elm Avenue to the Afro-American Student Union for use as a cultural center. The students called their new black cultural center the Wazuri House. "Wazuri" is a Swahili term for "beautiful people" — thus it was "the Beautiful People's House." The situation was an ideal one for the ASU: the rent and maintenance were paid from University of Oklahoma Student Association appropriations, there was space for study rooms and a library on the second floor, and the basement became a recreation and dance area. In essence, the ASU had acquired its own Greek-like house.

On November 1 the ASU held an open house that included a sensitivity seminar from 8 to 10 P.M. The panelists were Guinnevere Hodges, former ASU member and now an academic counselor in the University College; James "Jim" Kenderdine, associate professor of marketing; Paul Tharp, assistant professor of political science; and me. Our topic was "The Problems Black Students Encounter in Adjusting to Academic Life at the University of Oklahoma," but we didn't just talk about problems. We pointed out positive changes in the University's culture and the University's commitment to create more opportunities to become a culturally inclusive campus. Twenty-five ASU members and a dozen or so nonmembers attended the seminar. In addition to the seminar, black music was played to give nonblacks a sample of African American culture.

President Hollomon and David Burr had met with several black students and me early in the fall semester to discuss interracial issues. We told them that as long as the Greek organizations were racially segregated, weekends on campus would continue to be visual reminders of the racial chasm. White Greeks had their large, attractive houses where some of their members lived and all of them partied. The black Greeks had no houses on or off campus. They went off campus to locations in Norman or Oklahoma City for their parties. President Hollomon acknowledged that it was unlikely that segregation in the Greek organizations would end but promised he would try to do something about the situation.

Puffing on a pipe, Hollomon said, "We have inherited segregated organizations that involve many of the most powerful people in our state. I see no political capital that could be gained by me through an all-out assault on the white Greeks. There are bigger fish to fry if we want to lose our jobs over principles. . . . Maybe my administration ought to rail against racially segregated places of religious worship. And while we are at it, we could take on Masonic organizations, social clubs, country clubs, and Lord knows what else we can reform. But those are not my problems today. What can I do to give the black fraternities a little parity with their white peers?"

Alpha Phi Alpha house, Norman, 1970. Western History Collections, University of Oklahoma Libraries.

I said, "Help them to find some houses to rent."

David Burr was asked to inventory the University's properties and see if there were a few unused houses suitable for leasing to the black Greeks. He found only one available house. It was on Elm Avenue at the corner of Brooks Street. Hollomon decided to give the first black Greek organization on our campus, the Alpha Phi Alpha Fraternity, the first option on the house. The Alphas accepted the offer (although the house was torn down a few years later to make space for parking). Hollomon pledged additional houses, if they became available, for other black Greek organizations. It was a good-faith gesture, but nothing came of it.

Feeling appreciated and encouraged by the recent turn of events, the ASU circulated a petition to have a black studies program at the University and collected several hundred signatures. At the same time, President Hollomon appointed a special committee on educational opportunity to review University policies and programs that affected the lives of minority group students, low-income students, and students with disabilities. J. R. Morris chaired the committee. Its research and recommendations provided institutional documentation that was helpful later when the University created new programs and applied for research grants and student outreach funds.

The fall semester of 1969 was off to a good start. The new spirit of reconciliation raised my hope for a significant lessening of interracial conflicts. In November the ASU had its first Thanksgiving meal in its new cultural center. But that day my hope abruptly gave way to terror, fear, and a harder division between blacks and whites. After the ASU business meeting was held in the living room, we adjourned to the dining room to eat a home-cooked meal. Shortly thereafter someone shot a bullet into the living room. Based on where the bullet was lodged in the wall, one of us would have been injured or killed if the shot had come just two minutes earlier. Our positive mood and good fortune changed quickly. The church that was renting the Elm Avenue house to the ASU asked its members to leave at the end of the school year, in hopes of preventing further shootings. The Wazuri House was relocated to one of the empty dormitories in the Wilson Center on campus and renamed the Sequoyah House.

Closing Ranks

The push and pull between violence and nonviolence was always a factor. The philosophical debate was so heated it could barely be mediated. Even under the best of circumstances, which the recent shooting and its consequences were not, it was impossible to rule out the possibility of violence. It was fortunate for all of us that most members of the University community rejected violence as their conflict resolution strategy of choice. Consequently, the violence between blacks and whites that occurred after the Wazuri House shooting incident resembled scuffles more than major battles. Nevertheless, a single gunshot had torn open feelings of exasperation among the ASU members—and others—to the point of publicly expressed outrage. Some of the black students believed that the only things of major importance left for them to lose were their dignity and their lives, so they withdrew deeper into black enclaves.

As civility waned, countless students abandoned the usual cordial methods of resolving interracial conflicts. Simultaneously, name-calling and jostling increased throughout the campus between black and white students. Flurries of University initiatives tried to find common ground upon which to reestablish civility, but some ASU members would have none of it. For them, the time for diplomacy was over. The shooting evoked the anxiety and fear they had been repressing. Several students vowed to defend themselves and, if necessary, to respond in kind to violence against them.

The brashness of a few outspoken ASU members—and those who rebutted them—was occasionally laced with vulgarity, which frightened the genteel people among us who were caught in the crossfire. But the squabbling did not snuff out the black peoples' determination to redistribute institutional power, nor did it discredit our allegation of endemic racism in most of the University's academic and service units. The intermittent internal and external skirmishes gradually took a heavy toll on our morale. In the end, each of us had to decide if we would—or could emotionally afford to—continue the black rebellion. To their credit, the ASU members did not let ideological differences overwhelm them. Outside of the ASU, it was a different story, however. Driven by a need to extract a measure of payback, small bands of roving blacks cruised the campus and nearby areas at night, looking for white people to beat up. An equal number, or more, of white students and others reciprocated. Although the incidents were relatively few, any one of them could have sparked large-scale campus unrest.

This was a time of heightened group identity among the black students. Many of them proudly displayed their blackness—and unity. Colorful dashikis, crescent-shaped Afros, and elaborate male handshakes were prominent among some of them. Curious white people would stare at the set of clasps, taps, and touches that made up black male students' handshakes—and the meticulous rows of beaded hair worn by several of the black females. Most of the black students and their white allies decided not to mimic the conventional white society clothing styles; they established their own unique styles of dress. In this instance, I was the odd man out. I did not for a moment stop wearing tailored suits, expensive shoes, and appropriate accessories. In terms of dress, I was a black Anglo-Saxon to the maximum degree.

There was a very simple explanation for my refusal to give up "white attire." I had grown up poor, graduated from high school poor, and begun college poor. I had spent too many years trying to afford the kind of "white men's clothes" that my father held up for me as the standard of proper dress. No doubt he had been brainwashed by someone to emulate white people, and he in turn brainwashed me. We were classic examples of the white-indoctrinated blacks that Frantz Fanon wrote about. The students sometimes made fun of my clothes fetish.

Clothing aside, the combination of increased aggressive behavior, black and white militancy, and one-way communication between groups weakened some of our interracial coalitions. There were ample divertissements and too few encouragements to keep the coalitions going. All of those trends worried me. I did not want the ASU to splinter apart, nor did I want irreparable fractures among the black students or between them and their allies. Several people agreed with me. The original organizational structure of the ASU had been able to maintain a balance between moderate and radical ideologies and behavior, thereby bestowing an attractive eclectic identity on the group. The new organizational structure drifted too far from that core, exposing the fragility of our unity. There were defections, but surprisingly few.

I myself was briefly expelled from the ASU. In December 1969 a group of militant black students summoned me and other black faculty members to a closed meeting. The purpose of the meeting was to belittle those of us who were committed to nonviolence. My inquisitor was a big, stern-looking student named Calvin Taylor. It was rumored that Calvin had once beat up three U.S. marines. When he pointed a long finger at me and grimaced, I gave him my full attention. His dour demeanor poked holes in my self-confidence. "Doc-tor Hen-der-son," he mocked me, "we don't need Uncle Toms like you on this campus."

The other students were hushed by Calvin's voice. I was hushed by his icy stare. An eerie silence settled in the room as Calvin moved slowly toward the back row where I was sitting. His body began to shake as he moved to within a few steps of me. "You educated, token, proper-talking Negroes are afraid to fight for freedom," he taunted me. A couple of students yelled, "Right on, brother. Tell it like it is."

I stood up slowly, trying to control a nervous twitch. Then I looked past Calvin to the students sitting near me. "It's true," I said to them, "I don't believe in using violence, but I do believe in finding other ways to obtain racial equality. Obviously I'm not needed in your civil rights organization, so I won't stay here to be verbally abused."

As I walked out of the room, I was aware that I was sweating. I felt fear, sorrow, and anger. I was afraid that my relationship with the students had ended. I was sad because the students in the room would not accept those of us who would not advocate violence as our civil rights tactic. And I was infuriated that the students thought I was an Uncle Tom. I went home.

Four hours later I was awakened from a sound sleep by a ringing telephone. "Dr. Henderson," the voice at the other end of the line began, "this is Judge Elvin Brown. A student named Calvin Taylor has been arrested, and he has given me your name as a reference for him. If you vouch for him, Dr. Henderson, I'll release him on his own recognizance."

Without hesitation I said, "I'll vouch for him, Judge Brown. May I speak with Calvin?"

"Hi, Doc," a small voice at the other end of the line whispered. The bravado that I experienced from him earlier had evaporated.

"Merry Christmas, Calvin," I chuckled. "I've just given you a non-violent gift of freedom. If there is anything else this Uncle Tom can do for you, let me know."

He and I laughed as I put down the telephone receiver. It was a poignant reminder to me that the struggle to help black students would not be solely a black-versus-white confrontation. There would be conflicts among blacks too. I had been fired as an ASU adviser by the students and, within several hours, reinstated. Calvin and I became close friends. In fact, he became like a son to Barbara and me.

The fall 1969 semester ended in suspense. The process of rapprochement was slow and emotionally draining. At some point during our pursuit of building healthy multiracial friendships, we lowered our expectations for them. Perhaps it was unrealistic to expect large numbers of them. Even so, most of us blacks did not lower our expectation for total racial equality in the University. What mattered most in the long run were the actions taken by administrators and other people to make the University and Norman communities more culturally inclusive. But that expectation wasn't just about blacks. It was about all ethnic minority groups.

More Activism and Changes

The spring 1970 semester was a watershed in the University's efforts to come to terms with some of its most pressing racial and social justice issues. During that period so many things happened so fast that it was difficult for me to give all of them my full attention and maximum efforts. The students always seemed to be protesting something. I moved from crisis to crisis without any triage strategy. Instead of working with appropriate people to prioritize the various problems, I treated all of them as if they were top priority, thereby not maximizing my energy or results. Some of the problems that could have benefited from more study and less immediate action were given the same priority as those that were so volatile that immediate action was necessary to prevent a disaster.

In a letter to the editor of the *Oklahoma Daily* published on January 13, 1970, the ASU issued a tribute to the Black Panthers. It was signed by Dwight Sanders, minister of information; Jafus Cavil, chairman; Greg Watts, minister of defense; and Raymond Velie, minister of education. The tribute stirred up a ruckus between radical and moderate members of the ASU. It was a rift I could have done without. When approached by a school newspaper reporter for my reaction to the tribute, I said that there were numerous black heroes who deserved our remembrance, including Malcolm X. Apparently that was not the answer that she was looking for. My quote was not included in a follow-up story, but a tribute to Martin Luther King, Jr., in a letter to the editor signed by "Members of the Afro-American Student Union," appeared in the *Oklahoma Daily* on January 15, 1970. The ideological split in the ASU was now public. My earlier fear of deep fissures in the organization had come true.

I was ready for some good things to happen, and they did—for a little while. The 1970 ASU Black Heritage Week program featured, a poet and the founder of a black cultural center in Harlem; Gylan Kain, former player and coach of the Boston Celtics professional basketball team; and Curtis Graves, Oklahoma state representative. On February 7, Bill Russell was a dinner guest at my house. It was a magic moment for eight boys who supposedly dropped by to see my son George Jr., and—surprise, surprise—Bill Russell just happened to be there. The boys coaxed him to come outside and shoot a few hoops with them. Having the only black-owned home in Norman had definite perks for my children. When prominent black celebrities came to town to deliver speeches at the University, many of them ate dinner in my home. In the case of Bill Russell, his record for eating the most pieces of Barbara's fried chicken still stands.

Before he left my house, Bill told me, "Watch out, George. There are dirty players in this civil rights game. Don't you become one. It's better to lose with nonviolence than to win with violence." It was as though he had a hunch that things were going to get more tense for blacks and other minority groups at the University — and they did. A season of protests and demonstrations began a few weeks later.

In March the black residents of Cate Center filed a formal grievance after several white residents sang "Dixie" in the dormitory's cafeteria as part of "Western Night" festivities. Because of the complaint, it was not sung again as a part of any housing activity. That long-overdue ending of a culturally insensitive tradition sent a stern warning to other staff members who preferred Confederate music and flags to "Yankee stuff," as one of them boasted. Violators of the ban got their comeuppance and then some: they lost their jobs. Those episodes highlighted the importance of songs and symbols in racially charged environments.

On April 3 the ASU called for a boycott of classes to commemorate the second anniversary of Martin Luther King, Jr.'s death. Students who, for whatever reason, were unable to boycott classes were asked to wear black armbands. Scores of students participated in the boycott, and individuals who attended classes did so unfettered. It dawned on me that members of the University community, especially the students, were becoming quite competent at planning and carrying out nonviolent boycotts and other kinds of demonstrations. It was as though they were writing a noncredit course in demonstrations on the spot.

Four days later, several members of the ASU joined a dozen or so American Indian students to stage a sit-in in President Hollomon's office. They demanded that he accept the Human Relations Committee's recommendation to ban Little Red as the school's Indian mascot. It was one of the most contentious issues of the decade. A month earlier Professor Jerome "Jerry" Weber and I proposed at a public hearing conducted by the Human Relations Committee that a costumed American Indian become a permanent member of the spirit squad and no longer be a mascot. I was surprised by how relaxed and jovial the protesters seemed to be. This suggested compromise garnered little support among the fans or foes of Little Red. I did not fully comprehend that, to a great many people, Little Red was the highest-status American Indian student position in the University or that, to his critics, his being the school mascot was the greatest public insult. I was surprised by how relaxed and jovial the protesters on both sides seemed to be.

On that same day, the Department of English sponsored author Ralph Ellison as a guest speaker. The irony of the events struck me as being profound. Ellison had written about a man whose blackness made him socially invisible. American Indians, who for too long had been like invisible people on our campus, had through the sit-in become very visible to considerably more people. Ellison and the American Indian students displayed their anger about racial slights in the same way. It resided almost entirely in their eyes; from the mouth down, there was hardly a trace of anger. I had misread the demonstrators. They were neither relaxed nor jovial.

On April 16 more than 150 students staged a sit-in in the administration building to protest the Vietnam War, the U.S. military incursion into Cambodia, and the presence of army recruiters on campus. Several black students joined the protesters. Once again a staged demonstration was carried out without violence.

I said to Bob Bibens in passing, "I hope that our luck doesn't run out. I'm afraid that one day there will be violent confrontations." It was the first time that I told someone about that fear.

Also in April, on a positive note, Marthenia Miller, a black sophomore, was a finalist for Miss OU. She did not win the contest, but it was the first time that a black female competed in a beauty contest that previously had been exclusively white.

On April 30, William "Bill" Moffitt was elected president of the University of Oklahoma Student Association. Jim Todd, a Vietnam veteran, was elected to the student government, and Annette Gilliam was the appointed interim attorney general. These three black students stopped by my office to share with me their historic accomplishments. Bill's election defied the law of probability—he was the first African American to be elected student body president at a historically white college or university in Oklahoma. His win seemed to signal the readiness of a majority of the white students to share political power with black students. At first, I admit, I thought his victory was a fluke, but it was not. The campus culture was changing faster than I'd realized. For a few brief moments, the four of us were very full of ourselves.

Bill Moffitt *(right, second from bottom)* and University of Oklahoma president J. Herbert Holloman *(with pipe)* in a student advisory committee meeting, 1970. Western History Collections, University of Oklahoma Libraries.

In his own typical fashion, Jim said, "Today the University of Oklahoma — tomorrow the world!" He was a master of overstatement. Within a few days, we would have more than enough things to conquer in Oklahoma, and not all of them would be exclusively about race or ethnicity.

On Monday May 4 a tragedy struck that none of my colleagues or I expected. Four students were killed at Kent State University during a nonviolent antiwar protest. Shortly thereafter sorrow, fear, and anger oozed onto college and university campuses throughout the nation. At our school, a student group called the People's Liberation Front quickly mobilized to protest the deaths. I thought their planned activities were bizarre. They set up a booth in the basement of the Student Union and passed out leaflets to entice students to attend an antiwar protest on

Tuesday, May 5, and to bring Frisbees, toy water guns, and water balloons that would be used to mock the ROTC army cadets while they drilled on a field near the football stadium.

The proposed activities seemed more like what was appropriate for a fun day, not outrage over the deaths of four people. That certainly was not my idea of a way to dry the tears that I saw in the eyes of students who were shaken by the Kent State tragedy. But nobody asked me for my opinion. Hundreds of students and other people showed up at the drill field. Not all of them were against the U.S. war and other military activity in Southeast Asia. Some of them were pro-war; others were uncommitted; most were curious. The event was, in the jargon of hip students, a significant happening. From my perspective, the only thing missing was popcorn for the spectators. Several of the students frolicked on the drill field. They occasionally came face to face with stern-looking cadets and taunted them, but there was little seriousness in their mockery of the cadets. Suddenly, a student named Keith Green ran into the mass of people, waving what seemed to be a National Liberation Front flag. The fun and games came to an abrupt end, and all hell broke loose. A spate of fear came over me, but I fought it down.

Two University of Oklahoma police officers took the flag from Keith and arrested him. "What are you doing?" several people asked the police. The once-jovial crowd became a raging mob that demanded Keith's release from the police vehicle. I was wedged into a small space near the middle of the crowd, but I could see and hear most of what was going on. Several individuals standing up front were cursing the officers; others were trying to extricate Keith from the police car. Amid cries of "Pigs, go home," a couple of men tried to blow up the police car by stuffing burning rags into the fuel tank. Then, perhaps imitating movie rioters, several students shook the car, hoping, I suppose, that Keith would somehow roll out. I couldn't see all of the action, but I didn't have to see all of it to know that I was stuck in the middle of chaos.

Amid the scuffling, I could see students who had jumped on top of the car and were trying to smash it with makeshift weapons. Bill Moffitt jumped on top of the car too, but for a different reason. He quieted the mob before somebody was seriously hurt. He cooled them down long enough for the dozens of police officers to clear the area. Using their billy clubs and precision riot control movements, officers from the Norman

Police Department and the Oklahoma Highway Patrol augmented the University police officers. They secured the area and blocked it off; there were no serious injuries. I managed to push my way to the outskirts of what had become a blockaded area.

Everything was surreal to me. I thought that I was dreaming. What I saw, heard, and experienced could not have been real. It had to be a flashback of the 1967 race riot in Detroit that erupted two blocks from where I lived. But I wasn't dreaming and I wasn't in Detroit. I was in Norman experiencing a campus riot in real time. I shivered and felt nauseous, so I ran to a secluded spot at a building near the armory and vomited.

Jim Todd saw me meandering slowly to my car. He stopped me and asked, "Are you all right, Doc?" He seemed to sense my fear.

I managed to get my thoughts together long enough to answer him. "No, but I will be tomorrow."

Bill Moffitt organized a May 6 antiwar rally on the North Oval to remember Kent State, to protest the Southeast Asia military conflicts, and to calm the campus. More than three thousand people showed up. Anxiety about large-scale violence rippled through the University. Bill asked several people to be keynote speakers, including Professors J. Clayton Feaver and Shankar Dwivedi of the Philosophy Department, David Whitney of the Sociology Department, and me. He also invited students Jim Todd and Jafus Cavil to speak. But it was President Hollomon and Michael "Mike" Wright — president of the local chapter of Students for a Democratic Society (SDS) and an active member of the local Committee to End the War in Vietnam — who made the greatest impact on the audience. Several people in the audience asked them to speak.

Amid a few cheers and a lot of boos and jeers — including "Chicken!" "Cop-out!" and "Bullshit!" — President Hollomon tried to absolve his administration of wrongdoing during the May 5 riot. And he reminded the audience, especially the students present, to respect the opinions of people that were different from their own. Above all else, he said, the University had to be a place of peace, not violence. A few hecklers drowned out some of his comments that pertained to nonviolence. Someone shouted at him, referring to the three students who had been arrested during the riot, "Your people put them in jail, so you should get them out. Pay the bail." Hollomon said that he would not get them out of jail but he would support peaceful protesters. Then he tried to frame his remarks to address the significance of having and respecting diverse views on complex matters such as war.

Annoyed by the rude treatment several people in the audience had given President Hollomon, I felt compelled to try to blunt the sharp edge of the hostile words they had hurled at him. I did not deliver my prepared speech, which would have focused on moods of discontent that transcended race or gender or social class. Speaking from an emotional page of my heart's invisible script, I asked, "Why do you want to stop the dying abroad? Is it just so that there can be racial segregation, hate, and killing here?"

That wasn't what I thought. But all the same, I questioned them.

A chorus of "No, no" filled the oval. I had their attention.

"I didn't think so," I continued. "I ask all of you to follow the tradition of nonviolence that was established by Martin Luther King, Jr. All war is terrible, all deaths are tragedies, and all of us are brothers and sisters. Let each of us protest killing but show other people that we will not maim or wound them with our words, that we will not kill or hurt other people for peace."

The atmosphere among the crowd was still as I paused at the podium. If the people standing at the back rows could have seen my face, as those close to me could, they would have seen my pained expression. Then, in a gravelly voice, I said, "You give this sign [I made a V for a peace sign with two outstretched fingers]. I hope you mean it. You must love people if you are to be nonviolent. Whatever you decide to do, I will be with you because I love you."

But that was not the end of the antiwar protests. Wright urged the students to have peaceful strikes until the three jailed students — Keith Green, Bruce J. Pels, and David J. Rosenblatt — were freed. The crowd responded agreeably to his exhortation with chants of "Free them!" At that moment Mike's status as a student leader rose higher among the audience.

Around 10:00 P.M. Bill Moffitt called me at home and said, "Doc, I need you to come to the student government offices here in Walker Tower as fast as you can — in the next ten minutes or so."

Detecting the urgency in his voice, I didn't ask any questions. Instead I said, "I'll be there before you can say Jackie Robinson."

Bill, Jim Todd, and Michael "Mike" Kelly were waiting for me outside the building, each with a worried look on his face. As we walked up the stairs to the second floor, Bill explained, "We're a bunch of young kids, except for Jim, and we're trying to decide how to best protest the Vietnam War. Several of the student leaders want to shut the entire University down for a week or two. We met with Governor Bartlett today, and we have no doubt that if we shut the University down, he will send in the Oklahoma National Guard to reopen it. You saw firsthand what weekend warriors who play soldier can do to civilians like us."

We walked into the crowded area where the student government leaders had convened. I recognized a couple of them and nodded in their direction. Every face was visibly strained. When I reached the center of the room, Bill motioned for me to sit in the chair that had been placed in a central location. I chose to stand. Then Bill said, "Dr. Henderson was in Detroit when the race riot erupted there in 1967. I asked him to tell us what to expect if we decide to shut the University down and the Guard comes on campus."

I prefaced my remarks by telling them that I was committed to nonviolence. Then I described several of the hateful, destructive things that members of the Michigan National Guard did in Detroit to "restore order." Buildings were trashed, property was stolen, innocent people were beaten, and some were killed. I speculated that if any of the Oklahoma National Guardsmen were anything like the men I saw in Detroit, there would be casualties at our university. The students listened intently.

A female student asked me, "Are you suggesting that we do nothing to protest the Kent State University deaths and the arrest of OU antiwar protesters?"

"Of course you should do something," I assured her. "Honorable people are obligated to protest injustices. I'm suggesting that you protest nonviolently in a way that will not provoke the governor to send in the National Guard."

A couple of voices, almost in unison asked, "What should we do?"

I didn't tell them what to do, but I did tell them that I would support them in any nonviolent way I could. I thanked them for listening to me. As I walked toward to the door, the students seemed to be a bit older and a lot less sanguine. This was going to be a harsh test for them. Bill said he would let me know what they decided to do. Close to midnight he called to tell me that the Student Congress was going to let the student body vote the next day, May 7, on whether to hold a one-day nonviolent strike on May 8.

When put to a vote, the referendum failed. Anticipating that outcome, the pro-strike students agreed to picket classes on May 8, and they named Mike Wright chairman of the strike-coordinating committee. Under his leadership, classes were picketed but not disrupted. For most of the students, it was school as usual. But that was not the end of it.

With the antiwar coalition intact, Wright, who became the head student marshal, and Moffitt negotiated with University administrators the terms for a nonviolent demonstration against the ROTC during its May 12 Field Day officer commissioning ceremony on Owen Field in the Memorial Stadium. I was one of several faculty marshals. Larry Hill, a junior faculty member in the Political Science Department, assumed the lead role in organizing us. He convinced five professors to share the responsibilities with him: David Kitts, Jim Kenderdine, Donald Reynolds, Richard Wells, and David Levy.

Student and faculty marshals joined with a cadre of University administrators, athletes, and police to become a buffer between the protesters and the ROTC cadets. My assignment as a marshal was rather easy compared with what those on the field had to do. I was a floater who monitored the stadium and also the area west of the stadium. I took seriously Jim Kenderdine's directive for me to make myself give the illusion of multiplying by not spending much time in the same place. In my mind, I became Batman or some other comic strip hero looking like a neatly dressed black professor. I missed a lot of the stadium action because of my constant movement, but I was not the only one. I saw a couple of other faculty marshals zigzagging across the campus grounds too, hoping not to see any dangerous-looking people.

It was less tranquil inside the stadium, however. Five hundred or so demonstrators were confined to the south end zone. When the ROTC cadets marched past them, some of the protesters held up antiwar signs; others shouted obscenities and made vulgar gestures; and many of them chanted antiwar slogans such as "Hell no, we won't go!" and "1-2-3-4, we don't want your f—— war!" and "Peace now." Someone threw a firecracker in the midst of the cadets during the awards portion of the officer-commissioning program. The physical restraint of the cadets and most of the protesters was riveting. Miraculously, the buffer between the protesters and the cadets held. To the chagrin of hard-core radicals, the event ended without major incidents. It was one of the University's finest moments.

With the antiwar activities behind them for a while, the ASU changed the titles of its officers back to president, vice president, and so forth. Also in 1970, Pat Piercy was selected as one of eight Yearbook Beauties, and Claude W. Johnson, Jr., received the fifth annual Carl Albert Award. I was especially pleased when black students were recognized for something other than sports. At the public ceremony, I commended Claude for being the first black student to get the award. He told me that he was pleased to be a recipient, but he would be even happier when it no longer mattered what race the recipient belonged to.

I smiled. "Until then, I will remain proud of you as a black student recipient."

He smiled back at me. We had made our point: race still mattered.

The black students and I were not always doing serious protest stuff during that spring semester. We had frequent moments of fun and out-right nonsensical pleasure as we let the little kid hiding inside of each of us come out and play. Those were welcome respites from race relations battles that had become part and parcel of our University lives. We protested hard and played hard — giving balance to our lives. The Jekyll and Hyde–like activities were essential to our survival. Most of the students found ways to make their weekends mirror those they had back home. Indeed, the rest and recreation activities weren't just therapeutic; they were our lifestyle.

In June, President Hollomon asked me to chair a committee that would find qualified black applicants and recommend the best one to serve on his administrative team as a vice president or as an assistant vice president of minority affairs. The other members of the committee were Bill Moffitt and ASU president Jim Todd. We solicited nominations from members of the University's black community. After an extensive search, we forwarded Wilbur Walker's name to President Hollomon. Wilbur had served the University well in several different housing positions. Further-more, the black students and I trusted him.

On July 24, 1970, J. Herbert Hollomon resigned as president of the University of Oklahoma. He informed Barbara and me of his decision on July 22. Sitting in our family room, he said that his abrasive management style and the May 5–12 nonviolent antiwar protests on the University campus had galvanized his detractors, especially Governor Dewey Bartlett, to the point that he had become a daily distraction — a liability. Also, Hollomon's mood swings were perplexing to people who did not know him well. He was just being himself. Although his fiery temper seemed to show itself more frequently, I attributed it to the increased intergroup confrontations among University students and the rash of public protests. He was, from my vantage point, a decent president. But mine was undoubtedly a minority view.

Barbara and I were simultaneously sad and happy. We were sad that our friend was leaving the University but happy that he would not have to battle daily to keep his job. We hoped that he would find a friendlier place to help shape students' lives. Pete Kyle McCarter was named interim president, and a new chapter of my life began.

CHAPTER EIGHT

Too Little, but Not Too Late

My first three years at the University of Oklahoma had been filled with memorable race relations gains and missteps. For the most part, unfortunately, not enough positive things had occurred to cause me to believe that the long-running Afro-American Student Union's civil rights struggle would end soon. On whole, I found the University's efforts to be lacking. For all the promises and speeches about racial justice, discrimination was still quite evident throughout the University. I was beginning to wonder if the gains up to this point were too little and too late. It was hard for me to shake the feeling of frustration that was becoming my constant companion. I was also beginning to drift to the dark side of my personality. But as I prepared to launch the Human Relations Program at the beginning of the fall semester of 1970, my melancholy subsided.

The Human Relations Program

In August 1970, when the Human Relations Program offered its first master's degree courses, I beamed with pride like a new parent. Also like a parent, I hoped that the program would have a long and societally productive life. The twenty students who enrolled in the inaugural classes were attracted to them because of their unique blend of traditional and experiential instruction. They were different from anything else available in the University. In more pragmatic terms, the students were attracted to the program because it was designed to train professionals called change agents. Specifically, the program would prepare activists to work in organizations that prevented or abated discrimination in education, housing, and employment. The curriculum encompassed issues pertaining to race, gender, gender orientation, national origin, disability, and age.

Among the first class of human relations majors were seven blacks (Guinnevere Hodges, Emetta S. Jennings, Jerry G. Johnson, Amuleru Marshall, Williamson T. Phillips, La Frantz A. Shawnee, and Pearlene "Pat" Westbrook), one American Indian (G. Mike Charleston), and one Mexican American (Albert G. Mata, Jr.). That did not go unnoticed by people in other academic units. In fact, several of my colleagues, either in jest or in spite, referred to the program as the black studies program or the minority studies program; a few of them even called it the odd people's program. Whether playfully or in scorn, those descriptions spread throughout the campus. I gained a measure of satisfaction from having the most ethnically diverse students in the history of the University's inaugural graduate programs. It was an appropriately auspicious beginning for the first master's degree program in the University of Oklahoma founded by an African American.

Other aspects of the Human Relations Program were trendsetting as well. It was the first master's degree program at the University to admit students based on the grade point averages they earned during the last sixty hours of their undergraduate degree programs, not on their Graduate Record Examination scores and their overall grade point averages as undergraduates. Further, we recruited and graduated the University's first master's degree student who had cerebral palsy: Gail B. Dunsky. To accommodate Gail, we organized teams to get her to the classes and to all of our social activities. That included providing her with transportation to and from the campus as well as carrying her up and down the stairs in all of the buildings the program used because they were not wheelchair accessible. We didn't just talk about and read about disabilities; we accommodated students who had varying degrees of disabilities.

All of the human relations students were required to participate in classroom and community team projects. In fact, team assignments were an integral aspect of the majority of our courses long before they were required in other University master's degree programs. One of their

Students in a human relations class at the University of Oklahoma, 1970. Western History Collections, University of Oklahoma Libraries.

community projects consisted of working with me to design and conduct a pro bono human relations workshop for the entire staff of the Frederick A. Douglass High School in northeast Oklahoma City. In addition to teaching four classes a semester, I was the graduate adviser and recruiter. For the first three months, I had little time to fret about the slow progress in campus-wide racial inclusion initiatives. But the respite didn't last long.

Winners and Losers

In September 1970 the University had begun operating Project Threshold. Guinnevere Hodges helped design the project in 1969 after she graduated and was hired in the University College as a counselor. It was going to be a centerpiece in Hollomon's efforts to recruit, retain, and graduate more ethnic minorities. Now it would be Interim President Pete McCarter's signature program. Central to Threshold were information about academic advisement, financial aid, and scholarships; free tutoring; and career and personal counseling for all students from educationally and economically disadvantaged backgrounds. I thought Guinnevere would have been an excellent director, but her lack of a postgraduate degree and no formal administrative experience disqualified her for the position. My first doctoral advisee, W. Clifford Armstrong from Southern University in Louisiana, was hired as Project Threshold's first director.

In December, Guinnevere came to visit me in my office. She was in tears, and her sobbing was uncontrollable for about two or three minutes. When she regained her composure, she said to me in a low sigh, "I am enraged, disappointed, and my heart is broken. I have given my time, energy, and loyalty to this school, and it has slapped me in the face. I have no doubt that I can direct Threshold. You have seen me design and carry out ASU projects. And you have seen me work with other students. Why didn't the University give me a waiver for the educational requirements?"

I don't think she really expected me to answer her question. I believe that she came to see if I could make her hurt go away. I couldn't do that, of course. I told her that I admired her professionalism and her dedication to achieving equal opportunities for ethnic minorities. She already knew that I sincerely valued her many fine contributions to the University of Oklahoma, and she knew that I wanted her to stay at the University at least long enough to complete her master's degree in human relations.

She sat silent for a minute or two. Then, without the slightest hint, she abruptly got up and told me good-bye.

"I hope that you don't mean good-bye as in you are leaving the University," I said.

"Good-bye, Dr. Henderson."

She closed the door quietly behind her and went back to Project Threshold to tender her resignation. I felt sad. This had not been a good year. Several of my current and former students had said good-bye to me. From my perspective, our time together had been much too brief. Even though they went on to other organizations and made tremendous contributions, I wanted more from them, especially those who were like Guinnevere, at the University of Oklahoma. I felt like my world was unraveling. To some extent it was.

On November 20, 1970, close to noon, the Cross Center housing director was suspended. She had engaged in what the black residents of the four-dormitory complex believed was racist behavior. Twelve black students, along with six American Indian and white students, had staged a sit-in in the center's cafeteria shortly before the suspension. Calvin Taylor, one of ringleaders, called me at my office and asked me to come to the dorm to make sure that "nothing crazy" happened and nobody got hurt. He gave me an advance warning: "There are a bunch of wild people sitting in with us, but they won't do anything wrong if you'll just come and sit with us. They respect you."

The demonstrators had locked in the students who were eating their lunch, and they locked out anyone else who wanted to come in but did not have their permission. Only those people who were cleared by Calvin or one of the other sit-in leaders were allowed to enter the cafeteria. When I arrived, one of the leaders recognized me and let me in. The students in the room were glum. There was little talking and a lot of tension. Sit-ins had become a common ritual on our campus.

A couple of the trapped coeds were crying. "Let them go," I advised Calvin.

He walked over to the near-hysterical females, apologized for detaining them, and allowed them to leave. The frightened students ran to the door, screaming. After they got outside, one of them looked up at the sky and muttered, "What's going on? Why is this happening to me?" It was a confusing time for everyone involved.

The protesters wanted to settle their grievance quickly and get on with the rest of their lives, and the locked-in students wanted their dormitory back the way it was before the upheaval. I suggested to the protesters that they contact Jack Stout, director of resident programs, and negotiate a settlement. When Jack arrived, I called him aside and recommended that he assure the protesters of his intention to resolve the dispute "with all deliberate speed." (I borrowed that phrase from one of the U.S. Supreme Court public school desegregation decisions.) After nearly thirty minutes of haggling, the demonstrators believed that Jack would indeed conduct a swift, full investigation and take appropriate action. The protesters quietly disbanded.

In December 1970, Interim President McCarter appointed Wilbur Walker as his special assistant for minority affairs. Wilbur became the first black senior-level administrator on a University of Oklahoma president's staff. It was a bittersweet appointment, however. He did not have line authority or his own staff. He didn't even have a secretary. That was not what Hollomon had said he would do, but Hollomon was gone. Still, despite its shortcomings, the appointment was a crack in the exclusivity of the University's white male executive club. Also in December, the men's basketball team hosted Grambling State University, a historically black institution. Bits and pieces of the ASU 1969 demands were being fulfilled.

On April 15, 1971, I was one of five faculty members to receive an OU Regents' Award for Superior Teaching. The other recipients were Jack L. Kendall, professor of English; Maurice L. Rasmussen, professor of aerospace, mechanical, and nuclear engineering; Jack Renner, professor of education; and Gordon H. Deckert, professor of psychiatry at the University's Medical Center. Receiving the award was a good way for my academic year to end.

In fall 1971, Paul F. Sharp became the ninth president of the University. Before he was hired, he had promised the presidential search committee that he would finish the affirmative action initiatives started by Hollomon and McCarter. As the two blacks on the fifteen-member search committee, Steven Manning, a student representative, and I had no reason to doubt him. Based on our exhaustive background investigation of him, Paul Sharp seemed to be well qualified to fulfill his promise. The other committee members agreed with us. The excitement within the

University following his appointment was partially fueled by the prospect of the University getting past the rancor that had characterized Hollomon's brief presidency.

From fall 1970 to fall 1971, between the two of them, Interim President McCarter and President Sharp made several key black appointments. Thomas and Carol Carey ceased to be visiting professors and were made associate professors of music. Steve Manning was made assistant to the director of student activities; Glenn W. Shoate, placement officer in charge of minority recruitment; Harold Andrews, assistant to the vice president of the University Community; Wayne A. Long, coordinator of recreation planning; and Thomas J. Nolan III, extension specialist. Leroy Lloyd and Amour J. Andrews were appointed student placement counselors, and Elizabeth Holmes replaced Clifford Armstrong as director of Project Threshold. Also noteworthy was a public announcement by Leonard D. Harper, director of Personnel Services, that his staff was going to write a new affirmative action plan that would increase the number of the University's minority employees. There was much for me to feel good about, but not all of the black students shared my optimism.

Where There's Smoke

The smoldering fire of racial discord had reached a searing level by the fall semester of 1971. During that time, an increasing number of black students wrote letters to the editor of the *Oklahoma Daily*, spoke out in public forums, and held clandestine meetings to express their unhappiness with the slow pace of equal opportunity reforms on campus. Their protests were scathing, accusatory, and defiant. For example, in a letter addressed "Dear Sooners" and published in the *Oklahoma Daily* on September 22, Cassandra E. Smitters accused the University of exploiting black athletes while at the same time ignoring the requests of black students for a black studies program. She concluded: "We are tired of being used as pawns by bigoted white administrators and politicians who tell us 'you all go home and be good little niggers and cool it,' we'll give YOU YOUR CRUMBS IN DUE TIME."

As the rhetoric became increasingly anti-white, some of the black students, including Ruth Ann Walker, a senior, feared that a split between the black middle and lower classes, and another between black separatists and integrationists, were going to wreck whatever solidarity the black students had. On September 24 she wrote the following in a guest editorial aimed at the black male students in particular: "To separate within the black race, whether over integration vs. separatism or because of economics, would be a betrayal of that unity displayed and pledged to as [our] 'black brothers.' To separate in either way would be to repeat the sad mistakes made by whites in this country." The editorial publicly exposed the divisions within the black community. Now the internal fracturing was no longer a secret to be kept. Those of us who were involved in the affairs of our community had privately lamented a growing number of bad signs within it. It came down to this: somebody would have to put aside his or her need to publicly criticize rival black groups. Cooler heads prevailed, and several students from the verbally warring groups called for and got a truce, albeit a shaky one.

Nothing exposed the unraveling of black-white relationships more plainly than the seemingly rampant fistfights between black and white male students, almost all of which were triggered by name-calling. A considerable amount of media attention was given to six members of the Alpha Phi Alpha Fraternity who were arrested in 1971 for fighting members of the Phi Kappa Sigma Fraternity. No doubt white alumni reading the reports in the one of several Oklahoma newspapers wondered out loud what was going on at their alma mater. In fact, nothing new was happening; the same sorts of fights had occurred when they attended the University. This time, though, a greater number of black students were responding to racial epithets with their fists. Fighting within racial groups was deemed less newsworthy by the media, but whether the altercations were between or within groups in no way lessened their seriousness.

The extent of the verbal and physical conflicts on campus was grave, and because of it, black-white relationships were edging closer to the point of irreparableness. The erosion was described in a series of three special reports by Windsor Ridenour and Yla Eason in the *Tulsa Tribune* on October 25, 26, and 27, 1971. Based on interviews with 150 black students, the series painted a tense and grim picture of race relations. Two years had passed since the Black Declaration of Independence was publicized, and a dozen or so black interviewees were still asking for racially segregated housing and governance. Several of their other demands contradicted those of the separatists. For example, one of the demands was for permanent black cheerleaders. (As a member of an ad hoc committee impaneled by Anona Adair, I voted to add four black cheerleaders to the fall 1971 spirit squad through special auditions conducted in September.) The conflicting demands gave the unfortunate impression that the black students couldn't decide if they wanted to be with or apart from the white students. But that issue was not unique to the black students. Many of the white students wrestled with it too.

In one of my more lucid moments, when Ridenour and Eason asked me what could be done to reverse the negative trend, I listed some suggestions, which the reporters cited in their series:

> Dr. George Henderson, head of the Department of Human Relations . . . said it will take a change in personal attitudes for virtually all at OU. Some of the changes could almost be considered minor: stop telling racial jokes, invite black students into white homes and meet informally with students. Other suggestions that Henderson feels would help include hiring a black at a high level in the administration, possibly as a vice president or director of housing, accelerating recruitment of superior high school students and making a strong effort to entice black graduate participation in University alumni activities. "Placing a black on the [OU] Board of Regents would help a great deal," Henderson added.

Those things would happen in subsequent years, but for now they were merely wishful thinking.

The Tide Turns

The year 1971 was the University of Oklahoma's race relations watershed. Everything seemed to be falling apart. During the darkest hours, I wondered if our revolt would end in defeat. When people are angry at each other, separation can trump noble goals such as racial integration, and the University seemed on the verge of splintering into permanent black and white pieces. The black rebellion was ongoing; it had moved from the incipient protest against discrimination lodged by the black athletes in 1968 to the sporadic incidents of fistfights with white students in the

1970s. In a way, we were breaking new ground in race relations at the University. Nobody with an objective mind thought that the University had done all, or even most, of what needed to be done to mend the rift. It was going to take more than talk to turn the tide of bitterness into a happy ending for those of us who still believed in Martin Luther King, Jr.'s dream of racial equality.

Also in the October 27 piece of the *Tulsa Tribune* series, J. R. Morris, vice president for the University Community, in a sign of growing urgency, reiterated with conviction the essence of what former President J. Herbert Hollomon said in 1969 — that is, that the University of Oklahoma had to find ways to truly incorporate black people and their cultures into its own culture without physical, social, or academic segregation. That was exactly what the founding members of the Afro-American Student Union had set out to achieve in 1967 — nothing more, nothing less. It was the right thing for the University to do. The crux of the matter was always administrators' actions, not their promises. The decisive moment came shortly after the newspaper articles were written.

At the OU Board of Regents meeting on November 11, Michael DeWitty, representing himself and nine other black students, delivered a written statement that accused the University of perpetuating institutional racism. The statement cited, among other things, racially hostile classroom learning environments, racial slurs written on the sidewalk in front of the Alpha Phi Alpha Fraternity house, and physically aggressive acts aimed at black students. For good measure, the students documented an incident in which a black female was shot with a pellet gun while she was walking across the campus. Before the students left the meeting, DeWitty told the Regents to do something before someone was seriously injured.

The complaining students were frightened not only because of the sporadic violence against them but also because of what they believed was a lax approach to campus security. The Regents and President Sharp issued a written statement saying that they did not condone racial bigotry in any form or by anyone. Further, perpetrators of racial abuses would be punished. J. R. Morris promised to have weekly meetings with black student leaders to keep them informed of the University's progress toward preventing and abating racist acts. Although the verbal assurances had substantive and emotional value for the students, nothing short of positive action was going to please them. On November 17, around 1:30 A.M., someone fired a bullet into the Alpha Phi Alpha living room, the second time a building occupied by black OU students had been shot into.

Wilbur Walker, assistant to President Sharp, correctly summarized the deteriorating racial situation from the black perspective: "Many black students come to OU expecting to find an integrated campus. And they are disappointed to find the same racist elements here as those in their hometowns. Nor do they expect to find faculty and staff members who are racial bigots in a place where some of the most learned people in the world work."[1] His comments caused merely a slight stir within most of the departments. Except for statements from the usual campus activists, little outrage about the University's deplorable race relations situation was expressed publicly. President Sharp and his executive staff were paying attention, though. They had already initiated several positive programs and were planning more.

With student morale hemorrhaging, Sharp told his administrators to redouble their efforts to communicate with the black students, to hire more blacks in faculty and staff positions, and to broaden the curriculum to include more black history courses. But time was running out for reconciliation. Most of the campus residents who read about the accelerating fistfights between blacks and whites, as well as incidents of arson, shooting, and vandalism, were aghast. On November 18 four University buildings — the Walker Tower dormitory, the Wilson Center dormitory's cafeteria, a book storage facility near the Cate Center dormitory, and a wooden warehouse building near the South Campus married student apartments — were targets of arsonists. Twenty-six people, all of them Walker Tower residents, were treated at local hospitals for smoke inhalation, burns, and lacerations; the property damage amounted to more than two hundred thousand dollars. The culprits were not caught, but there was plenty of finger-pointing, as blacks and whites accused each other of burning the buildings in order to provoke a race riot. That was also the same day that someone fired a bullet into the Alpha Phi Alpha house, with no injuries. A less dangerous offense occurred in the University's main library, where vandals destroyed file cards on the third and fourth floors.

Almost unnoticed, but very important, was the establishment of the University's first biracial dormitory, housing fifty black and fifty white student volunteers. J. R. Morris was following up on his pledge to find ways to facilitate racial integration. The significance of the biracial dorm was underscored by its being the largest racially integrated student housing unit in Oklahoma. Thus, through that single initiative, a vestige of racial segregation was swept aside. But it would be several more years before integrated housing became the norm.

Although reconciliation was becoming more difficult to achieve, it was still a viable goal. The positive changes on campus gave me a profound sense of hope. My mentor Leonard Moss had been only partially right. In 1967 the University was a very hostile environment for blacks. It was less so in 1971, and the signs pointed to even less racism in the future. Paul Sharp, a president with a heart for oppressed people, and his administrators were finding ways for the University to become more culturally inclusive. That kind of restructuring always stands or falls on the commitment of the chief executive officer. To his credit, President Sharp did not try to sugarcoat his own missteps or stop making difficult decisions that might positively alter the University's culture.

Even though there were still more negative things for the ASU and me to criticize than positive ones to celebrate, an encouraging pattern of proactive decision making was very evident to us. The steps forward were being built on President Sharp's directives and J. R. Morris's actions. The two men endured setbacks, but they never accepted defeat. As for those of us involved with the ASU, this was not the time for pity parties. We still had too much unfinished business to attend to. Our initial sprint to racial and social justice had morphed into an unending marathon.

Beth Wilson's recollections provide a succinct summary of the many and varied aspects of being a black student at the University from 1966 to 1970 and a Norman schoolteacher in 1971. Her story offers insight to the racial intersections of the City of Norman and the University of Oklahoma — and how similar both communities were in their treatment of blacks during that period. It further illustrates the value of tenacity and mutual support within a cohesive ethnic group enclave. As I look back with her, I can see how far the University and Norman have come racially since that time. I can also see how much more still needs to be done to achieve truly culturally inclusive communities.

Beth Wilson, 1970. Western History Collections, University of Oklahoma Libraries.

Ida Elizabeth "Beth" Mack Wilson Reminisces

I graduated from Manual Training High School (MTHS) in Muskogee, Oklahoma, in 1966 and was second in my class. My older sister, Dolena, brought me to the University of Oklahoma campus in August 1966 for my freshman year. Two of my classmates from MTHS also enrolled in OU that year: Rosita Brown and Barbara Smith. We were assigned to old Cate Center, an all-girl dormitory that housed two girls to each room. None of the rooms were air-conditioned. Barbara and Rosita were roommates, so I was on my own.

Being a College Student

I moved into my dorm room in Sanger House, unpacked my things, and started to settle in. Late in the afternoon I heard a knock on my door. When I opened the door, there stood three people: a white girl about my age (eighteen) and a white man and white woman who I assumed were her parents. Without uttering a word, they turned around and left—never to return. I thought that was odd, but I was kind of relieved—I hoped to have the room to myself because the closet was so tiny and I needed more space. Unfortunately, some time later I heard another knock on the door. I opened it again and this time, there was a white girl there about my age standing alone. I said hello and she said hello back. but nothing else was said. She never stepped inside. She too turned and left and never returned. I had the room to myself that night and maybe the next three or so.

A few days later, I received a third knock on my door. I opened it and in walked Bennie Simmons, my roommate for my freshman year. Bennie was a black girl from Wetumpka, Alabama, who had an Aunt Sybil in Sapulpa, Oklahoma. Bennie was loud, friendly, and smoked like a chimney. I started smoking myself as a defense mechanism. I was a pharmacy major, and Bennie was a nursing major. I don't think either of us lasted in those majors much past our freshman year. Bennie and I got along really well, and it wasn't long before we met most of the other black students on campus. There were so few of us who lived on campus that nearly everybody got to know everybody else very quickly.

We soon discovered that almost all of the black guys who lived on campus were scholarship athletes. They lived in the Athletics Department dorm. We discovered that the housing officials had miraculously managed to put two black girls in each of the freshman dormitories. A few of us knew junior and senior students from our hometown. There were three from MTHS: Patricia Simmons, Tamarsha Herbert, and Guinnevere Hodges. Patricia was a beautiful and very serious student who, I believe, had finished first in her graduating class. She seldom attended the all-black parties that I soon discovered were weekend happenings. I saw Tamarsha occasionally, but she was already in a serious relationship and spent most of her time with Marcellus Buckner, her boyfriend whom she later married. I don't know what Guinnevere was doing, but I saw her around occasionally. (Sadly, both Patricia and Guinnevere died in early adulthood.)

Black sororities and fraternities were big on campus, and my closest friends and I joined Alpha Kappa Alpha Sorority. There weren't enough members or pledges on campus, however, for us to have our own chapter. So the graduate chapter in Oklahoma City sponsored a multicampus chapter with students from OU, Oklahoma State University, Central State University (now the University of Central Oklahoma), and Oklahoma City University. Those four campuses made up Beta Beta chapter, and we were pledges for what seemed like an entire year—from the spring of 1967, after we received our first semester grades, to the fall of 1967, when we "went over" that December just before the Christmas holidays began. My pledge class had to travel from one campus to another and "help" big sisters on each of the campuses. I recall that one of my big sisters at OU invited herself to visit me at my home so that she could see her boyfriend in Muskogee, the older brother of one of my MTHS classmates.

It didn't take me long to find the "man of my dreams." He was at a party given by members of the Omega Psi Phi (Q) Fraternity in a house someone had been foolish enough to rent to them. The Qs who lived in the house were members of the OU track team. The party was held before classes started, and we were served an innocent-looking punch. I soon discovered that the pharmacy students had spiked the punch with grain alcohol borrowed from the pharmacy lab. It was the first time I ever got totally intoxicated, and I was miserably sick. The pharmacy student culprit, Clarence E. Wilson, turned out to be "my man." I admit I was prejudiced against athletes, and Clarence was one of the few black undergraduates who were not athletes. He was really smart, and I have always been drawn to smart guys. The fact that he was tall and good-looking didn't hurt either. He seemed really mature to me. With the exception of one date that I went on at the request of my roommate, Bennie, Clarence was the only other guy I ever dated, and we eventually married.

Being an Activist

Life on campus was really interesting. Those were the days of panty raids, the SDS, the Black Panthers, the Socialist Party, feminist activism, protests against the Vietnam War, and civil rights demonstrations. A graduate student, Sterlin Adams, was pretty much the self-appointed leader of student civil rights activism on campus. One of my OU classmates, William "Bill" Moffitt, was elected student body president with the help of a lot of activist coalitions. By then we had formed the Afro-American Student Union [now the Black Student Association] in late 1967. We used to meet in a basement room in the Student Union. The most active members were twenty-five or so of us. Early on, we started drawing up lists of demands and discussed them with various University administrators. As I recall, we were concerned about black athletes being a part of the organization but not risking losing their athletic scholarships and maybe their future careers in professional sports. So they supported us, but discreetly.

Clarence was a dormitory counselor and he had an academic scholarship, but he didn't seem to be worried about being a University activist. I became one too. Even though I graduated second in my class and was a National Achievement finalist, I was not offered a scholarship or any significant financial assistance except loans. Therefore I didn't feel financially threatened by the University because of my involvement in the ASU. Many of my friends were in the same boat. None of the black girls, to my knowledge, had scholarships. But one of my friends and an AKA sister, Sandra "Sandy" Rouce from Tulsa, had a 4.0 the first semester and went on to graduate Phi Beta Kappa. As I recall, she was offered a scholarship, but her father turned it down. Sandy was this petite little girl who seemed a little on the ditsy side. So while we were all stressed about getting grades good enough to pledge AKA, we were shocked to learn Sandy had a 4.0. (She went on to earn a doctor of philosophy degree in clinical psychology, has a private practice in Houston, and teaches at Texas Southern University.)

I can only remember a few of our many demands: more black faculty; more black students; a soul food restaurant; a barber and beautician who could do "black" hair; a black church. I remember those things so well because somehow the administration actually made most of them happen for us. A few black faculty members were hired. Black student enrollment increased slightly. A black barbecue place was opened, and a black barber and beauty shop opened. Unfortunately for the restaurant owner, barber, and beautician, we didn't have enough money to support them. We had to eat in the dormitory cafeterias on whatever our meal plan provided, and we had our own hot plates, hot combs, and barber clippers by then, and each of us could either do our own hair or a friend could do it well enough that we just settled for that. The barbecue place and the barber and beauty shops soon went out of business. We were sad because we really wanted them to survive. But we were all constantly broke and barely scraping by.

As a freshman, I remember my first (and last) panty raid. All of the white girls were screaming and laughing and running around and having a great ole time. The other black girls and I were scared to death. We didn't have a clue about what was going on, and we just wanted to survive it. Later we all held our breath, hoping that none of the guys that got caught and suspended or expelled were black. Fortunately, either they got lucky and didn't get caught or they—like us—had no clue about what was going on and stayed out of it. Why in the world would any female want to give her panties to a guy? Few black girls could afford to give away panties and buy new ones. The whole idea seemed like a stupid rich white kid stunt.

What we, the black kids, did want to do, however, was to engage in civil rights protests. Some Afro-American Student Union members even wanted to collaborate with the SDS and the Black Panther Party and engage in joint demonstrations and demands, but they were both just too radical for us to deal with openly. They had been accused of violent acts with bombs and guns, and that just wasn't what we wanted to do. Most of us believed in nonviolence, but a few ASU members engaged in discreet activities with those groups from time to time. The SDS seemed to have more money than we did. We could barely afford the signs that we carried during protests. We made signs protesting the Vietnam War, and we carried them in marches on campus and at speaker forums where we gathered to listen to speakers protest the war. Most of us had relatives, friends, and classmates in Vietnam; and we wanted them out and back home whole and secure.

During my sophomore year, I moved to the new Cate Center, where the rooms were air-conditioned. Once again, I didn't have a roommate. By then my friend Rosita had married Wayne Long, her college sweetheart from the track team, and they had a baby daughter. My friend Barbara had dropped out of OU and moved back to Muskogee. My other friends stayed with the roommates they had. And my roommate, Bennie, moved off campus and got an apartment with another girl, Gloria Griffin, who later earned a doctorate and became the superintendent of the Millwood School District in Oklahoma City.

I was assigned a black girl as a roommate. She was dating a white boy and having serious emotional problems. I tried to get a job as a dormitory counselor so that I could have my own room, but the housing administrators wouldn't give me the position and they wouldn't give me a different roommate or my own room without paying more money. So I endured that roommate for a semester. Then I moved into a one-bedroom OU apartment in Niemann Apartments on campus. It cost $60 a month and the rent was hard to come by, but I could cook my own food and do what I wanted there, which was mostly to entertain Clarence. I didn't know how to cook, but I gradually learned to fix something edible.

I remember vividly when Martin Luther King, Jr., was killed. We were having a meeting of the Afro-American Student Union. It was the day before my birthday, April 5, 1968. We were all just devastated—angry, sad, restless, and wanting to do something. That may have been when we drew up the first list of demands, and it may have been why the administration tried to appease us by granting some of them.

Memorable Teachers

During the entire four years of my undergraduate year, I had only two classes with other black students: an education class and a math class. I had only one black teacher: Norish Adams, the wife of Sterlin Adams. She was a graduate teaching assistant, and she taught one of my math classes. My schoolmates had similar experiences. We knew of only two black faculty members on the Norman campus: Dr. Melvin Tolson, Jr., and Dr. George Henderson. I never had classes with either of them.

There was a white faculty member I will never forget. He taught early American literature during my sophomore year, when I had changed to a major in English. I had made As in every English class that I took at OU until then. I wrote well. I even won a citywide essay contest and competed statewide with white students while I was a high school student at MTHS (an all-black high school, as were my other schools), and I received honorable mention in a national essay contest. Also, as a high school student, I wrote a bill that was debated in the Oklahoma Senate during Youth in Government Day. Real legislators watched the debate, and ultimately (I was told) it led to the repeal of the miscegenation laws in Oklahoma. I was a very good student and a very good writer in that OU professor's course too. I worked doubly hard in his class because he made his racism so obvious. He laughed about slavery during discussions in class, and he would never call on me to answer his questions no matter how many times I raised my hand. He gave me a C on my midterm exam despite the fact that I was 0.5 points away from a B. I knew the paper deserved an A, but I didn't challenge him. Instead, I redoubled my efforts to get an A on the final exam. I know absolutely that I earned an A, but I didn't get it. He gave me a C for the class. I was devastated and upset, but I was afraid to challenge him since I was just this insignificant black student in a world filled with powerful white people. I never took another class with him.

Shortly before I graduated, I saw him at the library where I worked. I had seen him there before but never said anything to him. This time, knowing that my degree was all but in my hand, I confronted him. I was shaking and could hardly get the words out because even after more than a year I was still very emotional about it. I told him what he had done to me. He just looked at me and walked away. I could have saved my breath. I wish now that I'd had the courage to report him. But I had no confidence that anything would have been done to him. Instead, I feared that something bad would have happened to me. No doubt other black students had similar experiences.

There was another English teacher at OU, fortunately, who was very encouraging and very complimentary of my completed course assignments. I will always be grateful to him for validating my scholastic abilities. That teacher, along with my high school teachers and parents, kept me strong in the belief that I had what it took to succeed at whatever I chose to do if I had the potential and was willing to work hard to realize it. That is a lesson I learned early and well.

Married Life

Clarence and I got married on August 11, 1968. I had just turned twenty, and he had just turned twenty-three. I had finished my sophomore year at OU and become an English major, and he had finished the University of Oklahoma's Pharmacy School and was entering its Law School. He moved into my apartment, and we started our married life there. We still went to parties from time to time with our friends, but life did change. We wanted to live off campus and looked for a place to rent nearby. Directly across from the football field were several small brick duplexes. We noticed that one was for rent, so we went over and inquired. The person didn't want to answer the door, but Clarence was insistent and she reluctantly cracked it open. When we told her we wanted to inquire about renting the duplex, she wanted to know if we were African—I'm not sure why that mattered. Then she told us we would have to ask the people next door if it would be okay with them. We were surprised by that requirement, but we decided we'd go next door anyway. We knocked on the place next door, but notwithstanding our persistence, the person would never open the door and we gave up. We tried a couple of other places but got similar responses.

I was working in the Interlibrary Loan Department at OU, and I mentioned the problem to a fellow student worker, a white girl, and she offered to help. So she found a place that was vacant. But when the owner found out black people would be the ones to actually move in, it was no longer available. We eventually found a place on Elm Avenue, a duplex with one space upstairs and one space downstairs. We took the downstairs apartment, and we were very happy there until the summer rolled around and the air conditioning went out. The landlord would never fix it. I was pregnant, and we had to drag out the mattress to the living room, where it was cooler. The landlord then put the house on the market for sale, and we had to move out. We gave up and moved into Kraettli, an OU apartment complex.

While I was pregnant with our baby in the fall of 1969, Clarence and I joined a group of other college students from OU and other nearby colleges as well as citizens from Oklahoma City in the garbage workers strike. I remember that we drove in a caravan to the old St. John Baptist Church in Oklahoma City, where Reverend W. K. Jackson was pastor and where Mrs. Clara Luper gave us instructions on what to do. We had heard about the plight of garbage workers—their low pay and the filthy and dangerous working conditions—and we wanted to do something to support them. Clarence and I were happy to be able to join the march. As I recall, we marched from the church through downtown Oklahoma City. Mounted police officers surrounded us. I walked next to Clarence, who held my hand as we sang and walked and chanted and held up signs. I was wearing a brown and black checked maternity dress—probably shorter than it should have been, but that was the style then. Thinking back, I probably endangered my unborn child. If I had slipped and fallen or been kicked by a nearby horse, I could have lost him. But during that demonstration, and others that we had participated in, we seldom thought about the dangers we exposed ourselves to. We focused instead on changing the world, and we got caught up in the cause.

It never really occurred to me that something could have gone terribly wrong—a gunshot, a bottle thrown, or a police club that found a mark could have sparked a riot. I didn't think that we were doing anything spectacular. We just did what seemed the right thing to do at the time. There may have been marchers who understood the kind of history that we were making, but I did not. I was merely doing what my parents taught me in terms of helping other people. My parents were small business owners who worked hard and raised their five children to work hard, to respect others, and to take pride in themselves. We were the children of Mr. and Mrs. Dolvin T. Mack, Sr., and membership in their family came with very high expectations. My father didn't take crap from anybody, black or white, and he was among the most respected people in Muskogee—as was my mother, who kept the business going after my father died. My husband was a lot like my father, and therefore it never occurred to me that he wouldn't keep me safe somehow. Fortunately the strike brought about positive changes, and nothing bad happened to us during the march.

Having a baby at Norman Municipal Hospital was itself a memorable experience. Clarence E. Wilson, Jr., or "Gene," was born on February 4, 1970. I was put in a hospital room for two at the end of a long hall. I never had a roommate. I believe the candy striper, a sweet teenage white girl, felt sorry for me because I was alone and isolated, so she would stop by periodically to visit and bring me magazines. I started to feel concerned for my baby, thinking that if the hospital administrators didn't really want me there, they probably didn't want him there either. I was supposed to lie flat on my back for a certain number of hours, but I remember getting so anxious about my baby that I managed to get up and make my way down the hall looking for the nursery. About midway someone saw me and got a wheelchair just as I was about to collapse. She took me to see my baby. When I peeped in the window, I saw a nurse holding him and brushing his hair. His complexion was so fair that it was hard to distinguish him until I saw the mop of dark hair. He was one of the few babies in the nursery with hair. The nurse told me they liked to brush it. Satisfied that he was OK, I returned to my room.

If Gene was not the first black baby to be born at Norman Municipal Hospital, he was among the first. I wanted to take him home, where I knew he would be safe. I had saved up green stamps and got a rocking chair that was delivered just before I went to the hospital. I had forbidden anyone to sit in it until I could sit in it with my baby and rock him for the first time. When my husband and I got to our apartment with our precious bundle of joy, there was my mother-in-law and my sister and brother-in-law. My mother-in-law was sitting in my rocker. Of course I didn't say anything. Because I had insisted that Clarence and I bring Gene home together without any of the family, I gave his mother the honor of being the first person to rock Gene in the new rocking chair.

Being a Teacher

In 1970 the College of Education had initially assigned me a school on the south side of Oklahoma City for my student teaching, but I refused to be that far away from my new baby, so I was reassigned to Norman High School. That was another interesting situation. To the best of my knowledge, I was the first black student teacher at Norman High School. I worked with a team of American literature teachers there, but I had a lead teacher—Mrs. Mary Lou Willis. (Her name just came to me as I was writing, and I hope I got it right.) Because I did well as a student teacher, the Norman Public Schools offered me a full-time teaching position for the next year. I accepted the offer and thus had another interesting experience. I believe I was the first black contract teacher they ever had at Norman High School. In that school of two thousand students, I encountered only two black students: one was a black male who was in a special education class when I did my student teaching; the other was a black female in my American literature class when I taught as a regular teacher. She was a good student, but she left after the first semester. I never found out why.

In February, I decided to celebrate Black History Week by having my American literature students read black authors and then discuss what they had read. I didn't tell the other American literature teachers what I was doing, but they found out and questioned me about it. They didn't ask about the heritage discussion that I had with my students, but I'm sure they wanted to. As the literature discussion turned to the issue of race and color, an idea came to me. I asked the students to tell me what race they thought I was. They were somewhat perplexed because the answer appeared to be obvious. A brave student finally said she thought I was black. I said, "Okay. What else?" Finally, I disclosed that I was named after my great-grandmother Elizabeth, who was a white woman married to a black and Indian man; that my aunt Elizabeth—my father's sister—could have passed for white; and that I was Elizabeth III. I then asked them how many of their families had lived in Oklahoma for more than two generations. Several hands went up, and I then told them that chances were pretty good that they too were mixed with some other ethnicity and that maybe if we went back far enough we would discover our common ancestors. I'm sure I shocked them. I fully expected to be called into the principal's office, but I wasn't. I guess they just didn't know what to do with me. When my colleagues questioned me about it in the teacher's lounge, they only indicated they would have been happy to do something similar. Okay. Maybe.

While I was teaching my first year at Norman High School, my husband was finishing his last year in Law School at OU. His freshman Law School year was eventful. He decided to go to a bar on Main Street in Norman with a few of his white Law School buddies. When they got to the bar, the proprietor told them that my husband would not be served there because he was a "nigger." Well, thinking they knew the law and their rights and feeling self-righteous indignation, they decided to challenge the man. He called the police, and the students ended up in jail for a short time. At the end of the day they were released without an arrest record, but they had been reminded rather forcefully that Norman was still a "sundown" town and that blacks better stay on the campus and off the streets of Norman after sundown. We were expected to stay out of white people's places where we didn't belong. That was in 1969.

Later that same year, I drove my husband to class. We were running late, so I put a robe over my nightgown and drove him to the class. I dropped him off and started for home to get dressed before returning for him. A few blocks from home a Norman police officer stopped me. I don't recall why. He ordered me to follow him. I was in my husband's old Chevy, the one where you had to go under the hood to change the gears. Being partially dressed, I didn't want to get out of the car and go under the hood to change gears. I tried to explain my predicament to the officer, but he made me do it anyway. I was glad that my husband didn't see the incident; he would have gotten himself into more trouble. The incident occurred in front of students who were nearby and no doubt watching. I think the police officer enjoyed it. I never got a ticket, but I'm sure his buddies had a good laugh at my expense when he bragged about how he humiliated me.

Some of the good memories that I have are about the parties we had on the South Campus during weekends; the times we danced to the juke box tunes at the Helm Restaurant on campus; plotting and planning to get Bill Moffitt elected student body president; the feeling of power and purpose that came with my participation in several civil rights demonstrations; and even the minor but long-term hazing that I experienced while pledging AKA. I also remember the time my geology class went to Turner Falls and I fell into an icy mountain stream and then nearly froze in the air-conditioned bus on the ride back to the OU campus. I remember chats with my friends, attending football and basketball games and track meets, and all the good things that we accomplished as pioneers of sorts during the civil rights era.[2]

CHAPTER NINE

Adversaries, Bystanders, and Allies

From the late 1960s into the early 1970s, charges of racism had been troubling the conscience of many people on the University of Oklahoma's Norman campus. Sides were taken that pitted friends against each other. The antagonists were blacks who believed they were victims of racial discrimination and segregation, and whites who believed they were falsely accused of being racists. Holding fast to their beliefs, both groups refused to back down. There was no perceived glory in surrendering. It was a classic battle of perceptions and wills. Onlookers who wanted to remain neutral often found themselves wavering. Indeed, our emotions played out in the shadow of racial unrest. This chapter describes three of the most prominent roles played in this human relations drama: adversaries, bystanders, and allies.

Adversaries

Numerous individuals argued that racial segregation on the Norman campus was basically the same in the 1960s and early 1970s as it had been since blacks were first admitted as students in 1948. They also argued that racial discrimination was not more prevalent in our university than it was in other predominantly white institutions. Those arguments begged the

question of whether the University of Oklahoma's mandate was to become one campus, not two separate and unquestionably unequal ones.
The subtexts of legality and morality were frequently lost in the ranting of
the discussants—both blacks and whites. We seldom talked calmly or
behaved politely in mixed company when the topic was race. At times,
especially during arguments about white privileges, it seemed unlikely
that there would ever be enough goodwill to get beyond finger-pointing.
That angst was precisely what opponents of racial integration preferred
and perpetuated.

The black students and I knew that we had far more enemies than
allies. Our enemies came at us in many ways. Some of them were vocal,
others silent; some were direct, others devious. All of them were dangerous people who had a knack for peddling interracial dissension. Add
to that unsavory mixture of scoundrels the people who tagged along just
for the hell of it. As in the 1692 and 1693 Salem witch trials, there were
onlookers who enjoyed watching people suffer, but this time the victims
were not executed, and they were black instead of white. The increasing
frequency of verbal attacks against black students who walked alone on
campus and on the streets of Norman, coupled with sporadic physical
confrontations, gave the students reason to heighten their awareness of
racial predators. Consequently, whenever they could, black students
walked in pairs or larger numbers, and some of them almost never walked
alone at night.

Figuratively speaking, the Civil War was being fought all over again,
but this time in miniature. Still, the social, emotional, and physical casualties were life-size. As the struggle evolved, it became evident to astute
observers that the University was a mere trifle of what it might have
become if it was a racially inclusive community. The all too common tit-
for-tat exchanges of charges of racism and countercharges of demagogu-
ery added little insight to how reconciliation could be achieved. From
time to time, brief constructive dialogues took place. Although not a
panacea, those infrequent time-outs stopped the hostilities long enough
for concerned individuals to try to broker a permanent peace. Generally,
reconciliation efforts fermented, fractured, rebounded, and broke again,
often holding out to us promise and disappointment with equal measure.
At any given time, an initiative on the verge of succeeding was simultaneously on the verge of failing.

Successful and failed attempts to achieve racial equality were usually public knowledge. With each success there was always the question of whether it really moved our university forward or backward culturally. For example, did the other white Greeks follow the lead of Delta Upsilon Fraternity members and pledge black members in 1968? In the larger scheme of things, was it worth the effort if they did not? Clearly, rapprochement had a mountain of potential problems and a gaggle of critics. Throughout the nation, racial segregation and discrimination were the debris of abandoned efforts to achieve integration. Race-specific opportunities in any form challenged the moral underpinnings of colleges and universities, including our own, that claimed to be free of their antebellum roots.

Although our adversaries included some truly awful individuals, I do not mention their names. It was their behavior that I disliked, not them personally. The teachings of Gandhi and King, among others, led me to this decision. What is to be gained by painting a figurative *R* for racist or *B* for bigot on particular people? Besides, character assassinations often persist, even if their subjects change their behavior. The objective of this chapter is to emphasize how to treat culturally different people fairly. It is not to call out the villains. So, unlike allies whose meritorious behavior deserves personal recognition, hateful people are given the cloak of anonymity.

On the OU campus there were several types of racial bigots, most of whom had little in common except their disdain for black people. A few of them assumed whatever demeanor they thought would lure their black prey into a false sense of security. Disingenuous people were plentiful. They grinned and deceived us while their actions hurt us. Initially, the tiny bit of artificial sweetness they gave us was soothing, but that false gesture soon became bitter. Not all of their deceptions were transparent, especially when they publicly objected to other people abusing us. Those "friends" did not shed their crocodile tears for us because they were sorry we had been abused. To the contrary, they were upset because they had been denied the pleasure of being the abusers themselves.

People who made careers out of being hateful to blacks usually did it for all the wrong reasons. For example, they did it because someone told them to do it or because they needed a scapegoat or simply because they could. Disparaging the notion of sharing coveted opportunities with blacks, our adversaries worked hard to keep for themselves whatever privileges they had. For the most part they succeeded. The arrogant ones among them believed we were incapable forcing concessions from them. Therefore they saw no benefit in bargaining in good faith with us or with other ethnic minorities to peacefully share jobs, positions, or honors with them. Whenever we accused them of being unfair, they shrugged off our complaints as being groundless. And they chided us for seeing bigotry when, according to them, it did not exist. The minuscule amount of public concern about the heavy-handed tactics of our adversaries was disappointing to the black students and me.

The black students and I knew perfectly well what our second-class citizenship had cost us, but we were less sure of how to effectively counter the bigots who happened to be some of the gatekeepers of University opportunities. Frustrated and tired of trying to become accepted in mainstream campus activities, many of the students acquiesced. I was disappointed, but I understood why they gave up. Behaving like people typically do when continuously perched on the edge of the mainstream, the black students settled into their predetermined out-group roles and places. It struck me as bizarre that their critics blamed them for doing what the critics did themselves. both blacks and whites clustered together when they walked across the campus, ate in dining facilities, attended public events, and sat in classrooms. Although black students made up less than one percent of the student population, their critics expected them to somehow convince the others to integrate them into the mainstream.

When I joined the faculty, the black students' confidence in most University personnel was almost nonexistent. Wary of administrators and professors and weary of their white peers, the black students' morale had fallen to a new low, and an immobilizing despair had set in. Perhaps it was not so much despair but resignation that characterized the mood within the University's black community. There was not yet a groundswell of public opinion favoring racial equality. Furthermore, hatemongers did not take kindly to plans that might integrate black students into the University's mainstream. Thus in storybook fashion, foes of racial integration huffed and puffed until their hateful rhetoric and destructive behavior blew down the emotionally and educationally shaky black students' self-esteem.

Some of the black students became campus caricatures. They were made to appear stupid by teachers whose probing questions were calibrated to inflict maximum public embarrassment on them. It was a brazen example of bigotry. Far more often than not, those classroom charades of fairness were just the beginning of the black students' troublesome situation. The ending was usually even more depressing. Feisty black students who tried to deflect their teachers' dour put-downs often received low or failing grades even though their work merited higher grades. The students who were intentionally ignored by their teachers during question-and-answer sessions fared no better.

Upon closer examination, it was evident to me that some of the black students were set up to fail. Teachers who participated in that kind of discrimination were the equivalent of educational assassins. Generally, therefore, the black students had to protect themselves as best they could from those teachers who would, whenever possible, destroy their educational careers. Unfortunately, when those abuses were reported to administrators, the ensuing efforts to punish the perpetrators paled in comparison with the excuses that were made for them. That gave the black students little reason to be hopeful of fair outcomes. But that wasn't the only reason for them to be apprehensive.

Outside of their classrooms, especially in public places, black students were objects of racial slurs. As a whole, they demonstrated remarkable restraint by not retaliating when they were called "niggers," "coons," "spooks," and "apes," among other epithets. Most white victims of verbal abuse showed similar restraint when they were called "honkies," "white crackers," "rednecks," and other derogatory names. But there was a qualitative difference in the name-calling. Apart from racial epithets, very few of black students' campus experiences satisfied their expectation upon enrollment that they would be treated fairly during their time at the University. However, most of the white students expected to be treated fairly and, aside from being called derogatory names occasionally, they were treated fairly. Thus, for blacks more so than for whites, racial slurs and discrimination metastasized into isolation, defeatism, and low self-esteem.

Racial bigots did not all betray themselves in equal measure. Some held themselves aloof from their more vocal colleagues, preferring to remain above public scrutiny. Therefore it required a great deal of perceptiveness by the black students and me to flush out the hidden ones. We had no prudent adversaries, but there were plenty of discreet ones.

Their ability to hide from us was disheartening. Quite frankly, most of them managed to escape both public exposure and punishment. Consequently, they were able, with impunity, to hurt their black students.

To a great extent, life for black students, faculty, and staff on the University's campus was akin to being in Lewis Carroll's *Alice in Wonderland*. Like Alice, all of us at various times found ourselves down the rabbit hole, trying to get out of trouble that was not of our own making. It seemed to me that only a small number of University administrators, faculty, staff, and students were overt racists, but I had no way to determine exactly how many of them were covert ones. For example, what was I to make of administrators who chastised errant students for trampling on campus flowers but were noticeably silent about institutional racism? Whether their racism was overt or covert, hateful people played off each other, not only harming the blacks in their sphere of influence but also poisoning the minds of innocent bystanders with their prejudices.

Bystanders

I am inclined to support the theory that most white people did not give much thought to what was happening to blacks at the University, in Norman, or anywhere else. There might be more plausible explanations than that, but I doubt it. Unspeakable indifference swallowed up all but the egalitarians. Only a few of my white peers expressed even a small amount of outrage publicly or to me privately about the general absence of black students when University awards and honors were handed out. Nor did they decry the paucity of black faculty and staff. Those silent people were the bystanders. The opposite of love is indifference, not hate.

That there was tension and animus between the various racial groups on campus was not in dispute. Trust and patience were among the first things lost when the University was desegregated in the 1940s. That made it extremely difficult in subsequent years for concerned individuals to mediate or negotiate positive interracial relations. Although my verbal exchanges with bystanders increased the dialogue, they seldom moved it forward. Nor did they very often open the University to honest inquiry into the broader issue of social justice. Torn by conflicting beliefs, most of my white peers opted not to be fully engaged with me when the topic was racism. They took great care to hide their beliefs.

Several white students I got to know quite well told me what they thought was the major obstacle that prevented them from abandoning their fence-straddling position. In the absence of solid evidence that racism existed in the University, they said, they had no valid reason to support the ASU or me or, for that matter, to oppose us. Therefore their conversations with black people about race relations usually amounted to minutiae and never became anything more. Many students and others on our campus were masters of evasion. The decision to remain uncommitted during conversations that centered on racial issues was understandable. Backlash could be quite devastating for white people who publicly challenged racism within their own circle of friends, so they sat on the fence and waited to support the winners.

The rigid racial divide said something about the state of intergroup relations at the University of Oklahoma, though for the life of me it was hard to know what it said about how to turn bystanders into allies. My quandary was intensified many times over when my friends and I made intemperate public outbursts, which undermined our credibility as interracial bridge builders. Then there were the individuals who advocated racial integration in the University but who themselves had no friends from another race. The litmus test was not their grand statements but what they actually did to move the agenda of racial inclusion forward. As Sterlin Adams put it, with more than a touch of impertinence in his voice, "Talks about equality and racial integration are not only cheap at this school, they are dishonest."

Those of us who met with University administrators and faculty members to resolve racial problems often felt like we were scavenging for allies. We were sadly in search of additional supporters that we seldom found. Not many white administrators, in particular, wanted to be identified publicly as our allies, nor did they want us to label them our enemies. Being neutral was an organizationally compelling and a socially safe position for them to take. With their flanks closed, most of them gave us a few promises and very little helpful action. But if they wavered even a tiny bit, I would press the Afro-American Student Union case harder. I tried to recruit each potential ally one conversation at a time.

The black students, Melvin Tolson, and I knew that, to gain more supporters, we would have to compromise on some of the changes we wanted the University to implement. We were well aware that concessions made solely on our terms, while ideal, were an unrealistic expectation. In many instances, institutional changes were accepted or rejected through formal voting. Therefore bystanders were coveted political swing votes. Guinnevere Hodges used a religious analogy: "We need help to escape from this OU hell and go to some semblance of heaven — one that will let us in." Indeed. The black students and I could not say for sure that even if we had more white supporters, our academic lives were salvageable. We were reasonably certain, though, that without additional allies the status quo would not change much, if at all.

It was extremely difficult to convert people to our cause if they required that we reduce our proof of racism to algorithms and formulas. During those early years, not many studies of racism had withstood strict scientific scrutiny. But that did not deter us. The challenge was to find other ways to turn bystanders into allies. We learned how to use nonscientific arguments to show bystanders that people, including themselves, who were scorned, denied, and minimized as human beings were not shadowy abstractions of reality. They were real victims.

Only when that argument succeeded were we able to peel back a few layers of the bystanders' resistance to racial equality. Specifically, when proof-oriented bystanders grasped that bigotry defied logic, they also understood that it was morally inappropriate for them to remain neutral while entire racial classifications of people were being discriminated against. Even so, a noticeable gap usually remained between their knowledge of oppressive conditions and their actions to prevent or abate them.

White bystanders who believed that they were in no way connected to black people had to be convinced that they were very much connected. As an illustration, the shared fear of being hurt in a race riot was proof of a connection, albeit a negative one. One after another of them espoused half-baked rationalizations to explain their willingness to stand by while the racial tensions on campus mounted. Those who did not abandon their neutrality allowed themselves to be campus shields behind which ASU foes hid. The apologies these neutral bystanders made to us were not convincing. Livid after one such encounter, Lennie Marie Muse-Tolliver told me, "I wish they wouldn't even bother to talk to me about why they don't support us."

Notwithstanding the trickle of individuals who joined our side, the majority of the white people in the University remained neutral. An abundance of people pretended to be color-blind: they said that they didn't notice the race of ethnic minorities. That would have been an amazing feat on a campus of multicolored people. These individuals were delusional. Wrapped in a cocoon of denial, some of the bystanders also did not think of themselves as being involved in any way in oppressing black people or any other peoples. They did not understand that because they did not cry out against racism on the campus or in Norman, bigots were egged on by their silence. White silence and inaction were formidable counters to black rage and disgust. In numerous instances, properly focused sympathy from bystanders gave shape and sound to our plight. Nevertheless, their sympathy alone was no help in solving our predicament. It was, at most, a placebo. The solution resided elsewhere. The black students and I needed more true allies.

Allies

The University of Oklahoma was an extremely contradictory place when I arrived on campus. It was, in Dickens-like terms, among the best of places and the worst of places in the Southwest to teach. Faculty members who sought multidisciplinary relationships in order to become better teachers or researchers could find them here. There were slightly more than five hundred full-time faculty members on the Norman campus during the 1967–68 academic year. I got to know several of them quite well through committees, coffee breaks, lunches, dinners, and impromptu gatherings. Thus the University was an academically stimulating environment for me. Yet, for all the collegiality that I experienced, the University was a hostile environment for almost all of the black students. Their situation could have been much worse, however, if most of my white friends had not actively supported them too.

The men and women I mention here and elsewhere in the book — and those I do not mention — were relatively few in numbers but huge in University influence. My heroes have always been people like them. It was extraordinary for any student organization, particularly a black one, in the University to have so many allies from such diverse academic backgrounds. I would not fully appreciate the significance of this alliance until two or three years after our collaborations ended.

Our allies were anything but wishy-washy in their beliefs about racial equality and social justice. Most of them were effective brokers of peace in emotionally charged settings where black and white participants sometimes verbally attacked each other. Members of the Afro-American Student Union and I learned to differentiate quickly the several kinds of allies available to us. Some of them were totally committed, others were partially committed, and almost all of them were considerate, thoughtful individuals who were generous with their time.

Presidents Cross, Hollomon, and Sharp remained neutral in order to administer fairly to all parties during racial conflicts, but they provided the black students and me with whatever information and support they deemed appropriate. As an example, at a basketball game in February 1968, President Cross whispered to me, "You have been creating quite a stir on campus and throughout the state with your speeches about racism, inadequate educational opportunities, and open housing, Professor Henderson." He paused for a minute, looked into my eyes, and winked. Smiling, he said, "Keep it up. We need more professors like you." My activism caused him and Presidents Hollomon and Sharp a lot of grief, but they nevertheless protected me from many of my critics, on and off campus, who demanded that they get rid of me — the rabble-rouser from Detroit.

With that kind of support, a logical question was, why had so little progress been made to fully incorporate blacks into campus life? The answer was buried deeply in historical conditions of white power and black powerlessness. Before 1967 no potent black organization had challenged the status quo. Also, countless potential white allies were hidden in plain view. The black students and I simply overlooked them. White students with long hair, shabby dress, and other hippie looks were frequently designated as possible friends; while those with well-groomed hair, designer clothes, and other establishment looks were routinely written off as foes. Belatedly, we found out that some of our staunchest enemies wore counterculture clothes and some of our most supportive friends looked like models of mainstream America. The black students and I had cast too shallow a net when looking for allies. Even though the evidence against them was not cut-and-dried, I overlooked a number of potential allies among faculty and staff, including Pete Kyle McCarter.

Before his appointment as interim president, McCarter was not someone I counted on to help me push through changes that would open the

Henderson and Pete Kyle McCarter, 1971. Western History Collections, University of Oklahoma Libraries.

University to more ethnic minority people. After he took office, it became crystal clear to me how wrong I had been about him. He was more helpful than most of my flaming-liberal friends who merely gave lip service to my projects. His folksy manner was deceptive. My misperception of him bothered me so much that I sought him out in his office.

"I owe you an apology, Pete," I began humbly. "I sized you up all wrong. You are nothing like the person I thought you were."

He grinned at me like a card player who had already peeked at my hole card.

"I bet I know what you initially thought about me. Because I'm white and from Mississippi, talk with a Southern drawl, and take my time making decisions, many of my fellow faculty members think that I'm a dyed-in-the wool conservative."

He had nailed me to my bigotry, and that unnerved me. He had a unique way of knocking arrogance out of people and then saying something to allow them to regain their composure and dignity. I had already watched him do it ten times or more, but until now I had never been the beneficiary of his grace.

"Pete, I—"

"I'll accept your apology, George, if you will accept mine. I have a confession to make too. When I first met you, I sized you up as being nothing more than just another fast-talking, fast-walking, and too-fast-thinking hotshot from the North who came to Oklahoma to save us backward Southern people."

It was one of those gotcha moments. That brief exchange was yet another invaluable lesson to me about withholding judgment of people until I gathered enough factual information about them to come to an informed conclusion. After I got to know McCarter, I came to the sad realization that the black students and I had behaved in a way very similar to that of Pogo, a comic strip character popular at the time. Pogo spent several weeks scouring the countryside looking for an enemy to defeat. In the end, he came to this startling realization: "We have met the enemy and he is us." Pogo reminded people like me to look in the mirror when we set out to find our enemies.

Most of my white faculty and staff friends were colorful characters. Some of them did remarkably bold things. There was very little they could have done but did not do to help the ASU or me. For example,

David Burr and J. R. Morris identified and mentored numerous black students. In other chapters, I mention a few of the black students David mentored. J. R. was also successful in identifying, training, and promoting black administrators, including Paul Wilson, who became the University's first black director of intramurals. Then there were Ray and Martha Thurman, who opened their home to black athletes. Martha cooked the best black-eyed peas, rice, and cornbread west of the Mississippi. David Levy created and taught the University's first black history course in 1968. Because of his insistence, a few years later the History Department hired a black man, Jidlaph Kamoche, to teach the course. Steve Sutherland was one of few white men in the United States who was a member of a black fraternity, Omega Psi Phi. He gained a stellar reputation for his untiring work to improve the quality of life for all students at the University of Oklahoma, particularly those who came from culturally disadvantaged backgrounds.

A very public act of support for black students was carried out in 1968 by David French, who drafted a "Statement of Personal Intent," tacked it on his office door, had it published in the *Oklahoma Daily*, and encouraged other people to sign it. The statement, created to "cure the evils of discrimination," encouraged these private actions and beliefs: (1) extend to all people, without reference to race, creed, or national origin, the same respect, courtesies, and friendliness that we want for ourselves; (2) act without reference to race, religion, or national origin when renting rooms, selling real estate, or employing other people; and (3) do not join or patronize groups and establishments that refuse to extend equal services to people of all races, creeds, and national origin. Several individuals signed the statement.

Only a few of our white allies had been civil rights activists before 1967, but some of them became activists later. Those who disdained campus-wide activism worked at the committee and departmental levels to champion more educational opportunities for ethnic minority students. Whether center stage or backstage, their support was crucial to the black students' civil rights rebellion at the University of Oklahoma. There is no way to accurately assign a weight to their support. Suffice it to say that without it the ASU and I probably would have had only a negligible effect on the school. Our allies kept the reactionary and hostile members of their own departments at bay long enough for us to get a solid footing on campus. As a whole, our friends were men and women of uncommon passion for creating a just university. And so too were several students, including some I have not already mentioned.

In February 1968, President Cross's Committee on Student Organizations recommended that the University "should regard as an integral part of its structure only those student organizations which are open to all students regardless of race, color, creed or national origin." The committee specifically mentioned cheerleaders. On February 20, David Wise's *Oklahoma Daily* editorial got to the crux of the committee's report. "Will it apply to Greek organizations?" he asked. It was a salvo across the bow of the University's leadership. Paula Whiteside, an *Oklahoma Daily* reporter, said this about my April 16, 1968, Greek Week speech:

> Dr. George Henderson spoke to approximately 150 people Tuesday night. . . . Unfortunately the audience was too small and not strictly Greek. . . . The ones who were ready to join Dr. Henderson's crusade against prejudice were there. We were already on his side. His most valuable points should have been heard by the uncommitted and by those who will fight him. He would have challenged their prejudices. But those people were not there. They stayed home and watched TV, studied or just goofed off. They knew how they felt — for them there was nothing to discuss.

That same year, a dozen white students collected more than five hundred signatures on a petition that asked the University of Oklahoma Regents to name the new social sciences building under construction the Martin Luther King, Jr., Building. Although it was eventually named Edward Everett Dale Hall, after a popular history professor, the students' gesture pleased the black students. Often, just when it seemed to me that the racial divide was going to widen, something nice like that would happen.

What I wished for most, after the ASU was formed, was an organization of proactive white students who would relieve the ASU of the sole responsibility for mounting frontal assaults on racial bigotry. My wish came true on April 21, 1968, when approximately seventy-five white students formed the Student Action Committee (mentioned in chapter 7). Brooks Harrington, a junior, was the founder and first president, and I was the faculty sponsor. The organization was an outgrowth of an incident that occurred in the Student Union. More than a hundred white students jeered Ronald King, a black sophomore, when he tried to have a dialogue with them about racism in our University. Acting independently of the ASU, the Student Action Committee was formed to prod members of the University community to prevent and abate racially discriminatory conditions and to otherwise promote social justice initiatives.

Three days later, on April 24, freshman Anthony "Tony" Gilkey became the first black student at the University to pledge a white Greek fraternity, Delta Upsilon. Other Greek fraternities and sororities chastised Delta Upsilon for making that bold move. A week after he pledged, Tony came to my office for advice. "Did I do the right thing?" he asked.

He was extremely anxious. He had heard what several of the students were saying about him. Generally, the black students said that he was an "Oreo"—black on the outside, white on the inside—and the white students called him an overreacher. I thought that he was very courageous. This was not the time for me to tell him what he should or should not have done. He had to come to his own solution to racially segregated white fraternities.

I said, "You did the right thing if it was what you really wanted to do. There will be plenty of people second-guessing you. I am not one of them."

Tony was extremely mature for a nineteen-year-old, and he was extremely hopeful. Most pioneers are. If people could know in advance all of the bad things that would happen to them, I don't believe there would be nearly as many pioneers of any kind. I told Tony that whether his grand action succeeded or failed, he had cracked opened a door of opportunity that other black men might consider going through, and perhaps later a white sorority would follow Delta Upsilon's lead.

As Tony got out of the chair to leave my office, I said to him, "If or when things become too much for you, please feel free to call me. Better yet, feel free to call me anytime."

He didn't respond. What was he thinking? I wondered. Did he think the wrangling would end? The answer to those questions came sooner than I thought they would. Later that year, tired of being scorned by whites and ridiculed by blacks, Tony Gilkey dropped out of school, and we were left alone to contemplate another side of activism: remorse. The

University had lost another well-meaning student, and I was very sorry for our loss.

I now understood clearly that students like Tony would bear the brunt of the burden inherent in integrating our nation's colleges and universities. I had gained an added appreciation of the young men and women who didn't belong to any organized civil rights groups but who, through their own initiatives, overturned archaic, racist practices. It was not easy to do that as a member of a civil rights organization; it was almost impossible to do it alone. Tony's climb over one of the barriers that separated white men on campus from black men seemed doomed from the beginning. Those kinds of initiatives almost always required more than one trailblazer, and they required help from sensitive, powerful white allies within the organizations. Somebody had to watch out for the trailblazers' welfare.

A few of the ASU student allies that I have not yet mentioned include Sarah "Sallie" Burns, Allan H. Keown, Rosalyn "Rozzie" Katz, John C. Gatlin, Judith A. Blake, Gregory A. Vaut, and Teri L. Klausner. Sallie was involved in several sorority projects that attempted to foster positive black-white interactions. And under my direction, but through their own initiative, Allan, Rosalyn, John, Judith, Gregory, and Teri planned and conducted, with the assistance of guest speakers, a ten-week black history workshop for Norman High School students at the Stovall Museum, beginning October 9, 1968. The twenty or so students who participated in the workshop told me that they learned a lot about black contributions to our country.

There were other good student deeds for me to cheer as well. In 1969, out of respect to Dr. King, ten white freshmen proposed, in a letter to the editor of the *Oklahoma Daily*, the establishment of a Martin Luther King, Jr., Institute for Human Development at the University of Oklahoma. It was a thoughtful, practical proposal to create an academic unit where diverse students could study ways to combat racism. Earlier, out of anger, Sterlin Adams had suggested something else more inclusive: change the name of the University itself to the Martin Luther King, Jr., Institute for Human Development. His tongue-in-cheek proposal, while novel, was dead on arrival. The freshmen proposal was an appealing call for action, and it was discussed for several weeks in classes and in informal groups.

On January 9, 1970, the *Oklahoma Daily* did something no other edition had done. Patricia A. Piercy, a sophomore, became the first black OU female to have her picture on the paper's front page for winning an award — she had been crowned the 1970 Alpha Phi Alpha Fraternity Sweetheart. The mere printing of the photo told the University community that not all campus sweethearts were white. On March 4, through an invitation from Sallie Burns, members of the Pi Beta Phi Sorority heard me speak on "Human Relations in the World Today." During the discussion that followed, I noted the significance of the *Oklahoma Daily* article about Patricia Piercy. My closing plea for more recognition of the accomplishments of ethnic minority students was warmly received. Several members of the sorority — and others — became involved in campus activities that improved black-white relations.

In the late 1960s, scores of conservative and moderate white students, at the urging of a few religious leaders, came out of the shadows of bigots to support the ASU members at a time when it was not a popular thing for them to do. This shift was a harbinger of improved race relations at the University. In the front line of the ASU allies were several white students who predicted more academic success for their low-achieving black friends than most of the blacks predicted for them. This was especially true after Moffitt became president of the student government. There was hope in those predictions even if they did not always come true. Surprisingly to most blacks, when the predictions did not prove true, their white friends felt an unsettling sense of personal failure. Whites who had tutored those black students redoubled their efforts. The emotional baths of encouragement were tremendously soothing to the black students — and to me.

Association with the ASU was not for squeamish people. Paralyzed by the fear of being given lower grades than they earned if they were students or of being denied fair annual evaluations or promotions if they were faculty or staff members, a few of our allies dropped out and returned to the ranks of bystanders. They did not want to become direct or collateral damage in the war against racism. Many other factors propelled the unraveling of black-white coalitions, including an increase in racial conflicts nationally. Until they were tested, most black-white coalitions rested fragilely on blind faith. When tested, however, the relationships that survived were usually solidified. White people who were closest to the

ASU membership in 1971, four years after the organization's founding, from University of Oklahoma 1972 yearbook. Western History Collections, University of Oklahoma Libraries.

ASU members received the most public criticism, and that made their contributions all the more remarkable.

During the second week of August 1971, I eagerly looked forward to another year of teaching at the University. As was customary for a number of faculty members and students, I began the new semester by having lunch at the Library Bar, a local pub that was almost famous for its greasy hamburgers and cold beer. The room was filled with a noisy jumble of sounds. I could barely hear the music on the speaker that was perched above the bar. Midway through my lunch, I heard a loud shriek, followed by, "Dr. Henderson, I'm glad you're back." It was Rozzie Katz. She was now a graduate student. In her own forceful manner, she not so gently parted the sea of bodies in the crowded room and made her way to my table.

She bent down and kissed me on my left cheek.

Flustered, I looked around and saw half the people in the room staring at me, a black man in Norman being kissed by a young white female. Then, embarrassed and fumbling for words, I said, more loudly than I wanted to, "Rozzie, what will they think?"

She smiled, put her face close to my left ear, and whispered, "The kiss was for you, not them. The question is, what do you think?"

The pure humanity of my friends, most of whom were like Rozzie, defied clichés and stereotypes. I was moved by just how sincere they were. Individually, we were bodacious people, so to speak. When lumped together, our relationships added up to much more than the sum of the individuals. At the zenith of our friendship there was less than three degrees of philosophical separation between us. Our determination to challenge together the unjust practices of the University was a constancy that sustained me more than I ever told anyone. The hopes of our critics who expected our alliance to implode were soon dashed. During that period of my first years at OU, it was common for professors and students to form civil rights alliances. For four glorious years and beyond, we fought bigots and we won more battles than we lost. Along the way, I came to understand the deeper meanings of friendships that have no racial boundaries. When we were together, we felt a boundless sense of potential. Truth to tell, it was a time of cross-cultural enlightenment for me.

Postscript

After 1971 the torrent of black activism at the University of Oklahoma subsided to a slow drizzle of scattered, less holistic activities. We began to push the racial equality agenda forward at a less deliberate pace. I prefer to measure our success in terms of the quality of the achievements, not by the quantity of our efforts. Realistically, only so much could have been done within those first years. The bold tactics we employed then were precisely what we needed to jump-start our daring rebellion. But it was racial justice and human rights that became the guiding spirits of our efforts. Indeed, bold tactics, racial justice, and human rights were the threads that bound us into meaningful coalitions with other people.

The Winds of Change

We were determined not to leave the University under the cloud of failure. At the very least, we wanted to set in motion noteworthy changes that would someday result in a truly egalitarian institution. If we succeeded, those changes would be our main legacy to future generations of students, faculty, and staff. For some of us, activism was a calling; for others, it was an obligation; and for all of us, it seemed like the right thing to do. King Arthur had his Camelot; the University of Oklahoma was our place of noble challenges. My friends and I dared to envision a cross-culturally idyllic school — with or without ivory towers. We were not perfect crusaders, but neither were King Arthur's knights.

Although we did not always see eye to eye with our allies on tactics, we had no doubt that we were bound together in an epic search for racial equality. Despite false turns along the way, we were able to recalibrate our tactics and chart a new course. Thus we learned to appreciate each other's strengths and to recognize and minimize our own weaknesses. In the process, we kindred souls were able to muster the energy and commitment needed to seriously challenge whoever and whatever tried to prevent us from creating a racially just institution. Our battle lines were meticulously drawn.

Seldom were things so cut-and-dried that we were always the good guys. At times our grievances were extremely complex, and that caused people to misunderstand us. Of course in other instances they were straightforward, but our adversaries intentionally misinterpreted them. Most regrettable were the times when our self-inflated egos caused us to press our issues ad nauseam. Many of those tumultuous missteps still reverberate in my mind. Occasionally we turned racial oppression upside down and became the perpetrators; then we lost the moral high ground. Whenever we acted in unbridled anger, the outcome was less than we had hoped for. At such times, we were spinning out of control as we wallowed in our own self-absorption. Fortunately for us, someone among us always had enough good sense to remind us to not let our anger get the best of us.

Several generations of us knit together a string of successful strategies to combat racial discrimination. That effort was the longest consecutive campaign for equality ever waged by blacks and their allies at the University of Oklahoma. It lasted for nearly five years. Since that time, subsequent variations of the Afro-American Student Union (renamed the Black People's Union, 1972–87, and then the Black Student Association, 1987–present) redefined the organization from being militant to becoming mainstream. We were aided and abetted by our presidents, beginning with George Lynn Cross's last two years as president (1967–68) and continuing with J. Herbert Hollomon (1968–70), Paul F. Sharp (1971–77), William S. Banowsky (1978–84), Frank E. Horton (1985–88), Richard L. Van Horn (1989–94), and David Boren (1994–). Each of them made and kept promises to do something about the racially intolerable aspects of the University.

A few of the presidents did more than the others, but members of all of their executive staffs chipped away at disparate opportunities for minority groups in the University. It is worth mentioning that President Boren and his administration initiated more culturally inclusive programs and made considerably more substantive appointments of blacks and other minorities than the other presidents combined. All of these doings contributed to improved race relations and provided additional educational and employment opportunities for ethnic minorities at the University. Consider, for example, the following post-1971 actions that have positively altered the lives of black students, faculty, and staff.

The Black Declaration of Independence Revisited

The 1969 Black Declaration of Independence did not lead to all-black programs, but it circuitously advanced the Afro-American Student Union's racial justice agenda. In the end, the declaration accomplished what the ASU members hoped that it would. It caused the University to accelerate its efforts to do more to achieve ethnic diversity in general and black diversity in particular. The University has continued to move forward in fulfilling the promises made by President Hollomon and his successors. The outcomes of six of the black students' demands illustrate my point.

1. *Black Vice President of Black Student Affairs.* In 1991 Roland M. Smith, a black man, became the University's vice president for student affairs. He was responsible for University-wide student activities, not just activities for black students. He held the position until 1995, when he left the University to become vice president for student life at the University of Delaware. Currently, several black administrators and program coordinators are employed in OU's Office of Student Affairs.

2. *Black Studies Program with Master of Arts and Doctor of Philosophy Degrees.* In 1975 Jerry F. Muskrat, an American Indian assistant professor of law, became the University's first director of the Ethnic Studies Program. In 1977 that program was phased out, and American Indian Studies, Latin American Studies, and Black Studies programs were established. Jidlaph G. Kamoche, assistant professor of history, was appointed the first director of the African and African-American Studies Program in 1978. In 1994, under the leadership of associate

professor of education and human relations Charles Butler, the program began offering a bachelor's degree. When he retired in 2003, Jeanette Davidson became the program's director.

3. *Black Head Basketball Coach (or head coach in a major sport).* John Blake, the University's first black head coach, coached the football team from 1996 to 1998. In 2006 Jeff Capel became the first black head coach of the University's men's basketball team. He replaced Kelvin Sampson, an American Indian, who left the University to become head coach at Indiana University. Rodney Price was the first black co–head coach of OU's track and field team, coaching it from 1997 to 2005.

4. *A Constitution for the Student Body Acceptable to Black Students or the Right for Black Students to Function Independently Under Their Own Constitution.* The student body constitution that was approved in 1969 provided extensive policies and procedures to resolve conflicts that centered on racial discrimination. The student constitution is no longer an issue of dispute among black students.

5. *Scheduled Competition with Black Schools in All Major Sports.* To date only three sports have hosted teams from historically black universities. As noted in chapter 8, the men's basketball team hosted Grambling State University in 1970, and since then it has played several black teams. The women's basketball team hosted Mississippi Valley State in 1988, and the women's soccer team hosted Alabama A&M University in 2007.

6. *Student Year Abroad Program for Black Students at Universities in Black Countries.* The University of Oklahoma now has reciprocal exchange agreements with universities in sub-Saharan Africa. These programs are available for all students, and financial aide is available to students who need it.

The black declaration chided the University for not having blacks appointed to the top positions in its governance, faculty, and staff units. The following appointments have done much to remedy that situation:

OU Board of Regents. Three blacks have been appointed to the Board of Regents: Sylvia A. Lewis (1983–92), Ada Lois Sipuel Fisher (1992–93), and Melvin C. Hall (1992–97).

Office of the President. Wilbur Walker, Sr., was special assistant to the president (1970–73); Walter O. Mason was special assistant to the president and University affirmative action officer (1974–86); Beth Wilson was special assistant to the president and University affirmative action officer (1980–95).

College of Arts and Sciences. I was director/chair of the Department of Human Relations (1969–82, 1987–95); Betty J. Harris was director of the Women's Studies Program (2003–2006); Roosevelt Wright was director of the School of Social Work (2003–2004, 2007); George B. Richter-Addo is chair of the Chemistry and Biochemistry Department (2006–present).

College of Architecture. Abimbola O. Asojo is the director of the Interior Design Division (2005–present).

College of Continuing Education. Belinda P. Biscoe is an assistant vice president (2003–present). Within the college there have been two black directors of the Southwest Center for Human Relations Studies: Lonnie H. Wagstaff (1967–68) and Carole H. Hardeman (1981–85).

College of Journalism. Meta G. Carstarphen was an associate dean (2005–2006).

College of Liberal Studies. I was the dean (1996–2000).

Graduate College. Amelia M. Adams was an assistant dean (2003–2006).

Honors College. Christopher B. Howard was vice president for strategic and leadership initiatives (2005–2009).

Law Center. Stanley Evans is the dean of student admissions (2003–present).

University College. Adedeji B. Badiru was the dean (1995–2000). Within the college there have been four black directors of Project Threshold: W. Cliff Armstrong (1970–71), Elizabeth A. Holmes (1971–74), Anthony V. Bluitt, Sr. (1974–2005), and Deborah Binkley-Jackson (2005–present).

Provost Direct. Edward J. Perkins was senior vice president and the director of the International Programs Center (2003–2008).

Administrative Affairs. Oscar B. Jackson, Jr., was the minority recruiter (1974–76) and the manager of Employment Personnel Services (1977–79); Julius C. Hilburn is the director of Human Resources (2003–present).

Student Affairs. Paul Wilson was director of Intramural Sports (1976–2001); C. Don Bradley was the director of the Center for Student Life (2002–2004). Norris G. Williams has held three positions in Student Affairs: coordinator of Black Student Affairs (1977–80), director of Minority Student Services (1980–2003), and director of the Henderson Scholars Program (2003–present).

Athletics Department. Thomas Hill was an assistant athletics director (1989–93); Keith Gill was an associate/senior associate athletics director (2004–2007); Joe Washington is a special assistant to the athletics director (2007–present).

There have been increases in lower-level black appointments too. For example, in 1967 there were three black full-time professors (0.6 percent of the total); in 2007 there were forty-five black full-time professors (2.9 percent of the total). Seventeen of the black professors were tenured; twenty-eight were not. The gain in nonfaculty full-time black employees at the University is even more substantial: from 4 (less than 1 percent) in 1967 to 190 (5.5 percent) in 2007. The University must not only recruit additional black faculty but also retain them. This will require a better system of mentoring minority junior faculty. The University has a long history of being a revolving door through which junior black faculty come only to leave at the end of their probation period without tenure. This is proportionately truer for blacks than for their white peers. Also, the history of faculty members who have received tenure but not become full professors is considerably more dismal for blacks than for their white peers. Nor should we overlook that, despite the data I have presented, it is still considerably more difficult for blacks than whites to become a vice president, a senior or associate vice president, a dean or associate dean, or a department chair.

The University has been extremely successful in terms of recruiting black athletes and providing academic services for them. In 1968 the black athletes complained about the absence of black athletes in some of the varsity sports. The Athletics Department has become the foremost leader in cultural diversity on our campus. Although blacks have yet to win letters on the golf and tennis teams, the breakthroughs for blacks in University sports since 1968 have been phenomenal, including the following first blacks to earn a letter: men's baseball (Joe Oliver, 1978);

women's gymnastics (Shannon Gilbreath, 1982); women's soccer (Bridgette Smith, 1997); women's softball (Felecia Warren, 1983); and women's volleyball (Doris Stokes, 1974). In 1978 Thomas Lott became the University's first black quarterback. It is also worth mentioning that black athletes are now the majority of the scholarship athletes in football and basketball. With President Boren's support, Joseph R. Castiglione, director of athletics, is moving his department toward achieving nothing less than national prominence in the recruitment and graduation of all student-athletes.

Student Affairs

University of Oklahoma black students currently have some of the most outstanding support staff and learning facilities (including the Prentice Gautt Learning Center for athletes; and the Henderson-Tolson Cultural Center for all students) in Oklahoma, the Big 12 Conference, the Southwest, and maybe even the nation. In addition to Project Threshold staff (Deborah Binkley-Jackson, director), many of the black students receive staff support through the Black Student Association and the National Pan-Hellenic Association (Cordell Cunningham, assistant dean of students), Diversity Enrichment Programs (Brandon J. Brooks, director), the Henderson Scholars Program (Norris G. Williams, director), and the Athletics Department (Teresa A. Turner, assistant director of academic affairs and director of career counseling).

Black students now participate in a wide array of University organizations and formal activities. Several blacks have been inducted into the honor societies, become members of special interest clubs, and been elected to student government positions. Also noteworthy is that four additional black students were elected president of the University of Oklahoma Student Association after Bill Moffitt's ground-breaking election in 1970: Terry Carr (1987–88), T. Jabar Shumate (1997–98), Brandon Brooks (2001–2002), and Mary Milben (2003–2004). I was delighted when they came to me for advice and counsel. It is unlikely that many other historically white colleges and universities can match that number of black student body presidents.

Currently, many black students are standing between the hope for inclusion and the need to maintain their ethnic identities. An age-old dilemma still haunts them: do they want to be African Americans, Americans who happen to have African ancestors, or just Americans? Adding to this confusion is a growing number of biracial and multiracial students. What are they to be called? Undeniably the University's cultural issues are not correctly cast if we refer to them as being only black or white. (President Barack Obama's mixed-race identity has given this issue national attention.) Hopefully, all of these issues will be given adequate discussion and resolution as we move deeper into this century. In the end, the most pressing issue is not what any of us are called but how we are treated.

The City of Norman Revisited

In 1968 the Norman Community Relations Commission was established to seek voluntary resolution of housing and employment disputes. At the urging and persistence of the commission's chair, J. R. Morris, the City of Norman explored the feasibility of creating a commission with more authority and a broader scope. On October 16, 1969, unhappy with the very limited success of the Community Relations Committee in terms of racial disputes, several citizens of Norman established the first all-white NAACP chapter in Oklahoma. Not much came of the chapter, but it sure helped to keep alive the dialogue about a human relations committee.

In 1971 an election was held to approve Ordinance 2107, which established the Norman Human Relations Commission. In 1972 Ordinance 0-7172-104 was passed, changing the name of the commission to the Human Rights Commission. The first commissioners were Barbara Henderson (chair), Thomas Carey, Jean Galey, Dorothea Keller, Gary Rawlinson, Richard "Dick" Reynolds, Don VanMeter, James Weer, and Hugh Wilson. In 1975 the commission was given the authority to handle complaints of discriminatory practices in employment, housing, and public accommodations. Due largely to the tenacity and tact of Barbara and the other commissioners, with staff assistance from M. L. "Bud" Brownsberger and the support of Mayors William "Bill" Morgan and Gordon Masters, blatant discrimination began to recede. Today there are far fewer of such incidents. Once blacks were employed only in domestic household jobs, but that too has changed. There are even black realtors in Norman.

There have been several unanticipated consequences of greater ra-

Katie Barwick presents Barbara Henderson with Norman Human Rights Award, 1985. *Norman Transcript*, reprinted with permission.

cial integration, including one that I will mention briefly. When we were few in numbers, blacks throughout Norman and the University would freely acknowledge each other. If we were within close distance, we would exchange verbal greetings. If we were far away, we would make eye contact, smile, and nod or wave. There was a celebratory feeling when we saw other blacks. Today there is considerably less of that behavior. When I see other black people whom I do not know and try to greet them with a smile or a nod, I am most often ignored or silently rebuked. It is almost as though my presence embarrasses them or angers them. They sometimes glare at me before they turn away. I resist screaming, "Welcome to Norman! I've waited a long time for you." Alas, we are no longer brothers and sisters.

In 2007 blacks constituted 4,500 of Norman's 110,000 residents. That was a significant increase over the fewer than 100 blacks in 1967. In 2007 there were also about 7,000 American Indians, 4,000 Hispanics, and approximately 1,500 other ethnic minority-group residents. The community has undoubtedly become more multicultural. As my account of the black revolt enumerates, the road to this chapter in our history has had many twists and turns. Along the way, George Shirley became the city's first black human resources director (1977–2001) and Anthony Francisco became its first black director of finance (1996–present). For most blacks, Norman is a way station where they spend time before going to communities that are less white and more socially integrated. It is counterproductive for activists to help recruit blacks to Norman if the new residents become social isolates and then leave. More attention must be given to creating social networks for all newcomers to the city, but especially ethnic minorities.

Overall, despite my remorse about the loss of black newcomers, this onetime sundown town has undergone dramatic changes for the better. Do more changes need to happen? Yes. But it would be wrong to assume that the way forward is going to be easy. Many of the major antagonisms of the past still remain. If our past is prologue, and I believe that it is, there will soon be even more blacks in the University and in Norman. However, focusing only on blacks will not greatly alter the general public's perception of the value of desegregation. A more progressive approach would be multicultural. We must stop looking at society through a peephole covered with a black-white filter. Reducing discrimination exclusively to black-white issues does not serve our communities well. It would be prudent to widen our focus to include American Indians, Hispanics, Asian Americans, and immigrants. As the Hispanic population grows, for example, they could, without diligent oversight, become the "Negroes" of this century. Foremost among the unfinished business is getting more ethnic minorities in city government and public organization leadership positions. The city of Norman is much more desegregated now than it was in 1967, but complete racial integration is a more distant goal. This is true for the University of Oklahoma too. In the words of an anonymous author:

> We ain't what we want to be,
> We ain't what we ought to be,
> And we ain't what we're going to be,
> But, thank God,
> We ain't what we was.

In the twentieth century, activists pushed cultural diversity initiatives that focused on racial desegregation. Those were needed and bold initiatives, but they were also divisive. Charges of reverse discrimination became the battle cries of angry whites who sought to push back some of the gains minorities had achieved during the civil rights era. The twenty-first century ought to be the era of inclusion — of racial and cultural integration. This will necessarily require a focus on tactics and techniques to assist ethnic minorities to become integral, fully functioning members of previously all-white communities, schools, and jobs. Therefore programs that train activists need to place considerably more emphasis on minority-group histories and techniques that help individuals, groups, and organizations accept culturally different peoples.

Finally, it is important to remember that the desegregation process at the University of Oklahoma began in 1945 when Ada Lois Sipuel Fisher volunteered to be the NAACP's U.S. Supreme Court civil rights plaintiffs. Those of us who came after her are still trying to sort out the effects desegregation has had on our own lives.

Looking Back and Ahead

Through their interactions, our allies and adversaries became very different people from what they thought they would become. Goals pulled out of our intergroup conflicts frequently displaced those that were set initially with profound immediacy. All of us who were involved in the transformative process pertaining to the black students' rebellion were changed in significant ways. And all of us were scarred. Gnawing around the edges of the various black-white encounters has always been someone who tried to determine what we black people ought to be: African Americans or just Americans. Perhaps if we could have expunged from ourselves the cultures of our slave ancestors, by fair or foul means, then there would not have been a problem with our assimilation into the mainstream University of Oklahoma and Norman communities. That would have been too simplistic.

What could we have done to our physical features to smooth the transition? Maybe things would have been different if the race riots throughout the United States had not happened. Over the years the speculation has gone on and on: maybe this, maybe that. It has all been meaningless conjecture, however. In our own unique ways, we African Americans and our allies have placed our lives on at least a page of the University of Oklahoma's history. When I look back and grasp the significance of those accomplishments, whether small or large, I am filled with pride. In our own ways and in our own time, we brought about some positive changes in race relations. And, in many instances, we were changed in positive ways too.

Notes

Chapter 1

1. Hill, "All-Negro Communities of Oklahoma," 260.
2. George Breitman, *The Last Year of Malcolm X*; Stokely Carmichael and Charles V. Hamilton, *Black Power*; Harold Cruse, *The Crisis of the Negro Intellectual*; Martin Luther King Jr., *Where Do We Go from Here*; Carl Oglesby and Richard Shaull, *Containment and Change*.

Chapter 2

1. Lomax, *The Negro Revolt*.
2. Alinsky, *Reveille for Radicals*, 11.
3. Alinsky, *Rules for Radicals*, 80.
4. Ibid., 126–30.
5. Fanon, *Black Skin, White Mask*, 250.
6. Fanon, *The Wretched of the Earth*, 96–97.
7. Breitman, *Malcolm X Speaks*, 21.
8. Ibid., 35.
9. Erikson, *Gandhi's Truth*, 198.
10. Andrews, *Mahatma Gandhi*, 192.
11. Ibid., 190.
12. Lincoln, *Martin Luther King, Jr.*, 36.
13. Ibid., 29.
14. King, *The Measure of a Man*, 11.

15. King, "Bold Design for a New South," 260.

16. Boyd, *Human Like Me, Jesus*, 128.

17. Berger, *Invitation to Sociology*, 123–31.

18. Gilbert, *Clients or Constituents*, 26–27.

19. McSurely, *Hang-ups*, 1–3.

20. Bullock, "Morality and Tactics in Community Organizing," 140–48.

21. Minnis, *The Care and Feeding of Power Structures Revisited*, 6.

22. Mills, *Power, Politics, and People*, 25–31.

23. Hunter, *Community Power Structure*.

24. Banfield and Wilson, *City Politics*, 218.

25.Tullock, *The Politics of Bureaucracy*, 38.

26. Goffman, *The Presentation of Self in Everyday Life*, 17–18.

Chapter 3

1. In 1968–69 two American Indian students were listed in the ASU directory: Amy A. Tiger and Johnny W. White Cloud. Also, most of the African American students had multiple racial heritages.

2. After Norish earned an M.S. degree in mathematics, she and Sterlin moved back to Nashville, where he applied his considerable activist skills to improve the lives of black students at Tennessee State University and throughout the United States.

Chapter 4

1. Jim Weeks, "OU Report Clears MacLeod of Discrimination," *Norman Transcript*, February 14, 1969.

Chapter 5

1. The "Memorandum to President J. Herbert Hollomon from 175 Black Students" was presented to Hollomon on March 6, 1969. In the version of the memorandum reprinted below, which I received two days later from Guinnevere Hodges, spelling and grammatical errors present in the original had been corrected.

Chapter 6

1. Jim Henderson, "Angry OU Black Students Feel Unwanted, Left Out," *Tulsa Daily World*, December 5, 1971.

2. The newspaper omitted a line here: " 'The question is,' said Alice, 'whether you *can* make words mean so many different things.' "

3. Frey, "J. Herbert Hollomon," 125.

4. "Hollomon Urges New Attack on Racial Barriers," *Norman Transcript*, April 10, 1969.

5. Ibid.

6. In 1970 Sandy earned a B.A. (cum laude) in psychology from the University of Oklahoma. She also earned two degrees from George Peabody College (now Vanderbilt University): an M.A. in psychology in 1973 and a Ph.D. in clinical psychology in 1975.

Chapter 8

1. John Barth, "Walker Tells of Efforts for Minority Program," *Oklahoma Daily*, September 14, 1971.

2. Beth earned two OU degrees — a B.S. in secondary education with a major in language arts (1970) and an M.P.H. with a major in health administration (1975). She also earned a J.D. from Oklahoma City University in 1982.

Bibliography

Alinsky, Saul. *Reveille for Radicals.* Chicago: University of Chicago Press, 1947.

———. *Rules for Radicals.* New York: Vintage Books, 1971.

Andrews, C. F. *Mahatma Gandhi.* New York: Macmillan, 1930.

Banfield, Edward, and James Wilson. *City Politics.* New York: Random House, 1963.

Berger, Peter. *Invitation to Sociology.* New York: Doubleday, 1963.

Boyd, Malcolm. *Human Like Me, Jesus.* New York: Simon and Schuster, 1971.

Breitman, George. *The Last Year of Malcolm X: The Evolution of a Revolutionary.* New York: Schocken Books, 1967.

———. *Malcolm X Speaks.* New York: Grove Press, 1966.

Bullock, Paul. "Morality and Tactics in Community Organizing." In Jeremy Larner and Irving Howe, eds., *Poverty: Views from the Left.* New York: William Morrow, 1968.

Carmichael, Stokely, and Charles V. Hamilton. *Black Power.* New York: Random House, 1967.

Cruse, Harold. *The Crisis of the Negro Intellectual.* New York: Random House, 1967.

Erikson, Erik H. *Gandhi's Truth.* New York: W. W. Norton, 1969.

Fanon, Frantz. *Black Skin, White Mask.* New York: Grove Press, 1967.

———. *The Wretched of the Earth.* New York: Grove Press, 1963.

Frey, Donald N. "J. Herbert Hollomon." *Memorial Tributes: National Academy of Engineering* 5 (1992): 123–26.

Gilbert, Neil. *Clients or Constituents.* San Francisco: Jossey-Bass, 1970.

Goffman, Erving. *The Presentation of Self in Everyday Life.* Garden City, N.Y.: Doubleday, 1959.

Hill, Mozell C. "The All-Negro Communities of Oklahoma." *Journal of Negro History* 31, no. 3 (1946): 254–68.

Hunter, Floyd. *Community Power Structure: A Study of Decision Makers.* Chapel Hill: University of North Carolina Press, 1953.

Jones, Stanley E. *Mahatma Gandhi: An Interpretation.* New York: Abingdon-Cokesbury, 1958.

King, Martin Luther, Jr. "Bold Design for a New South." *Nation,* March 30, 1963, 196, 260.

———. *The Measure of a Man.* Philadelphia: Pilgrim Press, 1968.

———. *Where Do We Go from Here: Chaos or Community?* New York: Bantam Books, 1967.

Lincoln, C. Eric, ed. *Martin Luther King, Jr.: A Profile.* New York: Hill and Wang, 1970.

Lomax, Louis. *The Negro Revolt.* New York: Harper and Row, 1962.

Malcolm X and Alex Haley. *The Autobiography of Malcolm X.* New York: Grove Press, 1965.

McSurely, Alan. *Hang-ups.* Louisville, Ky.: Southern Conference Educational Fund, 1967.

Mills, C. Wright. *Power, Politics, and People.* New York: Oxford University Press, 1963.

Minnis, Jack. *The Care and Feeding of Power Structures Revisited.* Louisville, Ky.: Southern Conference Educational Fund, 1967.

Oglesby, Carl, and Richard Shaull. *Containment and Change.* New York: Macmillan, 1967.

Ross, Murray G. *Community Organization: Theory, Principles and Practice.* New York: Harper and Row, 1957.

Sjoberg, Gordon, Richard Brymer, and Buford Farris. "Bureaucracy and the Lower Class." *Sociology and Social Research* 50 (1966): 325–29.

Thoreau, Henry David. *The Variorum Civil Disobedience.* New York: Twayne, 1967.

Tullock, Gordon. *The Politics of Bureaucracy.* Washington, D.C.: Public Affairs Press, 1965.

Index